# FEATHER WHITE

## MICKEY MAGUIRE

SUNBURY
PRESS

Mechanicsburg, PA USA

Published by Sunbury Press, Inc.
Mechanicsburg, PA USA

**www.sunburypress.com**

For information about special discounts for bulk purchases, please contact Sunbury Press Orders Dept. at (855) 338-8359 or orders@sunburypress.com.

To request one of our authors for speaking engagements or book signings, please contact Sunbury Press Publicity Dept. at publicity@sunburypress.com.

FIRST SUNBURY PRESS EDITION: October 2021

Set in Adobe Garamond | Interior design by Crystal Devine | Cover by Lawrence Knorr | Cover photo of F/V *Little Infant* by David Meads | Edited by Lawrence Knorr.

Publisher's Cataloging-in-Publication Data
Names: Maguire, Mickey, author.
Title: Feather white : a 1970s memoir : commercial fishing out of Provincetown and the backwoods counterculture movement in Nova Scotia/ Mickey Maguire.
Description: First trade paperback edition. | Mechanicsburg, PA : Sunbury Press, 2021.
Summary : Feather White is a 1970s chronicle of a youth's emergence from an alcoholic family and search for his missing pieces as he builds a log cabin in Nova Scotia and struggles to break in as a greenhorn in the fishing fleet of Provincetown, Cape Cod. Battling storms, both asea and of the human variety, learning a perilous trade, finding solace by a crackling fire in a remote cabin, he must make peace with what drove him there.
Identifiers: ISBN : 978-1-62006-570-9 (softcover).
Subjects: BIOGRAPHY & AUTOBIOGRAPHY | BIOGRAPHY & AUTOBIOGRAPHY / Personal Memoirs | NATURE / General.

Product of the United States of America
0 1 1 2 3 5 8 13 21 34 55

*Continue the Enlightenment!*

For our Erin: May your compass always point True North.

# Contents

## PART IV: SHIP'S COOK

# *Acknowledgments*

**Many thanks to:** Beth and Erin Maguire who inspire me daily, without whose support and love none of this would be possible. Marie Maguire, for her spark, strength, laughter and ongoing example. Miss you, Mom. I am also indebted to: Art White for his mentorship through the years, editing advice and convincing argument to cut back on the f-bombs, Linda Gransby, Christopher Busa (Provincetown Arts Magazine), Ridley Enslow (Enslow Publishers), Jennifra-Hann Norton, Susan Renehan, David Meads, Julie Gillespie, Lawrence Schuster and all the great folks at Sunbury Press. For the early-read encouragement that helped me believe in the project: A.N. Dellomo, Neil Kugelman, Jeremy Szoc, Stephen Young, Diane Borders, Len Eisenberg, Joel Eisenberg, Bill Watson, Tom Lynch, John Anderson, Linda Rago, Gyasi Bramos-Hantman, Avis Johnson, Ricky Merrill, Bill Evaul, Tim Jeffryes, Alice White, Bob Brown, Lisa Showalter, Chuck Jacobs, Kathy and Bill Duke, Marie Brown, Mary Ziegelmeier, Pete Becker, Chris Scanlan, Marc Sicca, George Goodin, Greg Myers, Pamela Wood, George Sloane, Allan Sharpe, Jim Hale, and Suzanne Jaroszynski.

# *Prologue*

**Mostly because of** youthful self-absorption and the feeling I was treading across the pages of a novel, I kept a journal of my affair with going for the full-tilt boogie experience. At the time, I could not imagine anything more exciting than a February gale in the Gulf of Maine, more intimidating than trying to break in as a greenhorn on a Cape Cod offshore scalloper or more frightening than an angry drunken shipmate with a knife. I wrote it all down.

All related instances of the commercial fishing days were recorded soon after they happened, usually during the off-watch, if not soon after the trip's end. Most dialogue was written down by next watch and is reliably accurate. All boat names and most of the people depicted retain their real names, except for a few name changes to protect privacy.

There were many of us who took the counterculture express to early 1970s Nova Scotia. Beyond where the power lines stopped, young people were building log cabins and cottages, moving into century-old farmhouses, restoring, and making barns habitable. Fully committed to what we universally agreed was a better way, there were enclaves of us throughout the province. They are mostly gone now. I saw an article in a Canadian magazine by a writer who found the traces of one of those communities up on North Mountain recently. There were pictures of rotting geodesic domes and other structures, a "hippie" ghost town. The writer presented what we were all doing then as history. As the only surviving structure from that era past the power lines on our dirt road, the log cabin I built in 1974 still stands and makes me feel twenty again when I walk through that back door that has always dragged quite a bit. By God's grace, I am, so far, allowed to keep my tree fort.

Not cut out for the high school English teacher career I was studying for, I instead adopted the "Look what I stepped in" method of living life and, undeniably, prayerful surrender. I have come to believe living the way I did was my strong response to witnessing my father destroy himself with alcohol.

"Feather white" is a term sometimes used by fishermen to describe stormy conditions. The whitecaps on the ocean surface are often indistinguishable from the white feathered breasts of sea birds often on the wing during a storm.

M.

# PART I

~~~~~~~~~~~~~~~~~~~~~~~~

## Breaking In –
## F/V *Janet and Jean*

# Gone Fishing
## (meant to pick apples)

**Something was slapping** my foot. No. *Someone.* I was not in my bed—more like a narrow box. And there was this splashy water sound right near my head, foot-slapping again and a big engine droning in that unmistakable low growl of diesel, vibrating my back teeth like a tuning fork. Then, an unfamiliar voice: "Mickey. Wheel watch. Hey! Wheel watch."

The new reality cuddled up close, bad breath and all, a one-night stand first thing in the morning. *I am in a bunk on a 63-foot commercial fishing vessel I somehow managed to get aboard, headed down the backside of Cape Cod in the dark, bound for Great Round Shoal off Nantucket on a ten-day fishing trip.* Oh, man. The obsession with riding the edge was biting me in the ass again, but this felt like I might have finally pushed it too far. The splashy sound was the North Atlantic on the other side of the hull, breaking against the bow, just three inches of oak plank separating us and infiltrating all, the grind of a diesel engine driving us through the blackness.

"Get up. Wheel watch."

It was deckhand Skip Albanese. I pulled my foot back to avoid another slap. I later learned this was the way to wake someone on a boat. Some of these guys woke up swinging, so you wanted to be as far away from their arms as possible. But a greenhorn would not know this, nor that the greenhorn gets first "wheel watch" (whatever that was) if you put to sea at midnight.

"Wheel watch? What's that?"

"Just get up on deck and see Rick."

We were in the forward-most part of the boat, called the "fo'c'sle," shorthand for the forecastle of the tall ship sailing days. Below deck and dimly lit, bunks lined each side of the inner hull in the shape of a "V," being in the bow, and occupied by shadowy lumps of snoring men, ruffians who mostly, I remembered, resented my existence. *Oh, right. I'm a pariah. Nice.* I all but disappeared into the brand-new size 13 rubber boots that deckhand Chris Scanlan helped me purchase at Land's End Marine Supply in Provincetown the day before.

"What's your shoe size?" he had asked me at the store.

"Ten and a half."

"Size 13," he instructed the Land's End clerk.

"Why so big?" I asked.

"If the boat goes down or if you go overboard, you need to be able to kick them off. Otherwise, those boots will drag you to the bottom," Chris said, I thought too nonchalantly.

Great. A few days earlier, I was on a mission to make some money picking apples, the only risk—falling off a ladder. Instead, I was tumbling *up* a fo'c'sle ladder I swore was bucking me like a mechanical bull, my mind snagging on the rack of moose horns in Nova Scotia that put me on this Cape Cod commercial fishing vessel. Life sure was turning on the weirdest things. Most would consider this a dumb-luck coincidence, but I always felt there was a hand on my shoulder guiding me, sometimes downright shoving because of the always reliable thickness of my skull.

Headed aft toward the wheelhouse and Captain Rick O'Brien, my bewildered legs attempted to adjust to the boat pitching in swells, the deck consistently higher, lower, or more atilt than where my foot expected.

"Mickey," he shouted down over the diesel engine roar, startling me in the throes of my off-balance ballet, "You ever steer a boat before?"

"Not really," I said. "Canoes, rowboats . . ." Impressive.

"Come on, get up here," he said.

Climbing the steps, I entered the wheelhouse where the captain oversees the whole operation, darkened at night to allow for some degree of visibility outside and easy viewing of the radar screen, LORAN numbers (for navigational positioning), and illuminated compass. I was certain Captain Rick saw the twelve-year-old version of me standing there, awkward in Daddy's size thirteen boots, wide eyes just two little wet sparkles in the dark. He showed me our heading: 180 degrees due south. We steamed down what they called the "backside" or ocean side of Cape Cod for the Great Round Shoal, part of the Nantucket Shoals. The compass was a liquid-filled globe with a floating ball inside moving crazily, it seemed, in every direction. Rick showed me how to "steer into" the bearing. The wheel was an outsized wooden spoked prop they borrowed from a Popeye cartoon. He called my attention to the radar screen, its sweep revealing several orange variably sized blots of light.

"See those blips?" he asked.

"Yeah?"

"Those are other ships. Don't hit any."

Satisfied this ten-minute tutorial was sufficient, he turned and headed for his bunk in the after part of the wheelhouse and was snoring in seconds. OK. Standing there with a locomotive engine grinding below my feet and a ship's wheel shivering in my hands, it was the second reality-check in ten minutes: *You don't know jack about any of this, and everyone aboard is asleep? Are they out of their freaking minds?* Caught between fear of orange blips and the implausibility of how I wound up here in the first place, I stewed and gripped the wheel.

The bread crumb trail traced back to that rack of moose horns in Nova Scotia. How I had gotten *there* starts with an eleven-year-old New Jersey kid trying to figure out the "What's wrong with this picture?" quiz about his alcoholic family. With the terms dictated by addiction, "peace" was merely a concept, a word relegated to Christmas cards and carols. A winter Boy Scout trip to a log cabin gave me my first taste of peace, and I decided there would be more of that in my life and a log cabin of my own. For the next nine years, the thought of this cabin I was going to build became the desert island I clung to in the vodka ocean that dictated our existence.

In 1973 at age nineteen, I sold my car to my parents, made three trips to Nova Scotia, and bought six acres of forest for $300. Returning the following year, I cut the trees with an ax and built the cabin.

It was still the '60s in the early '70s. Throughout the province, pockets of young people flourished, building rustic homes, growing vegetables, exploring the old ways with good food, good dope, good music. At one point, there were eight handmade cabins on Fraser Road, six of them log. These were not perfectly symmetrical build-by-numbers log cabin kits with their lathe-turned uniform logs. These dwellings were imperfectly beautiful "piles of sticks" in the woods (my friend Bill's term) built with a touch of the random exquisiteness a bird might build a nest. We were off the grid, burning candles and kerosene lamps, heating with wood, and using outhouses.

Frasertown was a well-known and notorious "hippie" haven, though we never called ourselves hippies. *Freaks.* That's what we were. A steady stream of like-minded folk from the states coming to the Annapolis Valley and Bear River area joining turned on locals, carving out their idea of a better way in the woods. Some had plans other than dying for their country in Viet Nam. Others were trying to break off from the pack of lemmings, all looking for something more, closer to the earth, and more substantive than cookie-cutter lives waiting for them after college. One such couple became the catalyst for my fishing days.

Arriving in a gray 1950s model U.S. Army truck, Rick and Deb O'Brian bought thirty acres less than half a mile from my place. Rick was an imposing

The Nova Scotia log cabin in 1977, three years old.

figure—tall and authoritative, there was gravitas in everything he said, warranted or not, and a deep, resonant voice grating past a Sam Elliot mustache. He could make, "Please pass the salt," sound like he just gave the order to proceed with the Normandy invasion. He and his wife Deb hailed from Provincetown, and I filed it away as "Providence," as in Rhode Island, committing my first annoying Cape Cod offense.

The Frasertown freaks welcomed them into our small enclave, much like they had done me a few years earlier. During one of the road's epic parties, we all somehow decided to strap a big-ass rack of moose horns to the front grill of Rick's army truck, mainly because it looked cool. Now it looked like it ought to belong to some comic book hero: Sgt. Cragface of the Yukon, maybe. That rack of horns got me into commercial fishing nine months later.

With the cabin construction behind me, the rest of the '70s was all about making a little money and returning to Nova Scotia to resume my primitive peace. Two Fraser Road friends told me about autumn excursions picking apples in North Brookfield, Massachusetts, and making $1500 to $2000 in a few weeks. A fellow could live like a king off the grid for quite a while on that kind of money. That's what I would do.

The plan was to hitchhike as usual since I had sold my car to buy land, but an acquaintance from college offered to take me from New Jersey to North Brookfield if I didn't mind going first to Cape Cod National Seashore for a few

Pilgrim Lake (East Harbor), Provincetown, Massachusetts.

days. Coming from a Jersey Shore town where they bulldozed the dunes flat to build their Atlantic City, I was curious to see natural seashore.

So, in September of 1977, I departed for the apple orchard with a bit of Cape Cod vacation scheduled to kick it all off. The spectacle of the great dunes to the east of Rt. 6 at the end of Cape Cod forced a stop. To a kid from coastal plain South Jersey, these were mountains. I trudged up the face of the giant dune fronting me. On reaching the pinnacle, a rolling sea of dunes stretched for miles. Many approached a hundred feet in height and were bald, evincing Sahara-like visions, like the one I was astride. Some were peppered with salt grass, while others were wooded and could have passed for some landscapes of the American West. These "Province Lands" were surrounded by Cape Cod Bay and the formidable Atlantic Ocean, a deep September blue. The Cape itself, here near the tip, felt like a ship, its prow plowing the water.

After tearing myself from the dunes and a ripe beach plum feast, we proceeded toward Provincetown and the first intersection with a traffic light where we would turn to enter the town. Waiting for the light from the opposite direction was a gray 1950s military truck . . . with a rack of moose horns mounted on the front grill. There were few models of that era that came with the moose horns option. Behind the wheel, a Sam Elliot mustache. No mistaking. I hopped out of the car and trotted over to the truck while the red light held us.

"Rick?" I asked.

"Province Land" dunes.

"Mickey!" he said. "What are you doing here?"

Going over it in my mind, I realized I had taken a wrong turn to Providence. Rick lived in *Provincetown, Massachusetts*. I told him about apple picking my way to a year in Nova Scotia. He told me he was skippering an offshore scalloper headed for the Nantucket Shoals at midnight.

"Need any help?" jumped right past the Stupid Idea Police.

"Well, we do need a shacker." A shacker, I would learn, is an unskilled greenhorn, paid half as much as regular crew for slave-like labor.

"I'm in if you'll have me," I responded. The Stupid Idea Police must have been a block away on a bender in a sour-smelling neighborhood dive.

Telling my ride I wouldn't be going to Brookfield, I retrieved my gear from the car and threw my fate onto that big ol' army truck with Sam Elliot. Within ten minutes of my arrival in Provincetown (actually, we hadn't even made it into town), I was hired onto a fishing boat. In a heartbeat, I went from prospective apple picker to greenhorn commercial fisherman.

We headed towards the harbor. Rick was pulling on a Camel (of course, he smoked Camels) and telling me about our fishing vessel, the *Janet and Jean*, built by a famous wooden boat builder from Maine. I was getting my first look at Provincetown, my new homeport, peering out over those moose horns I helped strap on that front grill in a significantly challenged state of sobriety.

## Provincetown and the Fleet

**Provincetown was bright** and vibrant on that crisp fall day. Having landed here first before heading over to Plymouth, the Pilgrims are to blame for the local phrase "where New England began." The Mayflower Compact was written and signed in Provincetown Harbor.

Colorful (OK, weird) people were everywhere, and it was apparent this was a place where anyone could feel comfortable. P'town rests at the very end of the curl of Cape Cod. Once you are there, there is nowhere else to go, reinforcing the sense that you are indeed at the end of the earth. Poets, painters, writers, and thinkers from Thoreau to Eugene O'Neill have recorded their musings about Provincetown. Still, no one described it better, I submit, than the legendary fisherman I had the privilege to fish with, Richard Dickey: "My boy, Provincetown is like the trap in the drain of the world. All the sediment winds up here." Not even halfway to the harbor, I began to feel like I belonged there.

Provincetown, Massachusetts.

I was getting sedimental. Noted to be an outpost for rogues, smugglers, and a mélange of fringe elements in the 19th Century, artists discovered the sublime beauty and light of Provincetown and the Cape around the 1890s. Always tolerant of social outcasts, P'town is a welcome mat for those who avoid conforming to norms, and in the 1970s, there were still a lot of freaks.

Rick drove down the middle of MacMillan Wharf, the main wharf in town. In the 1970s, P'town had a thriving fishing fleet, and crews were all busy with gear work. If the crew was out eight to twelve days fishing and in port for three, two of those "in" days would be occupied by gear work. On each boat, men were mending nets or working on the chain bags of scallop dredges. Welding trucks and pickups full of groceries jockeyed for position, the crew passed grub down to the cook in the fish holds where he would ice it all down. Some boats took on fuel, some receiving tons of ice, while others were offloading their catch, packing the fish into ice-filled wooden boxes.

Although there were a few steel boats in the fleet, the wooden vessel dominated Provincetown harbor. Boats of many sizes and purposes were tied up three and four deep at the pier, a practice called "rafting." There were "day boats," smaller vessels that did their fishing close by all in a day, and trip boats that went out quite far from three to fourteen days. Colorfully painted and appearing well-maintained, these boats reflected the pride of captains and crew.

As we did the slow drive toward the wharf's end, you could look down onto the busy decks of each boat, the crews all looking like hard cases. I would be joining ranks with some of them imminently, the whole scene intimidating. The tourists stood on the wharf and gaped at the fishermen: polar bears in natural habitat cages. Man, what had I gotten myself into?

# Greenhorn

**Our rack of** moose horns on wheels pulled to a stop at the end, and Rick said, "There she is." The F/V (fishing vessel) *Janet and Jean* was a 63-foot eastern-rigged offshore scalloper built in Maine by Harvey Gamage, revered among boat builders. She was blue with white trim, her wheelhouse aft, and a big bow forward. Eastern-rig vessels all have the wheelhouse aft and deep hulls designed to ride out the storms of the North Atlantic.

Some rangy-looking crew worked on her dredges, also called "rakes" or "drags." One guy was splicing the metal tow cable using a big marlin spike, although, at the time, I didn't know what a marlinspike was. Others were using big metal cutting jaws to cut worn-out rings and links from the suspended chain bag of the dredge with loud snaps. *How am I going to fit into this?* I followed Rick down the ladder to the boat, a spaceship touching down on a strange planet.

The captain announced me as the new shacker. Whatever a shacker was, I could tell it wasn't good. It might have been a little better if he had announced me as the new toilet bowl licker. Most of the crew treated me with cold indifference. A few glared. There was no "Hi. I'm Todd. I'll show you around the dorm." No. "Todd" would have a dredge dropped on him about two days out.

I was out of place and dressed for the forest with a buckskin jacket, a leather hat, and a leather backpack. Ain't no log cabins this far out on the Cape. I might as well have been wearing a tutu. All my cred as a hard-working log cabin builder went right overboard in a greenhorn shacker splash.

Rick took me forward, past these leering shipmates to the *folk's hole* (that's what I thought he said) where I could stow my gear. I learned this "folk's hole" was not a place where the folks hole up. It was the "fo'c'sle," an abbreviation of "forecastle." Hell, I wasn't even saying "forward" then. Ignorance of nautical nomenclature makes being a greenhorn excruciating. You don't know what to call things, and your every idiotic utterance reinforces the fear that your less than impressed shipmates will drop a dredge on you about two days out.

I needed to learn a language first: "Greenhorn, go get the gaff by the gallous."

"The what? By the who?" Yeah. Impressive.

During this highly technical/technique-laden portion of the trade called gear work, I was utterly useless. The presence of unskilled labor on board invited resentment: *This douchebag greenhorn who don't know fuck-all is taking part of my hard-earned share. And he's asking me stupid fucking questions all the way through. It's criminal.* Nice.

Rick was fair to me. He knew me from Nova Scotia, where I had built my cabin at age twenty. He figured I wasn't afraid of a bit of work and would give me every opportunity to succeed. Not everyone takes to the rigors of commercial fishing. It was still a gamble.

The engineer, Dan, said to be a former motorcycle club member down south, clearly would not be one to cut me any slack. Dan had long scraggly hair, a matching beard, and various crudely executed tattoos of the kind guys do on themselves when they're in prison. His pale blue Alaskan huskie eyes looked right through me, beyond me. Hell, they didn't even acknowledge my existence. A tough guy who was not shy about bringing up my inadequacies for all to hear, Dan used his position as engineer to fuel his arrogance, a guy who enjoyed being on the "ins" when somebody was on the "outs." We run into people like this throughout life and do our best to avoid them. On a boat, this tactic is not an option.

There was Bobby Reed. With long blond hair and a beard, Bobby was chill. He seemed like a laid-back, "everything's cool" stoner to me. He was quiet and would probably watch me have my liver cut out, that being cool with him, too.

Chris Scanlan, the fellow splicing the tow cable with the marlinspike, was a surprise. He was from Atlantic City (Ventnor, actually), too. Chris was the son of a well-known local doctor, our parents knew each other, and our sisters went to school together. Dr. Scanlan had performed an experimental operation on my father's kidney, saving his life in the 1950s. Man, the "coincidences" kept on rolling. Chris was the silent type but with a lot of stuff going through his mind. Kind and patient with my greenness, he took me to Land's End Marine Supply and helped me buy the essential equipment like oil gear, boots, gloves, and scallop knife. He was smart too and, as it turned out, brighter than all of us.

Stocky Skip Albanese, his long dark hair pulled into a ponytail when he worked on deck, had eyes that took everything in and always seemed to be searching for a joke or an angle. His smile could be characterized as a shit-eating grin punctuated by several missing front teeth. His thick Popeye forearms, tattooed by central casting with nautical themes, suggested great strength. Loud, raucous, and funny with a cackling laugh, he was the boat's Falstaff. Under this layer of "Let the good times roll" was a thinker and a schemer. I learned he had done some time in prison, but he never told me his crime. He had a young wife and baby and was trying to make a clean go of it. Though not above breaking greenhorn balls, Skip helped me connect my willingness to work to actual tasks at hand when no one was looking. I learned I could ask him questions of the how-to variety on the sly, although he would not openly help a greenhorn if he could help it. He knew a lot about the trade and to watch him work the gear on deck was like watching someone play an instrument.

There was Lobster ("Lobstah" in Cape Cod speak). I never did find out his real first name or his last. Lobster, during this *Janet and Jean* portion of my fishing days, became my friend and companion. He looked like his name should be Lobster. Red of hair and beard, freckled, a flush to his cheeks, a beneficent glassy-eyed smile that I have seen on so many barflies, he looked like a happy hour Irish Santa. He was warm, talkative, fun to be with, and, I think, a caring soul.

He was up from the New Bedford/Fair Haven scene, which was widely known as the home of the big-time commercial fishing industry. All fish prices reflected New Bedford pricing. Lobster had some experience on a boat but not scalloping, which put him a little closer to me in the vessel's hierarchy. For instance, if they treated Lobster like an old boot, I was like a clod of dog shit that gets scraped from the boot.

John was the ship's cook. Weighing around 300 lbs., he produced a re-markable series of unremarkable meals—"cream of wet sneaker soup" being his specialty. John was a pretty nice guy. I think a lot of cooks on boats are decent humans, their very jobs about nurturance.

Rick took me forward and below to what would be my home for the next couple of months: the fo'c'sle. There is no downstairs or upstairs at sea. It is above or below. No front and rear; it's forward and aft. There is no ceiling but an "overhead." Not a floor; it's a deck. There are no walls on a boat, only bulkheads. Consistent with my penchant for learning the hard way, the crew called me a *dipshit good for nothing buttwad of a shacker* whenever I did not use the proper terminology. There would be no trophies for merely participating. There is, however, something to be said for this kind of treatment: It motivates you to learn fast. Buttwad.

The fo'c'sle is forward of the mainmast, and to get there, you must climb down through a narrow doghouse-like structure aptly named "the doghouse." The steep ladder leads you below to the fo'c'sle in the bow section of the boat and is traditionally the crew's quarters. Being in the bow, it has a "V" shape with upper and lower bunks on each side, and a "V" shaped galley table with benches on either side for mealtime, shooting the shit, or playing cards.

Just aft of this table on eastern rigged vessels is the galley. The *Janet and Jean* had an old cast iron cook stove that looked like it belonged in a log cabin. Instead of wood-burning, it was kerosene fed and had a blower on it to regulate temperature. In addition to its cooking chores, this stove was called upon to heat the fo'c'sle, glorious in winter but god-awful oppressive in warmer months. But it stayed lit, even in summer, for the whole trip. What distinguished this from land-lubberly stoves were the metal rails that enclosed the stovetop and the stainless-steel springs with hooks like metal bungees for securing pots

Scallop dredge coming over the rail with scallops (courtesy David Meads).

during rough weather. These worked well until we got an unusually wicked blow that could change an ambitious menu to cold cuts in a heartbeat. If it's rough enough, ain't nuthin' staying in a soup pot.

The galley had a sink with a hand pump and an icebox the size of an industrial refrigerator. When the ship took on ice, a good portion was fed down to the icebox via an opened, round bunker plate up on deck. There were shelves for food and condiments, all with rails to prevent spillage. Everything on board was designed to avoid spillage and continue to function despite the world's end. I learned the hard way (my usual methodology) you don't pour more than half a cup of coffee in a full gale.

The rest of the food was stored and packed in ice down in the fish hold, and its care was solely the cook's responsibility. The fo'c'sle/galley of the *Janet and Jean* was beautiful. Rick had stripped some paint in the fo'c'sle and found fine-grained mahogany underneath. He had studied art and had artistic sensibilities, and he appreciated and respected the craftsmanship of yesteryear.

# Gear Work

**After stowing my** stuff in a bunk, it was up on deck for gear work with the crew. I arrived there with the formidable task of contributing with no clue as to how to do so. Much of the gear work on a scalloper involves getting the dredges right. The dredge, or rake, is a large triangle made of steel. Ours were 12 feet wide at the base. Suspended from this triangle is a bag made of chain, made by the crew ring by ring. Each steel ring has four links attached, which connect it to the rings to either side and above and below. The dredges dragged across the ocean floor, so these rings and links take a beating and wear away quickly, requiring frequent maintenance.

The dredges, suspended in the air during gear work to allow access to the chain bag, are corrected and repaired by the crew. While most of the crew work on the dredge, the engineer is in the engine room, making sure the engine is tip-top or on deck, greasing blocks, and checking other gear. He has an auxiliary engine going called the lister so that electronics and pumps will work without starting up the main diesel. Most guys called it the popcorn machine for its pop-pop-pop sound. I stood there trying to figure a way to help and not just be a horse's ass. Unsuccessful, I got many compliments on being the best horse's ass ever to set foot on a boat.

When working on the chain bag, the two tools used most often are squeezers and cutters. The cutters were long two-handled tools with powerful jaws used to cut through thick rings and links. Heavy and requiring considerable strength to operate, their jaws were always rusty, constantly exposed to salt water, making their use even more challenging. Though a few squirts of WD-40 would go a long way toward making them more user-friendly, I think they were left in this condition so they could also function as a prop to degrade greenhorns.

"Here, *shacker*, cut this link."

I picked up the heavy cutters and had trouble even opening the jaws. Then I tried to cut through the link, coming onto it with all I had with these arms that built two log cabins, veins popping, arms trembling—nothing. The crew laughed. My self-esteem went flaccid.

"Here! Give me those!" biker/engineer Dan barked at me, more than pleased to highlight my uselessness.

I swore someone welded those cutters shut as a joke on greenhorns. Over the years, I've seen animal crew with biceps the size of rump roasts cut through a link just using their arms on each handle. But usually, one arm of the cutters is laid across the upper thigh or lower gut, and both hands are used on the other handle to pull it toward the body. This bit of useful information was conveniently withheld from me. Snap! A piece of the broken link goes flying. I guess he showed me. I felt my status on the boat sinking even lower, hard to imagine, having started as a clod of dog shit on the bottom of an old boot.

# The Fo'c'sle Bar

**Having no place** to live, Rick offered to let Lobster and me stay on the boat. Oh good, a place to live. It surprises me today how little attention I paid to such details. As the sun set, Rick called an end to gear work. The married crew usually went home. The rest of us hit the bars. In a strange town, I had to rely on the crew to suggest what came next. There were three fisherman/townie bars near the wharf: The Old Colony (the "OC"), the Governor Bradford, and The Fo'c'sle. The *Janet and Jean* crew went to The Fo'c'sle. It was blissfully unadorned, homey, and presided over by beneficent bartender Mike Moon. Moon made everyone feel welcome, even slime-ball-good-for-nothing-dip-shit-idiot greenhorns. The two newbies stuck together. A few beers went a long way towards dispelling the notion that I was making the biggest mistake of my life.

The Fo'c'sle had none of the trappings that would attract a tourist. Sometimes a moneyed, well-groomed couple would wander in, look around, and wander right back out. What the Fo'c'sle had were heart and hearth. Not just a fisherman's bar, it was a townie meeting place to relax, drawing locals, poets, and artists who lived in Provincetown. There was always a thematic conversation going on that Moon would shepherd along, and if you didn't want to get into that one, there were conversations at the wooden tables and from one table to the next. The folks here were gritty, down-to-earth, and generally agreeable. They were either from P'town or, as my friend Avis Johnson likes to say, "Importegees," people who wound up living here like the "sediment" in the trap that Dickey so colorfully described. Usually, they (we) are called "wash-ashores."

Purchasing the necessary gear left my finances on life support. This venture was a quest for money, but now I was so far from an apple orchard the money part seemed like a fume or a memory of one. Even though I was a good-for-nothing piece of shit shacker, after a day of gear work, I was a good-for-nothing piece of shit shacker on the *Janet and Jean*. My mates made sure I had plenty of beer to drink. When it all wound down, and everyone went home, Lobster and I made our way out and down Commercial St. and hung a left at the wharf where the *Janet and Jean* was tied up.

During this long walk down the pier, I first became aware of a sound that would color many of my thoughts in the coming years: the Long Point foghorn. At the tip of Cape Cod, Long Point lighthouse stands guard, its foghorn bellowing a single note mournfully into the night. For years, it has serenaded fisherman's wives waiting for their men to come back from Georges Bank or men about to put to sea and even drunken greenhorns staggering their way to their bunks in the bow of a Harvey Gamage-built eastern rigged scallop boat.

"Boooooooooop."

"Wow, what's that?"

"That's the Long Point foghorn," Lobster told me.

"Boooooooooop." Good God, I was walking right through the pages of a Melville novel. This doleful wailing in the night sure set a nautical tone. There is a twelve-foot tide in P'town, so if the tide is out, negotiating twelve feet of wharf ladder down to a boat in the dark, aided by copious amounts of beer, is an adventure. Once we landed on deck without killing ourselves, we made it over to the doghouse, trying not to trip on the gear in the shadows. Using the key to the padlock Rick had given us, we climbed down into the strange quiet of the fo'c'sle, interrupted only by the water of Provincetown Harbor lapping up against the hull. Maneuvering into our respective bunks, we drifted off to sleep to the tune of "My God, What Have I Gotten Myself Into?" which was a big hit that fall.

## The Race

**The next day,** we finished gear work by mid-day, so Rick told me to hop in the truck. We went to Herring Cove, known as New Beach to townies, overlooking the northernmost part of Cape Cod, Race Point. It was sunny but windy that day. We got out of the truck and stood on the beach looking out to sea off Race Point. I saw mountains out there, islands like the Porcupine Islands in Bar Harbor, Maine.

"What are those islands out there, Rick?" I asked.

"What are you talking about?"

"See those land masses sticking up out of the ocean?"

"Those aren't islands," he said, "those are the Race Point Rips." I heard the reverence in his low tone.

There before me was one of the most wicked tide rips in the North Atlantic, caused by the confluence of four forces: Cape Cod Bay, Massachusetts Bay, and, from the other side, the North Atlantic. With a wind blowing from just the right direction, the result is mountains of water in a violent conflict that every Provincetown vessel must pass through on the way in and the way out of port. It could make for sloppy seas for about fifteen minutes, even on a beautiful, calm day.

But, on a night when it was blowing 70, it was the final insult to be endured before you could consider yourself safe in port. It was known to fishermen simply as "The Race." On that windy but gorgeous day near Race Point, those rips induced a sense more of dread than awe, perhaps because Rick reminded me we'd be coming through "The Race" later that night. Years later, in my bluegrass days, I wrote and recorded a banjo instrumental with String Fever, inspired by those rips titled "Rifftide."

We had gotten the vessel ready to go, but nature was not in a cooperative mood and provided a northeasterly blow for about three days. Sometimes the *Janet and Jean* rocked and rolled pretty well, merely tied up at the wharf.

On the afternoon of September 18, 1977, we finally took on ice. The boat maneuvered over to the building where they offloaded the catch, and a long

Race Point rips looking like land on the horizon (known simply as "The Race").

pipe/chute about ten inches in diameter, fed down each bunker hole, filled the fish hold with several tons of crushed ice. It was a noisy affair, but most guys enjoyed doing this. The cook had been busy at the supermarket filling the entire back of a pickup truck with grub for the trip. The fuel truck paid a visit, filling her massive diesel oil tanks. The water tank had to be topped off, too. Grub, water, ice, and fuel—the crew pays for that off the top.

The way the split in P'town went in those days was thus: the boat-owner(s) got 50% of the catch. The captain got two shares and sometimes a percentage. The engineer and cook got a share plus a $100 "pur" or "per" (purse?). The rest of the crew got a share. If you had a good-for-nothing piece of shit greenhorn shacker, well, he got a half share. Expenses like fuel and food came out of the crew's portion. They had to make $5000 to $7000 or more before they could make a dime. So, if you were ten-handed at full share, that's eleven shares because of the captain's double share. You made 1/11th of 50% of the catch *after* expenses. The fishing had better be good.

# *Bound*

**Plans were to** steam at midnight, which I thought was a God–awful time to leave. But most skippers want to make the first set out of the gear in daylight. It looked like we were the only vessel putting to sea that night. MacMillan Wharf was dark except for the brightly lit *Janet and Jean*. The lister was pop-pop popping, and the deck was abuzz with crew who knew where they were going and what they were doing. The aroma of strong coffee wafted up through the open doghouse doors. I contributed my spot-on impression of a horse's ass.

Rick gave Dan (who loved me so much) the order to fire up the diesel engine. In a moment, the beast came to life; the entire vessel vibrated from the backbone up. The roar coming from the belly of the engine room felt like a final warning: *Last chance to go apple picking.*

Someone on the wharf threw the lines down to the deck where they were neatly coiled and stowed until we made port again. We were the inside boat with three other vessels tied to the outside of us. It takes piloting and line skill to extricate your boat from a three or four-deep situation and leave the other vessels safely tied up.

With a degree of frigging around, the *Janet and Jean* was free of the wharf and slipping past the black shadow of the breakwater. The breakwater was a later addition to Provincetown Harbor. Made of huge rocks (in Atlantic City, we would call it a "jetty"), this was not attached to land and was put there to slow the buildup of silt in the harbor and act as a buffer to rough water for the tied-up fleet. Once clear of that, Rick pushed the diesel a little more. We were heading with a purposeful momentum into complete darkness. For the time being, I left my second thoughts about this venture dock-side. I was going wherever this boat was going.

"Booooooooop."

We steamed past the Long Point light and foghorn, louder now that we were so close. It was relatively calm, and the *Janet and Jean* had a nice easy roll to her. A few minutes later, we were pounded by seas. She was rocking and rolling, unsecured gear skittering around the deck.

"What the hell?"

One of the crew laughed and said we were going through the Race. Yeah, that's right, the Race Point tide rips, those "islands" I saw with O'Brian from the beach off Race Point. I had forgotten them and thought some freakish storm had hit us. Fifteen minutes later, it was all over and back to the gentle roll again.

The deck lights were on, illuminating my way amidst the gear, but ten feet beyond the vessel was pure black, and that was where we were headed: into the black like it was outer freaking space. I stayed on deck alone for a while, sucking in the sea air and the moment. *Well, we've really done it this time, Stanley.* Making my way down the doghouse ladder to the fo'c'sle, I joined the crew, where Skip was holding forth with that cackle of a laugh. There were wagers on how long the new shackers would last, which had an ominous feel. The crew had fun with this, playing their advantage of knowing something we didn't. I wondered what they did with you if you didn't "last"—over the side?

A card game gathered around the fo'c'sle table. Usually, it was a game called "Spit" or "Screw," and like everything else on this blasted boat, I didn't know the rules, and it was out of the question to bother explaining them. For the next hour, before we all turned in ahead of our arrival on the fishing grounds, what transpired would have passed as a fine example of tribal shunning. The crew barely looked at me unless I was in someone's way, and then I'd get barked at like some dumb animal. I'm outgoing by nature. OK, I can't keep my mouth shut, but here, the worst thing I could do was to have something to say, unless it was, "I quit," which was what most of them wanted to hear anyway. This "Mr. Verbosity Takes a Vow of Silence" chapter was an unusual read for me, but even I knew it was practically suicidal to be my chatty self. So, most thought me the quiet type.

The smart ones were in their bunks, already sleeping. An even smarter one was back in P'town somewhere. Chris Scanlan did not make the trip, heeding the inner voices that warned, "This Boat Will Never Make Any Money."

You could hit the icebox and make any kind of sandwich at any time except when Cookie was preparing a meal. There had to be five pounds of every type of cold cut and cheese. Between meals, snacks were called "mug-ups" and did not involve the cook. Any dishes used during a mug-up had to be cleaned by the crew and not left for the cook.

I crawled into my casket-like bunk when everyone else turned in and managed to somehow drift into a deep sleep, only to have my foot slapped by Skip, telling me I had to do this thing called wheel watch.

So, that's the fractured math that added up to how I had gotten to that darkened wheelhouse, clinging to the ship's wheel while every soul on the vessel slept, doing my first ever wheel watch. After a standard two-hour watch, during which time I had managed to avoid hitting any other ships (always a plus), the sun struggled to poke through a gray day. Someone relieved me from my watch, and I got my first look at being at sea far from shore. That 63-foot scalloper didn't look so big anymore.

## The Work

**It turned out** we were seven-handed after Chris had left the boat, which made the watch system (six hours on, six off) impossible. Captain's watch was 6:00 A.M. to noon and 6:00 P.M. till midnight. The mate's watch was from noon to 6:00 P.M. and midnight to 6:00 A.M. The latter was often referred to as the dog watch. You must wash, bag, and ice down the scallops in the hold, eat, poop, hang out and sleep during your six hours off. Sometimes, when the situation called for it, the captain would "break watch" and do a six and three (six on and three off), and at times we have even endured the nine and three, but you can't do that for very long before you risk someone getting hurt. So, with the six and six off the table, the boat could not fish the standard twenty-four hours a day. We got up at 5:00 A.M. and worked till 11:00 P.M. I say "worked," but it was more like being pushed to the limit of endurance. It made me laugh and shattered my previous concept of hard work. After 11:00 P.M., we shut down and dropped one of the dredges to the bottom using it as an anchor, a procedure referred to as "laying to" on the rake.

During the actual fishing operation, the port and starboard side dredges were set out when Rick had a good head of steam going. They rested on the outboard side of the rails with the pelican hook, a releasable shackle, keeping them tethered to the vessel. The captain rang the bell, alerting the deckhands, who pounded the pins out of the pelican hooks with a maul. Each dredge splashed into the water while the winchmen stayed by the spinning drums of cable paying out. A typical tow was twenty minutes to a half-hour.

At the end of the tow, the skipper backed down the engines and rang the bell for "haul back." The winches hauled the tow cable back, grinding and snapping until the dredges were in view. The hookup men and winchmen worked together to get the dredges up over the rail and emptied on deck. We were fishing the Nantucket Shoals, so it looked like we were trying to catch rocks, deck-loads of them with a few scallops mixed in. Getting the loaded dredges over the rail is dangerous and gets exponentially more hazardous with worsening weather.

The crew, including the shackers, then attacked the pile after another set out of the dredges. You set a wire basket on the deck between your legs, bend over and dig at the pile for scallops. The captain would yell, "All I want to see is assholes and elbows," a common phrase in the fishing vernacular. Scallops went into the basket behind you. Everything else, rocks of all sizes, crabs, mud, and other debris were shoveled or thrown over the side.

It was here that I made the point that I intended to pull my weight, or rather, be worthy of at least a half-share. Though I did not have much to offer by way of skills, I knew how to be an animal, flying through those rocks like a beast. The deck had to be cleared for the next haul back, coming in twenty minutes. Some rocks were so big they had to be removed from the deck using rock chains and the winch. And so it went, haul back after haul back, digging, clawing, and throwing rocks like maniacs. I knew that the ridicule would have been worse had I not proved willing to dive into that rock pile with everything I had. I worked at a frenetic pace I am sure everyone thought unsustainable. But I never slacked off. When the scallop basket was full, I went aft to the shucking boxes and dumped the scallops where the crew was shucking them, a skill yet beyond me. But I sure knew how to pick the pile, shovel, and throw rocks. I was a rock star.

# *Full Gale*

**Unless our goal** was to acquire the material to build a castle, the fishing was not so good anywhere we went on the shoals. Rick left the rakes on deck and decided to steam to a different spot. Most of us were work-tired, so we hit the bunks for a snooze. The sky had been darkening, and Great Round Shoal started to chop up as we turned in.

Sometime later, the ship's horn blowing in groups of three startled us to consciousness. From my Boy Scout days, I knew that a group of three of anything was a universal distress signal. Rick must have been ringing the bell with the other hand as that was clanging too. Even I knew something was wrong: we were not moving forward—only severely rocking side to side. A fierce autumn gale had kicked up while we slept; I heard a shout from the wheelhouse down into the fo'c'sle.

"All hands on deck! All hands on deck!"

It was the Cap. We all jumped out of our bunks, slipped into our boots, and raced up the doghouse ladder like ants out of a burning ant hill.

"We lost the steering! We have a battery fire!" Rick barked from the open wheelhouse window.

The *Janet and Jean*, without steering and unable to head into the seas, naturally laid broadside to the gale. She was gut-punched, and violently rocking from port to starboard, so much so we all knew we could roll over. Gale force winds shrieked through the rigging. The stays, the metal cables running from the mast and booms, are of various lengths, producing different notes in the scale when storm winds cut through them. They are not usually harmonious, a chorus of demons howling some tortured opera. All this coming out of a nice nap.

I managed to put myself in the thick of this situation. Maybe it was the Boy Scout training; we were always preparing for some sort of emergency. I went aft with everyone and learned that a couple of bolts had let go on the port side that secured the metal steering cable housing to the hull. It had detached, and the cable was loose, scraping across the top of the battery banks, causing an acid fire. The quadrant, a quarter pie-shaped piece of wood that sits atop the rudder shaft and the terminus for the steering cable, was swinging back and forth erratically. Whatever the quadrant was doing, so too was the rudder. It could snap off, not built to withstand such treatment. Guys were slipping and falling all over. I went below with Rick, and he did not discourage me.

Skip shouted above the wail of the wind, "Green water on deck!"

I learned that clear, foamy water on deck might be only a few inches deep, certainly within the ability of the scuppers to let it through and overboard. Green water on deck is deep water, a foot, maybe more. The scuppers cannot handle that kind of water, and the boat is in imminent danger of capsizing. It was blowing about 50 mph. I got my first look at twenty-foot-plus seas coming at us like two and three-story buildings, one behind the other.

They would be manageable heading into them, but we were vulnerable laying broadside. Though I would see taller seas than this in the years to come, this greenhorn initiation was humbling. The elements are indifferent.

The engineer was already there and told Rick he managed to get the acid fire extinguished. They were trying to figure a way to secure the housing of the steering cable to the hull. Each extreme roll of the vessel laid us over more than before, the pendulum of a clock he had to beat. Tools from the engine room and anything not tied or bolted down were flying and crashing everywhere, heavy projectiles. I grabbed a flashlight and lit up Rick's work area, trying to remain steady and upright. At least in this, I found a way to be useful.

Rick yelled to Dan, "Get me bolts!" Dan disappeared into the engine room.

"We've got no bolts," he hollered back.

"Then shit the goddamn bolts!" Dick became a force of nature himself. I marveled a little that he would say such a thing. What's Dan going to do with that?

I had forgotten at this time that the engineer didn't like me and thought I was a threat to his well-being and financial solvency. What I cared more about was that he knew his shit. Dan disappeared into the engine room and came back a few seconds later with some "C" clamps. What a dope I was. I thought they were "sea clamps," you know, because they were clamps, and we were at sea, right? A "C" clamp looks like the letter "C." The bottom part is adjustable, screwing up and down like a vise. Rick grabbed them and clamped the housing back to the hull with some difficulty, given the pitching back and forth. He ran back up into the wheelhouse, started the boat forward, and headed into the seas. The insane rolling from side to side stopped. Now it was just the usual mayhem of a full gale. Rick gave the wheel to one of the crew and came back down below to where I was still standing, a horse's ass with a flashlight.

"Mickey," he said in his craggy-voiced Sam Elliot, "I want you to crawl in there between the battery banks and keep that flashlight on the "C" clamps. If they let go, yell. And keep an eye on the quadrant. If the cable slips off, yell."

I crawled into a narrow space between two open wooden casements that held the batteries. Knees tucked up under my chin, acrid fumes from the battery banks wafted up into my eyes. The quadrant, my new word for the day, was threaded again with the steering cable. When Rick turned to starboard, the quadrant swung from right to left about an inch from my face. It is in this way I entered Nantucket Harbor in a full gale. I could be no lower or further aft on the *Janet and Jean*. Once in the shelter of the harbor, things calmed down with the rocking and rolling. I wiggled and contorted out of this narrow space one limb at a time, untying the knot of me, bound by the battery banks and the moving quadrant, thinking of Houdini performing one of his trademark escapes.

Up on deck, I sucked in the fresh air that went down a lot better than acid electrical fire air. Rick thanked me for having squeezed into that tight space during the gale. If we had indeed capsized, apparently the plan of our friend Gale, I would have had the worst chance of making it to the surface. But I walked straight into the situation instead of watching on the periphery like a good little greenhorn. No one would have faulted me for that. I didn't know much, but I was skinny and sure knew how to point a flashlight. You go with what you've got.

# Nantucket Liquor Run

**We made it** into Nantucket harbor alive. Good. I went up on deck to gaze upon this old seaport, the home port in Melville's classic *Moby Dick*. Nantucket, like Provincetown, seen from the harbor, looked like it was the year 1889. My Ishmael fantasy was kicking into high gear now. But this was not "the trap in the drain of the world." This was a fine spring where the elite slaked their thirst. The harbor was full of expensive yachts with their perfectly coiled lines. Even though I was a greenhorn, I knew we did not fit in at this squeaky-clean mon-eyed port of Nantucket, we scroungy scallopers from P'town—roaches crawling across a fine linen tablecloth.

All my recollections worth telling about fishing trips have two parts. The first recounts the perils, adventures, tight spots, and near-death experiences at sea. The second almost always recounts the perils, adventures, tight spots, and near-death experiences ashore in a strange port. This first time was no exception.

When you get "blown in" to a port, the usual procedure is that the captain will sell off a few bags of scallops so the crew can go out on the town, or rather "hit" the town . . . hard. This trip was aborted early by the failed steering and bad fishing, so there wasn't much to sell.

After the *Janet and Jean* was tied up and secured, many of the crew headed for the nearest bar. Being typical fishermen, they had little or no money in their pockets when they started on this trip. I tagged along, feeling like a puppy, asking how we were going to pay for drinks. Dan waved off the question.

We entered an upscale establishment. A lot of "Todds" here: neat hair-cuts and cable-knit sweaters, trophy girlfriends with hair just so, and perfect makeup. There were four of us. Skip and another crew member split off and went for the tables at the far end of the room, and sat down. I was near the bar with my shipmate and was told not to move. Obedient puppy stayed.

Skip and the other mate began arguing loudly over something, drawing everyone's attention. Then they threw punches, seriously beating on each other, escalating to turning over tables, tossing chairs; it was pandemonium—glasses breaking, people diving out of the way, girlfriends screaming. The bartender vaulted over the bar and ran to the end of the room where my shipmates were fighting. A coiled spring releasing, the shipmate next to me bounded over the bar, grabbed two bottles of hard liquor from the top shelf, jumped back over, and ran like hell out the door. I stood there in a daze for a few seconds trying to digest what had just happened. A small voice in my head was saying I ought to consider leaving too. So, like I was on satellite delay, I took off, a few seconds behind the bottle thief.

Eventually, we all met back at the boat for a drunken card game and lots of laughter. I had made an excellent start to my initiation. I had been through my first gale, my first equipment failure, my first near-death experience, and my first maritime lapse of judgment. I was on my way.

# *Inroads*

**There were a** few little things that helped elevate me up the food chain a speck. The first was the crazy, animalistic way I attacked the "pile" on deck. The goal there was to suggest that I wasn't afraid of a little work. I believe they noticed. That is currency on a boat.

The second resulted from being a lifer in the Boy Scouts and Eagle Scout: I had experience working with rope. It raised a few eyebrows that I knew how to tie some basic nautical knots that luckily happened to be scouting staples.

But the most significant lift I got from the crew of the *Janet and Jean* was from having friends in Nantucket via Nova Scotia. First was Mike Phillips, part carpenter/part wizard, who had a degree in "Wood" from Goddard College. Getting shot at in a steaming jungle came in low on his priority list, so Mike built a log cabin on the Fraser Road in Princedale, Nova Scotia, about two years before I did. He was from Nantucket and brought two of our Nova Scotian friends back with him. Greg McEwan, his father Chief of the Mi'kmaq tribe at the Bear River reservation, was soon to be Chief himself. On a quest to make some money, he was cooking in a restaurant. Rhonda McCauley was there, too. Rhonda was with George Goodin when he built the first log cabin of the hippie era on the Fraser Road after living in a treehouse on Vancouver Island. She was kind, knew how to rough it, liked good music, and had a lovely singing voice. I honestly don't remember if it resonated with me then, but all of us had been at that Nova Scotia party when we mounted the rack of moose horns that connected us all now in Nantucket.

Mike was on a carpentry gig in New York, but we found Rhonda babysitting a swanky house owned by affluent summertime residents. O'Brian and I went to see her.

"Bring the boys from the boat over," she said at the door. "They can all get showers, and I'll whip up something to eat."

The boats in the '70s mainly were older boats from the '40s, '50s, and '60s, so they did not have showers like all boats do nowadays. If you were on a 12-day trip, you didn't shower till you got back to port. The crew jumped at the opportunity, and soon we were all clean and rid of that "just been picking the pile up on deck" smell. Rhonda threw together a bottomless rice, ground beef, and onion thing that we all just shoveled down. Greg joined us at our multimillion-dollar house on the waterfront. Guitars and drinking happened. This kind of situational improvement rarely happens on a fishing trip, and I could feel my standing on the *Janet and Jean* tick up a little, a slight easing of the initiation rite. Otherwise, we would have been stuck on that putrid boat. Boats smell worse when they are tied up. A working vessel always smells better because the engineer pumps its foul bilges regularly when at sea, and the deck gets washed clean continually.

The storm that blew us into Nantucket was a stubborn system, but we finally made ready on the morning of the third day. The harbormaster took the long walk down the pier, looking like he had something to say, and was having a tough time holding back till he reached the *Janet and Jean*. He told the skipper he never wanted to see our boat in Nantucket again. We stood there on deck, delinquent schoolboys looking down at our boots during a scolding, shuffling back and forth, suppressing smiles. We were proud of that. It seemed quite a distinction. I decided I wanted to be a fisherman.

## Poet Laureate of the F/V Doggerel

**One other thing** helped elevate me from dog shit on a boot status towards something resembling humanity. Near the end of our stay in Nantucket, I began writing a poem about our exploit at sea without steering in a full gale. Guys were curious about what I was writing, and I think if it had been poetry about anything else, I would have been further ostracized. But I let them see what I was doing and that it was a poem about *them*; well, that made a difference. Rick, a hopeless romantic, was excited that I was writing about his boat.

Just a rhyming piece of doggerel; it was an accurate account of what happened. Started in Nantucket, finished on the bow of the *Janet and Jean* in Provincetown Harbor; the guys thought it was great. I had gone from piece of shit shacker to Poet Laureate of the *Janet and Jean* in a short time. I could safely say it was less likely I'd have a dredge dropped on me.

# "*The Voyage of the* Janet and Jean"

**Part I**
A renegade crew chasing their dreams
steamed out of P'town on the *Janet and Jean.*
She was named for two sea witches who haunted the shoals
plundering sailors in times of old.

The crew they were seven, though they worked like nine.
They were far from heaven, and most had done time.
John and Bobby, Lobster and Mick,
Skip and Dan and Captain Rick.

They steamed at midnight on the tempestuous sea,
and each one wondered what their fate would be.
The wind, she blew and kicked up the sea
she tossed and turned the *Janet and Jean.*

The captain decided early that day
to steam to safety in Nantucket's bay.
So she chugged and tugged up and down the swells,
each tried to waste her and send her to hell.

The storm was hand-picked from the lair of Thor
with the wrath of Poseidon 'tween them and the shore.
About two hours out, the steering broke free,
sending the ship wild, just a leaf on the sea.

**Part II**
"All hands on deck!" Rick shouted aloud; his voice had just gone hoarse.
"This ship is in trouble, I hate to say, I can't keep her on her course."
The men, they rushed up to the deck. The atmosphere was frantic.
The swells seemed bent on sending the ship to the bottom of the Atlantic.

The boat was rocking with incredible force; we all thought we might die.
One moment we were looking at sea, the next we were looking at sky.
The captain went aft and tore up the boards exposing the unleashed rudder.
He looked at her swaying back and forth, and in his heart, he shuddered.

"Get bolts!" the captain yelled from b'low to the grease-covered engineer,
and when he couldn't find those blasted bolts, his concern had turned to fear.
"I have none, Rick!" the engineer shouted, "There are none about I fear!"
"Then shit them!!" the captain promptly replied, "And bring them to me here!"

He jury-rigged her good and tight—the steering was restored—she knifed right
through those mammoth swells just as she did before.
They made it to the harbor clean before they could have sunk, so the pirate crew
of the *Janet and Jean* got really fucking drunk. 9/27/77

# Feather White

**We got hit** by a magnificent nor'easter on our second trip. One of the deckhands jumped down the doghouse ladder in full oil gear, the last sea he took in the face still running down the front of him.

"It's feather white out there," he said, pulling back his dripping hood as he went for the coffee pot.

I had no idea what he was talking about; its meaning was evident when I made it topside. This is a term sometimes used by fishermen to describe very stormy conditions. Whitecaps, the tops of wind-sheared seas, are indistinguishable from the white-feathered breast of a sea bird. When it's "feather white" out there, there is more white than blue. Even in a full gale, sea birds manage to take to the air, preferable to angry seas, with their white breasts painted, it seems, with the same brush that feathered the seas.

My journal relates a series of busted trips, primarily due to *Janet and Jean*'s poor condition. Once we were steaming back to P'town during some sloppy weather, she lost power during my wheel watch. We were only four miles off the beach around Nauset, a place that has claimed vessels for hundreds of years. The engineer had little margin for error in getting the engine going again as the seas pushed us toward the bars off the beach. It turned out it was a leak in the fuel line. Dan patched it up, and we, as they often said on the boats, "headed for the barn."

The steering on the *Janet and Jean* was more of a concept than an actuality, breaking new ground for use of the phrase, "play in the wheel." In later years, after a few more boats, I realized just how bad it was. On a calm night, I had my two-hour watch, steering us in the blackness. The course was 180 degrees due south and the Nantucket (Great Round) Shoals again. Alone in the wheelhouse with the faint glow of the instruments, every other soul on the boat was sleeping. That 180 on the compass ball kept eluding me. The bearing was swinging too far to port. I turned the wheel, steering into the bearing as instructed, but nothing happened. I turned harder. Nothing. *What the fuck*. I turned the wheel even more, and finally, that 180 started to come right. I eased up so I could slow the turn and return to our bearing. Now the bearing was swinging to starboard with a vengeance, so I turned the other way. But 180 was so far to starboard we were making our way to Iowa. There was so much play in the wheel I had no idea where the rudder was in relation to the wheel. Meanwhile, everyone slept; outside, I saw nothingness. Inside, the orange radar blips I was not supposed to run into were poking me in the eye, and that maddening compass toyed with me.

*Fuck it.* I turned the wheel hard over as far as it would go to port. I had to figure out where the wheel and the rudder synched. I proceeded to steam the *Janet and Jean* in a 360-degree circle. With the full circle nearing completion, I was able to ease the wheel early enough that I was able to bring her back to 180. I never told anyone what I had done while they slept, and no one ever knew, except perhaps for someone on another vessel, paying too much attention to their radar screen.

The longer I was on the *Janet and Jean*, the more I realized that she was a well-made boat that had been allowed to deteriorate. The boat owner spent a fortune buying the boat but would sometimes come up cheap on the upkeep. The result is unsafe conditions. Chris Scanlan was looking more like a genius every day.

We made a short trip often referred to as a "pirate run" and lost the steering again. This time the metal steering cable just snapped. Rick and Dan jury-rigged it with rope adding even more play in the steering. Not good, but, hey, it got us back to port.

# *Blood and Rust*

**After finishing gear** work one afternoon, most of the crew left the boat to go home. I stayed because, well, it *was* my home. Engineer Dan decided that it was a good idea to fight for the "fun" of it, perhaps a vestigial form of amusement from his biker days. I was never much of a fighter. The only fights I ever won were ones where I completely lost my mind and went, as my childhood friend Tom coined it, "animal." That is, to go batshit berserk and overwhelm my opponent. So, Dan started our little recreational diversion by smashing me square in the mouth and laughing. The laughing was my cue that this was all quite a lot of fun. Cool. I was so glad to be having fun again, tasting the iron in my blood. I was obliged to hit *him* in the mouth now, this being a pissing contest with fists. Confident I understood the rules, I hauled off and pounded his face. But he got mad and hit me again, only this time he was more passionate, more

Scallop dredge on deck (fun to roll around on while fighting).

committed to putting a hurt on me. *What did I do wrong? You're mad that I hit you back? This was your fucking idea.*

Soon we were rolling around on deck on the gear and cables, blood and rust mingling. I was fighting for my life, but Dan was laughing. *Gee whiz, isn't this fun?* What hurt more was a toss-up, the punches or the dredge and gear as we rolled over them. Tourists on the wharf gaped at the polar bears in their natural habitat, trying to kill each other. Dan, having the time of his life, played to the crowd. Me, not so much. I think this was about him coming to terms with accepting me but saving face somehow, keeping the power. But when he got a headlock on me, I kicked it up a notch and went "animal." He didn't know what to do with that, so Dan decided he'd had enough, and soon we were swilling beer at the Fo'c'sle bar through our swollen bloody lips. Yep, buddies now, buying each other beers. Fat-lipped, stupid freakin' blood brothers. I wondered what the apple pickers were up to right about then.

# *Deb vs. the* Janet and Jean

**Lobster and I** continued to live on the boat in Provincetown Harbor since we weren't making enough money to afford a place. The cast iron stove operated only when fishing, so the fo'c'sle of the *Janet and Jean* was chilly.

Rick O'Brian was a dedicated man, and he threw all his effort into making the boat do well. Unfortunately for him, his wife, Deb, thought that a little more dedication should be coming her way and a little less to those bitches Janet and Jean, for they were genuinely needy girls. Deb resented anything that took Rick away from her, so the boat became her enemy. She started by putting sugar in the gas tank of that old army truck so he wouldn't be able to drive to the harbor. There was discord and arguments. But none of us were ready for what would be a step up in the duel between Deb and Janet and Jean.

Lobster and I were sleeping in our floating home. We awoke well after midnight by what sounded like a fight on the wharf and a woman screaming obscenities. We made our way up the doghouse ladder in a haze, having only recently fallen asleep after an evening at the Fo'c'sle bar.

The first image that made its way through our sluggish brains was a police car's blue and red flashing lights. Rick was there. And, oh yes, Deb was there, fighting to free herself from the police and hurling obscenities at Rick and the boat. Lots of "F" bombs. Boy, the mouth on her.

Lobster and I thought the whole scene interesting. Then our depth perception kicked in, wait a minute, the boat, the scene on the wharf, weren't we a lot farther away than we should be? What was in Deb's hand that the cops were trying to wrest from her? It was a knife of the butcher variety. She was screaming bloody murder, cursing the boat.

Then it dawned on both of us. Deb had *cut the lines* to the *Janet and Jean* and cast us adrift in the black of night. We were bound on the outgoing tide toward the breakwater. She had decided to rid her life of her chief competitor. So what if there were a few souls aboard? They were part of this conspiracy, too, dammit.

By then, we were too far out to throw anyone a line. A skipper from one of the other boats quickly got his vessel going and pushed us back to the wharf where we tied up. I had thought all the craziness happened when we were *out* to sea, but we were not immune at the waterfront. What if she had gotten away with it? We'd have been sound asleep, adrift in the darkness with no running lights, a hazard to ourselves and all shipping.

Between the first and second trips, the crew agreed to make me a full share crew member. Though not unheard of, most shackers did at least another trip half share. I guess it didn't matter much. A full share of nothing isn't much more than half share of nothing. I was learning, and that was certainly worthwhile. In the meantime, I fell in love with being at sea.

Provincetown seemed the next step in the salt water progression of my life. The Atlantic Ocean was the very reason for my hometown's existence, the city itself water-bound on Absecon Island. Our house in Atlantic City was right on the bay and four blocks from the ocean. We were always scavenging at low tide by the bay year-round. We tempted the salt water ice by walking on it when the bay froze in winter. Kids who lived near the bay in Atlantic City were "Bay Rats," and we all grew up in rowboats, speedboats, body surfing, and mudflat digging. You could always hear the ocean wherever you were. We crabbed and fished year-round. I loved the way a good nor'easter would whistle through the ill-fitted storm windows of my bedroom at night. Now I was riding the high seas, something it seemed I was in training for my whole life.

P'town and AC shared a similar dynamic. I came from an ocean town that was a great place to grow up but had the unfortunate blight of being inundated with hordes of tourists we had to cater to because they were the town's economic lifeblood. There wasn't a townie alive in Atlantic City who didn't yearn for Labor Day, after which we could have our home back again. Mom used to say they "rolled the sidewalks up" after Labor Day. We went to the beach year-round: tackle football in the fall, during storms in January, hand in hand with your girl.

## Hookup Man

**I began to** work with the gear as a hookup man for the winchman, a position requiring some skill and a definitive promotion from lowly "shacker." With two rakes aboard, there are starboard and portside winchmen and hookup men. When the skipper rings the bell for haul back, he puts the engine in neutral, and the "power take-off" part of the engine is used to power the winches as the two drums reel in both rakes. Nylon line, spliced into the cable at intervals of ten fathoms, allows the winchmen to judge when the dredge will break surface. The hookup men wait for this at the gallous.

Yes, I found out what the gallous was. Sometimes called gallows, they are heavy metal frames with a block suspended in the middle through which the tow cable runs. When the dredge breaks surface at the gallous, the hookup man takes a heavy Gilson hook, the business end of the block and tackle, and puts it through the bull ring at the top of the rake.

I am told my description of how the dredges are brought over the rails and dumped is about as exciting as studying a gearbox schematic of a Mack truck transmission. So, I have conscientiously spared details. Suffice it to say, the choreography between the winchman and hookup man is nuanced and quite dangerous, every haul-back a potential opportunity to lose life or limb. Wanna lose a foot getting sucked into a deck block or get your skull pulverized by a wayward dredge? Not today.

It all worked reasonably well in the calm but was a real rodeo in foul weather. Two years later, and on another boat, we would fish in winds up to 55 mph. Those dredges, loaded with rocks, coming over the rails in that kind of weather were some of the most frightening things I ever saw. As a deckhand, you had to be agile and extraordinarily alert to get out of the way while your work surface undulated with the sea. The dredges weighed almost a ton empty and were considerably heavier when filled with rocks, mud, scallops, and debris.

Once the dredges were dumped of their contents and set out again, the mad scramble to attack "the pile" began on deck. Dig out the scallops, throw rocks over the side, and shovel the mud. The sand and mud could be the worst because they seemed suctioned to the deck. Then shuck the scallops, and haul back again in twenty to thirty minutes. This routine was repeated hour after hour, twenty-four hours a day for seven to fourteen days, depending. Yeah. No banana daiquiris on this cruise.

After some instruction, I got to be OK at hooking up. Instruction consisted mainly of yelling and OK being defined as hooking up for several watches without getting killed or maimed. One of the takeaways from this boat that is still a part of my constitution is a phrase Captain Rick would often use during the commission of some assigned task. A crew member might question one of his instructions or the feasibility of its completion. Rick would say, "Whatever it takes." On a boat, there is no room for "That's not part of my job description." We were all trying to keep this thing afloat, fill the hold and get home alive. Just do whatever it takes to get the job done. Next.

# *Shucking*

**So if you** manage to hook up correctly, set out the gear without getting killed, attack "the pile" like a wild man, and get the deck cleared, there is still an area of this whole operation that every scalloper is judged by: how fast can you shuck scallops? The quicker you shuck, the more 40-pound bags of scallop go down to the fish hold. That is where the money is. Shucking scallops efficiently and quickly requires skill. Those who are good at it are respected. Those who are otherworldly at it are revered. In the 1970s, the two best shuckers in the fleet were Jo-Jo and Richard Dickey. I had the opportunity to fish with both.

The part of the scallop we eat is the muscle that the scallop uses to open and close the shell to jet propel itself. I learned that, on average, only one in ten scallops get swept up in the dredge. The rest swim out of the way. A scallop can swim for miles in this way. If you are fishing for small scallops (we called it fishing the "peanut pile"), it can take about 1600 scallops to fill a standard gallon bucket. Average size scallops take a lot less. Occasionally, we would find a bed of huge scallops. We called them "pie plates" after the outsized shell.

The trick to shucking fast is to shuck efficiently. It's easy to *look* like you are shucking fast with furious hand motion, but the efficient shucker will beat the fast and furious every time as there is no wasted motion. The results are in the bucket, nowhere else. Jo-Jo was the fast and furious type, but he was efficient enough that he was a remarkable sight: flash and efficiency together. He held the scallop out, away from his belly. Dickey had a completely different style, wearing a black rubber bib in addition to his oil gear because he held the scallop right up on his stomach. Dickey didn't even look like he was that much better than a decent cutter. But man, could he fill up those buckets. Not a wasted move. I think he was the best in the fleet, and there were a lot of guys who agreed.

The buckets were all dumped into a stainless-steel washer and at the end of the watch. While the next watch took over the towing, hauling back and shucking, you wash the scallops with seawater from the deck hose. Once cleaned, they were poured into 40-pound capacity cloth bags and tied tightly with wire using a twisting tool. And like anything else in this trade, there is a specific skill to crimping up the overloaded cloth bag and twisting the wire, a two-person operation. There was always competition between watches. Each watch wanted to put more bags in the hole than the other.

# *The Fish Hold*

**Storing the bags** in the fish hold was serious business. The fish hold consisted of several pens below deck, separated by a middle walkway. One pen was designated for the bulk of the food. Roasts (beef, lamb, pork, and ham), ground beef, many gallons of milk, a turkey for the last night, and various other perishables were all buried here in ice. Keeping the food iced properly was the cook's responsibility. His daily commute included the fish hold to retrieve that day's meals.

Scallops must be chilled on top of the ice for a watch before the next watch could pack in them. Just a few light shovels full sufficed for the first six hours. If packed tight right away without chilling, the bag would melt some of the packing ice around it, creating an air pocket and a less than optimal temperature. Anyone storing the scallops had to make sure none of the bags touched the wood of the pen. Wood catches bacteria, so a good ice buffer separates the bag from the bulkheads and pen boards. Nobody wanted to risk their life under ridiculous conditions and show up in port with a catch that had gone bad.

# Off-Watch

**After bagging and** storing the scallops, it was oil gear off and down to the fo'c'sle for breakfast, lunch or dinner. All storage chores and mealtime took place on your six hours off. So now you are down to five and a half or even five off. You are awakened a half hour before your next watch so you can eat your meal and make ready to go back on deck for another six hours. If you were lucky, you'd get four hours of sleep before the craziness started all over again.

Meals were usually a lot of fun. The off-watch would rehash what had just happened on deck the last six hours. Lousy weather, lousy gear, funny situations, near injuries, inept greenhorns, stories of wrecks, past trips, and the female body's nuances were all discussed with gusto over the meal. The food, no matter how good or bad, was wolfed down at an alarming rate. These men had worked their bodies to the brink of exhaustion, so the caloric requirements were significant.

Some guys were misers with their off-watch time. Once they had eaten, they popped right into their bunks for much-needed sleep. Others would be too wound up and could be counted on to hang at the table for a while and tell deranged jokes or play cards. Up on deck, the boat was fishing, and you could hear the other watch working the gear. If they were having a problem with something on deck, it was not uncommon for an off-watch guy to climb up the doghouse ladder part-way and offer annoying criticisms.

Most guys slept like stones on the boats, but for a greenhorn, sleep could prove elusive. Though the vessel was wooden, the deck, amidships where the dredges dropped, had thick steel plates bolted to its surface. Dropping the dredges and working the gear sounded like a car accident on deck during the haul back/emptying process. Picture trying to sleep through two locomotives dropping on the floor above you every twenty minutes. After several days of slogging around in a sleep-deprived state of pain, I was snoring away through train wrecks on deck, just like the pros.

# *The Railway*

**The boat had** a breakage or malfunction issue with every trip. Rick had been pleading with the owner between trips that the vessel was unsafe and required critical repairs. After yet another "busted" trip (a trip where we made little or no money), Rick informed the owner he would no longer put his crew at risk.

"If you don't make the necessary repairs, you'll be looking for a different captain," he said.

The owner knew full well he wasn't going to get any captain with half a brain to set foot on this disaster waiting to happen, so the *Janet and Jean* went up on the railway. Thank you, O'Brian.

When Rick told us the boat was going "up on the rails," I had no idea what that meant, but I soon learned that P'town had two boatyards: Flyers and Taves. Each yard had what looked like railroad tracks that went straight down into the water. On these tracks rested what they called a cradle. The cradle had railroad wheels that sat on the rails, and the whole thing had a metal cable connected to a winch in the boatyard.

I was on the boat when they hauled her out of the water. We brought her from the wharf over to Flyer's Boatyard, where a cradle awaited us, submerged in the high tide. Wooden ribs stuck up out of the water on either side of it. Rick piloted the vessel in between these ribs and tied up. Then we waited for the tide to go out. As the water lowered, the boat would sit squarely in the cradle, no longer afloat. A powerful winch hauled her out of the water and into the boatyard.

It was an odd sensation, taking this little train ride on a boat that gained altitude as she gained the boatyard. Finally, when she was up and out of the water, it seemed we were three stories tall. One of the yard workers laid a tall ladder against the boat amidships, and, whether you had issues with height or not, you'd have to commit to a bouncy wooden ladder to terra firma below.

I have always loved the lines, look and feel of an eastern rigged wooden fishing vessel with its wheelhouse aft and big bow forward. But you can't fully appreciate it until you see one hauled up out of the water. Most of the boat on an eastern rigged vessel is below the waterline—deep hulls that make for seaworthiness in the storms of the North Atlantic. On the rails, it is here that you could see her depth and gorgeous elliptical lines, a signature feature of all Harvey Gamage's works. Skip and I remained with Rick working on the boat in the shipyard for $25 a day. I was never good at math, but right around then, picking apples was looking like the more lucrative career choice.

But I was hooked: the sea, fishing, Provincetown, adventure in abundance. Apple picking could not compete with this, the only danger being the possibility of falling off a ladder in an orchard. No sir. It's a pirate's life for me.

The men who worked the shipyard were characters who very often had fished themselves, especially the old-timers. Here in the boatyard, older artisans were valued for their knowledge and experience. When work shut down at the end of the day, we would go inside the shop where they had an old potbelly stove cranking with hardwood. We'd hang out there with the ancient mariners in their worn coveralls, and someone would break out a bottle of whiskey, everyone taking a pull off the bottle. That's when the tales began to flow, stories of storms fifty years ago, boats and men lost, talk of unforgettable characters and their exploits, funny anecdotes, and memorable ships.

And then the conversation turned to the inevitable: the loss of the *Patricia Marie*, a fresh wound in the psyche of everyone in town. This Provincetown scalloper was headed for the barn during a storm in October of 1976. Other boats last saw her going down into the trough between seas. Instead of popping back up on the mountain before the next valley, she never emerged. All hands lost and a town with a big hole in its heart. I heard the names of these much-loved men who had gone down with her the whole time I was in Provincetown. A close-knit fishing town never gets over a loss like this. Adding to the difficulty of grieving this loss is that often there are no bodies to say goodbye to, no burial at a graveside, or not with an occupied coffin.

Within two years, one of my close friends in Nova Scotia lost a nephew, Joey Milner, on a scalloper. I went to the memorial on the pier in Annapolis Royal, N.S. All the grieving family had was a wreath with their loved one's name written in flowers: *"Joey."* At the ordained time, the family threw the wreath to the outgoing tide and watched it fade on its journey to the sea.

These men, standing around the wood stove, speaking of grave matters, were sacred, were druids. I just listened during these sessions, feeling privileged to be there. The shop looked like it could be the 1880s, cluttered with all things nautical: hawsers, blocks, machinery whose purpose was a mystery to me. A boatyard incense of rope, sawdust, oil, and wood smoke consecrated everything.

During one of these sessions, a gale blew outside. Rick had brought a bottle of whiskey. The old-timers took a pull or two from the bottle, but that was it for them. When the session broke up, there was much of the bottle remaining, so Rick and I climbed back up the wobbly ladder in the dark and went into the wheelhouse of the *Janet and Jean* to do our level best to polish off the bottle.

The wind shrieked through the rigging, but the boat was perfectly still. I had a little trouble walking. My brain was telling me to reengage my sea legs when I didn't need them. Rick had a good heart and a playful sense of humor. But what I remember most about him was his passion for everything. We talked of the sea and things we were going to accomplish. He wanted to get the *J&J* back into shape and make her one of the most productive boats in the fleet.

## *Bilge Work*

**So began the** next and least glamorous phase of my nautical education. There were a lot of things wrong with the *Janet and Jean*, many best left to the experts. However, the shit jobs suited me perfectly. One of them was working in the bilges. At the bottom of the boat, where the ribs meet the keel, the vessel's backbone, is the bilges: foul, oily water. The bilge needs to move between the lowest parts of the ribs. Here the wood has holes drilled through called limber holes. Blockage of the limber holes impedes pumping out the bilges properly, and the space between the ribs becomes stinky sludge.

My new work home was down in the engine room, in the cold and damp-ness, reaching into the awful smelling, slimy bilge water with a teaspoon, dig-ging at stones and scum that clogged the limber holes. The worst was trying to clear the holes under the diesel engine in a prone position, reaching into black muck at awkward angles, trying to unclog holes I could not see but only feel. The cold crept deep into my bones, and at the end of the day, only a long soak in an almost scalding hot tub would put a dent in it. Stretched out in an oil spill, contorting and digging at a stubborn stone in a limber hole under the diesel engine with fingers and a spoon, I had an epiphany. *BA in English. Yeah.* The journal entries from this time are smudged with grime and oil scum.

# The "Bethel"

**It was around** this time I fell in with a cast of characters, fisherman all, who had rented the upstairs of a house at the East End and called it "the Bethel." A true seaman's bethel is a port in a storm, a town-subsidized mariner's hostel for out-of-town fishermen who get blown in. Our bethel, however, was a house of rowdy, partying fisherman who kept the doors open to stranded men of the sea.

Lobster and I were looking for a place because the boat, our home, was "up on the 'ways." Dan was already living at the Bethel and suggested we crash there for a while until we found something. At this stage, he had gotten past my greenness and was a lot more civil to me, dating back to when we pounded each other senseless. Looking back on it, I was almost always just a half-step ahead of homelessness.

The Bethel was presided over by Ralph Meyer. Ralph was a complex character, and he became a true friend to me. He was older, I guess in his 30s, articulate and well-read. He was possessed of a cynical view of the world and had a matching well-developed sardonic wit. Philosophically, he was the Byron to my Shelley. I think a cynic will sometimes connect with a dreamer, seeing something of their former selves in them. They may criticize the dreamer's ways but will secretly revel in them. The pain of innocence lost still stings. We took to each other at once.

Ralph loved to sit at the kitchen table in his dark clothes, puffing slowly and dramatically on a Lucky Strike, like in a '50s noir film, sipping a beer. Mostly, he would listen. Then, if a conversation interested him enough, he'd take a pull on the Lucky, eyes squinting a bit as some of the smoke wafted up and say something that meant more than met the eye. Sometimes he might think something was funny, and he would burst forth with a loud belly laugh that went on longer than you thought it should. *Man, I guess he thought that was funny.* Although I never knew what he was going to find amusing, I made him laugh a lot. Ralph liked poetry and was interested in hearing my stuff when I told him I was a poet. Cynic that he was, his favorite poet was Charles Bukowski, whose work was a revelation. I devoured *Mockingbird, Wish Me Luck* in a sitting.

Ralph, though a fisherman by trade, avoided fishing studiously. Only when the bills had to be met or were alarmingly overdue would he extricate himself from his kitchen chair/throne, where he observed and commented on the world, to make a trip. His lack of desire for work earned him the nickname Captain Drive. He would occasionally go as cook on the *Connie F.*

Dan got a site on the *Cape Star*. A "site" is a job, a position on a fishing vessel. Usually, that site was yours until you told the skipper you'd be "getting through" and moving on. There were many parties, not just here but at different houses. The lobstermen brought lobster, scallopers, scallops, and so on, assuring that we ate the very best seafood all the time for free.

Evenings at the Bethel were always an event. The kitchen table became the altar for beer and whiskey bottles, card games, pot smoking, tales of our fishing trips, plans, and raunchy jokes. One (dark and stormy) night, we were hosting a crew from New Bedford that had gotten blown into P'town by a wicked nor'easter. The crew was very shaken by reports the fellow New Bedford eastern rigger *Navigator* sank with all hands that night. Having been through the *Patricia Marie*, our Provincetown guys were very sympathetic.

The Bethel did not have a shower but rather an old claw-toed bathtub. The water pressure consistently low; it took an eternity to draw a bath. One of the New Bedford crew was filling his tub for a much-needed cleanse. There were a bunch of us drinking at the table and playing cards. We all seemed to be having a great time when the guy waiting for the tub to fill picked up a beer bottle and threw it across the table, hitting one of our guys, a fellow named Jerry Auk, hard on the cheekbone. *What the fuck?* There was no argument, no provocation.

A bunch of us grabbed the guy, who was incoherent by this time. Although the bottle didn't break, Jerry had a good-sized egg growing on his cheekbone. We ushered the drunken New Bedford guy off to his bath. Matt Russe, a much-beloved P'town character, had just come back from the bathroom. After we left the assailant to his bathwater, we brought Matt up to speed.

"Man, what an asshole. That guy hit Jerry in the face with a bottle."

"That's alright," said Matt, "I just pissed in the bathtub."

Boatyard repairs continued on the *J&J*. Once she was up out of the water, her needs were so much more apparent. One of the planks on the starboard side near the bow needed replacement. If she popped a plank at sea, there would be very little time to react. That is what happened to Joey Milner's boat up in Nova Scotia. So, I got to see how a straight piece of wood becomes this curved, perfect plank that seals up the ship's armor against the elements. The men in the boatyard were experts at this.

A long cylindrical metal tube, a foot in diameter, was placed near the side of the boat and hooked up to a steam-making machine. The long plank is inserted into the tube and sealed off with canvas. I was way up on deck, observing from above. After the allotted time, a team of workers removed the plank and lifted it into place on the hull. The steam made the thick plank malleable and is bent right into the curve of the forward section of the hull.

I was making $25 a day and spending most of that at the Fo'c'sle bar. The *Janet and Jean* was getting to be a very expensive girlfriend for the owner, so he decided to save $25 a day and let go of one of the hired hands from the crew. Of course, that had to be me. Skip was a real deckhand, and I was simply a greenhorn. So, Rick reluctantly let me go.

"When this boat puts to sea again, you'll have a site on her," he said.

This sudden unemployment was not what I had in mind; I was now thinking "cabin." My original plan was to have $1500 to $2000 from apple picking and spend the winter, at least. Instead, I was learning a trade, but I had only lint in my pockets.

My book, "Whirlwind," was finished. I had written an idiot's guide to log cabin construction with poems and a short story between chapters. It had taken me two years to write and get into shape to send out. I had typed it on a portable typewriter four times and had done all the illustrations and photography but needed to sit down and figure out which publishers might be interested. My Writer's Market book was in Nova Scotia, and I figured I'd have the winter there to work on it with my earnings from apple picking. Now my winter was going to be spent somewhere else, and I needed the book. Great excuse, right? *Guess I have to get it.* Maybe I could even get a site on a boat up in Nova Scotia.

The book, written when I was 22, was rejected by ten publishing houses. I re-read the thing after fishing for six months and decided it sucked. But it had three things to be proud of: a beginning, a middle, and an end. I dedicated the book to Dad. If he had done something like building a cabin or writing a book, he might not have felt like he had lost himself. He might not have had to destroy himself.

With very few greenbacks, I set off for Nova Scotia. Deb gave me a ride as far as Hyannis, a nice jump. I hitched to Boston, where I spent a night with friends John and Linda, setting out the next day, hitching to Bangor in a cold rain that absolutely sucked. Snow is preferable if you are out on the road.

I made the midnight crossing from St. John, getting into Digby at 3:00 A.M. While on the boat, I chatted up a ride as far as Clementsport and walked the five miles up Guinea Hill and across the back end of the Fraser Road to Princedale in the dark. A hard hike, but every step reeked of freedom.

## Me and Robert Service

**There was no** lock on the cabin, just a latch from the outside and a welcome note inside. I kicked open the front door and was home. It was November, so the first order of business after lighting a few kerosene lamps was to get a fire going in both stoves. John and Linda had given me an ornate hardcover version of "The Lord of The Rings," and it was here in my little Shire that I was to discover the magic of Tolkien.

I decided to put in a loft while I was there since I had plenty of four-inch-wide spruce left over from the second flooring put down the previous summer. I cut down four poplar trees and used them as joists for the loft. Instead of sitting on a collar beam and calling it "the loft," I could sleep up in an actual loft where it was warmer. In addition to Tolkien, I read tons of poetry at my retreat, notably Wordsworth, Coleridge, Shelley, and Keats, with a particular interest in Shelley. But my friend Bill had broadened my horizons by introducing me to Robert Service.

Robert Service was working for a bank in British Columbia around the turn of the 20th century. The Klondike gold rush had started in 1898, and adventurous dreamers were still making the trip as late as 1910. Service was bored with his life and decided to do something about it. He quit the bank and made the trip to Dawson City, but the gold he was looking for was not in the ground or streams. It was all around him: the people of the gold rush. He experienced the harrowing trip to Dawson through the arduous Chilkoot Pass and lived among the prospectors, saloon keepers, dance hall girls, gamblers, killers, and mountain men. He lived in a log cabin that you can still visit today and explored many rivers by canoe with the very fringe of society. And he wrote about them in poetry.

Service made millions of dollars writing poetry. But not the heady legit stuff of the time like T.S. Eliot, Yeats, or Pound. These were rhyming bawdy ballads of the North, of the characters who lived and died on the edge, chasing their wispy dreams in the frozen Yukon. It was accessible poetry for the everyday person, the daydreaming bank clerks, shop keepers, and day laborers who dreamed of adventure that would never come to them. Service was a man who understood the riches of living in a camp in the ice and snow, the wealth of no coin. Although his most famous poems are the ones that made his reputation ("The Shooting of Dan McGrew" and "The Cremation of Sam McGee"), my favorites are smaller works like "The Joy of Being Poor":

> Although my pockets lacked a coin
> And though my coat was old
> The largest of the stars was mine
> And all the sunset gold.

It felt like this guy was sitting across the table with my kerosene lamp, looking at the log walls with the same sense of wonder. When you construct your own log cabin, you build a journal that you read for years after. On a frame house, the walls often rise in a day, but a cabin must go up log by log, layer by layer, all the way around. Because they are natural forest logs, each log goes through a litany of fitting adjustments, often raised to the wall and lowered to the floor for each modification. After several of these adjustments, you eventually arrive here: *Fuck it, it's only a cabin.* Spike it, then on to the next log. Staring at those walls is one of my favorite hobbies. Up close, I can still spot my pencil marks near each removed bump or knot. It is an old journal I never tire of paging through, and on November 12, 1977, I wrote this little rhyming lark in tribute to my cabin mate, Robert Service, borrowing heavily on his style:

### "Light As A Feather"

> It's been some time since I was young
> and ne'er knew anything
> 'tho I think for a while, I'm still a child
> I'm still a bud of the spring.

> Just give me a pack and a pair of boots
> And a winding mountain road
> And I'll sing all day on my merry way,
> It's Freedom that lightens the load.

> I've stood upon mountains, I've climbed rocky falls
> And braved the treacherous seas,
> I've brushed the sawdust from my hair
> And worn many holes at the knees.

I've sung many songs to my old log walls,
I've read my poems to the breeze.
I pray to God with my feet in the sod
And He lets me go where I please.

My pot is full, the cabin's warm
I'm wealthy beyond all measure.
Isn't it funny I haven't any money
And my heart's as light as a feather?

Chillin' at the cabin. Poplar joists to loft above.

# Lunenburg, Nova Scotia

**Staying in Princedale** from October 22 to November 17, I turned 24 on November 2 and walked the four miles to Clementsvale to pick up my mail. My journal entry at the time says, "Mom sent me $15 for my birthday. Got $17 worth of groceries." During this time, I hunted rabbits, with an occasional porcupine or squirrel to survive. My land is on the Bay of Fundy side of the province. Although there were fishing fleets in Digby and other smaller ports, I was told the big fleet was based out of Lunenburg on the Atlantic coast about 70 miles across Rt. 8. Being a greenhorn, I thought my best chance to get on a boat was in a bigger fleet instead of a small-town port whose crews have been solidified for years. I set my alarm clock for dark, got up, and started the trek across Rt. 8 to try to get on a boat in Lunenburg. The journal reflects that I had nearly walked a third of the trip when the nails started to come up through my boots and dig into my heels. I put some cardboard into the boots and pushed on.

Nova Scotia is about three times the size of New Jersey but still has less than a million people living there. Most of that population lives around its craggy coastline. The interior of the province is aptly called "The Interior," a wilderness. There are only a few roads that cross it, Rt. 8 is one of them.

After a combination of hiking and hitchhiking, I arrived in Lunenburg at dusk. Like almost all coastal towns in Nova Scotia, Lunenburg looked like a painting. I made my way to the waterfront and discovered no fleet. Some wharf rats said the whole fleet set out that morning because the forecast showed a few days of favorable weather after a bit of snow. Great.

So, another reality check—almost broke, hungry, and it is *cold*. It's hard for me to imagine now, traveling around like that so often with so little money. All that mattered was the goal. If I just walked toward it, everything seemed to take care of itself. I leaned on a phrase from the Bible a lot in those days: "Seek ye first the Kingdom of Heaven, and all these things will be added unto you."

Nova Scotia feels like fall on August nights, so November at night is brutal if you don't have a warm hearth. It was dark, and I had to shelter somewhere and found the Lunenburg equivalent of the Fo'c'sle bar in Provincetown. There was hardly anyone in the place owing to the fleet being out. I sat at a table and ordered a pint of draft beer, a ticket to shelter from the cold. It was an hourglass, not a beverage. When it was gone, if I didn't buy another, I was a vagrant and would have to move on. I didn't think it was possible to drink a single beer for an hour and a half but somehow managed this minor miracle.

I learned from the bartender that a job on a boat here in Nova Scotia is known as a "chance," not a "site." All I was looking for was a chance. If I had shipped out on a fishing vessel, I wouldn't have to worry about food and might even make a few bucks at the end of it. But instead, I was staring at my hourglass running out and the frost visibly creeping up in tree branch patterns on the windows. The bartender gave me the phone number of a captain. I called, and his wife said he was at sea and did not expect him for several days. It snowed.

With my beer/hourglass empty, it was out into the snow with me. The town shut down tight, probably since dark. Anybody with any sense at all was sitting near a woodstove. You could smell the wood smoke in the air, reminding me of folks sitting around their hearths. I looked for shelter around the shipyard, alleys, anywhere. In a gravel lot next to a shipyard, an old wreck of a school bus with most of the windows smashed out looked like the best bet. The doors were open. Though most of the seats were gone, about a third of the windows were still intact toward the rear. Something moved in the back and startled me. It was a fellow vagrant sheltering from the snow. He was thirtyish and seemed polite enough when I asked him if he wouldn't mind sharing the bus for the evening. I brushed the snow and broken safety glass off a couple of torn-up seat cushions and bedded down. That night on a busted-up school bus became a lifelong benchmark for "How cold can you get?"

I traveled with a kick-ass warm Army down sleeping bag and an equally warm down jacket. My bus mate was cold too, so I gave him the down sleeping bag, figuring the jacket would keep me warm enough. Faulty logic would come to fruition within the first hour when whatever heat I generated got sucked away through unprotected legs. I learned cold could prevent sleep, giving me lots of shivering time to dwell on the dude who was warm and sleeping soundly in *my fucking sleeping bag. So this is the meaning of "dire."* I also had teeth-chattering hours to redefine the definition of "stupid."

At sunrise, it had stopped snowing, leaving about three inches accumulated, considered a flurry in Nova Scotia.

I collected the sleeping bag that had done me no good and bid my bus mate goodbye. When the stores opened, I went to a five and dime and bought not food but a "Magic Marker," ancestor of the "Sharpie."

Since the fleet was going to be out several days and, having no way to eat or shelter that long, I had to beat it back across the province to Frasertown. Hitchhiking sucked in Nova Scotia as a rule, but a good legible sign always improved your chances. Around the back of the store, I found a suitable piece of cardboard and made a hitching sign with the marker.

Getting good rides across, I walked the ten miles or so from Rt. 8. When you drive to a place you love, that's pretty nice. But when you hitch sixty and walk the last ten miles to get there, arrival is most dear. Before the trip, I felled some maple, beech, and birch and junked up about a week's worth of wood. The appreciation for that first fire I still recall. A neighbor shot a partridge on the way over, so partridge stew for supper. A day later, he shot a deer, and it was fat city on the Fraser Road for a while—deer steak, roast, liver; it was a kingly existence.

I called Rick from a neighbor's house. He told me I should come back to P'town in about ten days and that the boat should be ready to fish by then. More rustic time. Greg McEwan was back in Bear River from Nantucket. We read poetry and held what Bill and I liked to call "High Council" through many lamp-lit nights.

The cabin, my "pile of sticks" in the woods, 1977.

## US Customs and the Citrus Conspiracy

**When the time** came, I tore myself away from my pile of sticks in the woods. Money had to happen to stay a long time as per the grand plan. The hitching was good, but I had to cross the border back to the USA on foot, making my entrance into the US Customs building in Calais, Maine, in buckskins with a caseless guitar. Two customs officers were busy with someone else, but the look they threw at each other would have been hard to miss. They motioned for me to throw my backpack on the table, and they would be with me soon, so I did and sat down for a long time. They were indeed breaking hippie balls, but I could be a douche, too.

They were thinking drugs. I pulled out a baggie of tobacco (there were no smoking bans then) and lovingly rolled me up a real nice-looking cigarette, getting their attention since the only thing getting hand-rolled out of a baggie in those days were joints. They were talking to someone else, but their hawk eyes were on me. Pulling out a strike-anywhere wooden match, I ignited it with my thumbnail for a bit of bravado, kicked back, put my feet up on an adjacent chair, and smoked my cigarette, bringing them over to me a lot quicker.

A customs officer approached. "Do you have any *marah-wannah*?"

"No, sir," I said. "I have nothing to hide from you."

"Open the backpack."

My backpack, made of hand-tooled leather, was a gift from my sister Kathy. Since I would rather have my eyes plucked out with rusty spikes than spend five minutes in a laundromat, the backpack was most certainly not contaminated by anything clean. I warned the Customs Officer that all he'd find was nasty underwear and smelly shirts. I admit it was enjoyable watching him root around in there with no gloves on, in a pit of my filth. Root, root, root, and then his eyes lit up like he found a key of heroin. He pulled out an orange that I had planned on eating on the road along the way. With a "now I've got you" smugness on his face, he held the incriminating fruit up in triumph between us and said like he had been practicing all his life for this moment: "You can't bring this into the United States of America!"

Wow. He emphasized the word "America" as if it was *his* country and not mine. I could hear "The Star-Spangled Banner" playing loudly in his head, like his headphones were up too loud, smell the apple pie coming out of his oven and feel the deafening roar of the Blue Angels making a pass overhead. Awesome.

*Great. They're gonna steal my fucking lunch.* I only had $7 to my name, and that orange was part of my meal plan. I owned a Buck knife, the classic folding 110 model with the four-inch blade. I learned that if you open the blade a speck with one hand, with a hard flick of the wrist, the knife will snap open for a switch blade-like open. It's a nice effect. So, snap! The four-inch blade was open between us. He was momentarily stunned.

"That's OK," I said, the epitome of nonchalance, "I'll eat it here."

I snatched the national security threat from his hands before he could react, used my Buck to cut into it, and ate it right there in the customs building. I guess we were both being pricks and deserved each other. He did have a particular advantage over me, however, with the guns and all. Since I didn't have any *marahwannah* and the fruit threat was now extinguished, I was now free to enter my own freaking country. They never treat you this way going into Canada.

I caught a ride across the dreadful Rt. 9. A guy near my age driving a pick-up took me across and down 95 a few miles south of Bangor. His name was Tim Hardy from Hartland. He was a brakeman for the railroad and was living a similar adventure only on the rails. We swapped stories and tales. I tuned up my guitar and sang him that great ghost train song by Merle Haggard, "The Miner's Silver Ghost." I rolled us up some cigarettes, and we had a nice ride.

Before leaving P'town and during one of our kitchen sessions at the Bethel, I suggested to Ralph that it would be cool to all get hammered and act out a Shakespeare play. He loved the idea. We decided on that old favorite of intoxicated fishermen, "Othello." While in Boston, I went to a used bookstore and picked up nine paperback copies of "the Moorish play."

I arrived in Provincetown on Sunday, November 20, and headed straight for the Bethel, having no real place to live. Ralph was there and told me to throw my gear in his room for the time being. Chris Scanlan gave me a ride down to the harbor. The boat was off the railway, but not because repairs were complete. The boatyard had to let another vessel in front of her down off the rails. Rick greeted me with an almost pressured enthusiasm.

"Boy, you are just the man I wanted to see."

Why did this worry me? He told me that Skip wasn't working out, and the steady job fixing up the *Janet and Jean* was mine. Skip was too good a hand to be not working out. Translated: *Skip, who has this functional organ called a brain, has decided that he could probably make more money selling pencils and had better get the hell off this boat before it bleeds him dry or kills him.*

To prove this point, Rick and I offloaded five and a half tons of pig iron ballast by hand off the *Janet and Jean* and onto Buddy Johnson's boat, the *P'town Queen*. Gee, I enjoyed that. 25 bucks a day. About $5 per ton.

And so began Part Two of the struggle that was trying to fix up the *Janet and Jean*. Bitches. The work got colder. Boats were starting to come in from trips with ice in the rigging. In the meantime, I had to find a permanent place to live. I wound up at a divey rooming house known in P'town for its cockroaches and fringe. To be thought of as fringy in P'town was quite an accomplishment. It was called "Mom's," but this place hadn't seen anyone's mom in fifty years, not unless "Mom" was a junkie. I was using most of my pay to stay there in hopes that the boat would get fixed and be productive. Dickey told me P'town was the trap in the drain of the world. "Mom's" was the trap in the drain of P'town.

On my first night "home" from bilge diving on the *J&J*, I headed for the shower. I opened the shower curtain and was greeted by a cockroach climbing up the tile wall. Next to the shampoo was a bottle of trusty old "Pyranate A-200" used for crab and lice infestation. *Oh, man, this stuff is a regular here, like salt and pepper shakers on the kitchen table.*

But all was not bad at "Mom's": I met a cool guy named Neil from City Island, NYC, who worked on racing schooners. He was now employed down at the fishermen's Co-op and would return every night with a delectable fish to cook up. He shared his food with me, a good thing because after my beer allowance, I could barely afford food.

# Othello *Comes to the Bethel*

**I stopped back** at the Bethel, and Ralph told me that they would like me to live there and that I was a good influence. Even my number one detractor, Dan, had voted in the affirmative. This was a most welcome development, renting the closet for $55 a month. The closet was just wide enough to get a cot mattress down on the floor, and that became my comfy shoebox to sleep in, living like a hamster. I was affectionately known as the "closet case" at the Bethel.

Our rehearsals for *Othello* began in earnest. We commenced with the entirely improbable occurrence of a bunch of drunken fishermen acting out a Shakespeare play. What happened amounted to a staged reading of the play at the Bethel. It was a thing of deranged beauty to see the bard's words come out of those grizzled mouths. Thinking on the day I arrived on the *Janet and Jean* as the new shacker, I envisioned Dan's ridicule and firing back at him, "OK, mother fucker. I'll have you reciting Shakespeare in three months." Ralph relished the role of Iago, arguably the best role in the play. We sat at the kitchen table well into the night, Ralph with a copy of *Othello* in one hand and a beer in the other shouting as Iago.

"Proclaim him in the streets! Poison his delight! Plague him with flies!" Then he would chase that with a swig of beer and a fit of laughter that would sweep me up too. Ah, commercial fishing.

# Jo-Jo

**As one of** the two fastest shuckers in the fleet, everyone in town knew Jo-Jo. Besides his speed eviscerating mollusks, he was great on a boat, handling the gear well and working hard. He was of average height with a stocky, solid build that announced his considerable strength. His hands were paws, leathery and cracked, rock crushers with unusually short fingernails. But Jo-Jo was also well known for something besides his shucking: he was a notoriously loud, out of control, obnoxious drunk. If he were auditioning for the role of drunken fisherman, the casting director would pass him over for being too over the top. It was simply not believable that anyone could get that obliterated. But Jo-Jo won the role here in over-the-top Provincetown.

On a boat, he was the nicest guy in the world and a man you'd want by your side when the shit hit the fan. (I can rightly say that, having fished with him two years later.) Ashore, you would want to be at least a time zone away. Shouting at an almost earsplitting level, laughing, slurring, drooling, staggering—I have never seen anyone get that drunk so consistently and with such commitment since. Jo-Jo's pattern was typical of the one Richard Dickey once described to me. I fished with Dickey the following summer. We were on deck watching the rest of the crew find their way back to the boat after three days of some gear work and a lot of drinking.

"Look at them," Dickey said, "They all made a couple grand four days ago. Now here they are: broke, tired, hungry, and ready to go fishing."

Jo-Jo epitomized this model. He always had to have someone with him when he drank to ensure he would survive the binge. His settlement money would fall out of his pockets as he reached for bills to buy everyone in the bar a round. His laughter would overpower any other noise or conversation, like a car alarm no one would shut off. I mostly stayed away from him until he took up residence in the Bethel.

Since the Bethel sat on dry land, the only Jo-Jo I would ever see (or hear, oh my God) was drunken-screaming-obnoxious-put-a-helmet-on-him-before-he kills-himself Jo-Jo. I worked at the boatyard every day; the wet, cold work was exhausting and started to wear on me. Sleep was the only thing I could do for myself, and now that Jo-Jo moved in, that was no longer an option.

He would get in very late at night, screaming at people who weren't there. Drunk-hungry (defined: would eat cold, canned beef stew with just *hands*), he'd cook himself up some kind of hideous-smelling concoction on the stovetop, stuff you would never consider putting in a frying pan, like liverwurst. When he left the kitchen, I had to get up to turn off the gas burner he regularly left on.

Rick would be there at 7:00 A.M. sharp for my ten to twelve-hour day, and I would be absolutely fried ala Jo-Jo. Something had to give. But I caught a break or a chance at one. Jo-Jo got a site on a boat out of New Bedford and had to catch a bus first thing in the morning. A reprieve was coming at last.

The night before, Jo-Jo prepared for his early morning shuttle to New Bedford by tying on a big, fat, loud, obnoxious, leave the gas burner on, drooling, word-slurring, liverwurst-burning bender, which I had no choice but to share every moment with him from that closet. *He had better make that fucking bus to New Bedford.*

After managing only an hour and a half sleep, I made a pot of coffee, mainly for Jo-Jo, and tried to wake him at 6:00 with no success. 6:15 went no better. When it got to be 6:30, desperation set in. Jo-Jo became aware of an annoying person on the periphery of his fog, a mosquito whining in his ear. I ramped it up at 6:45 and yelled at him that he had better make that ride to New Bedford.

Now *that* woke him up but instead of saying, "Gee whiz, Mick, that's really thoughtful of you. Thanks a lot. I owe you one," what he said was, "Don't bother me."

*Don't bother me?* I decided to let him know just who the "bothered" party was and how his unwelcome drunken screaming lullabies had never come close to lulling me to sleep each night. I had his attention now.

His response was simple, direct, disarmingly honest: "You mother fucker. I'll fuckin' kill you."

In a flash, his well-ripped compact body was up and *running* after me. Wasn't this guy drunk/unconscious two seconds ago? Fishermen. And just in case I was not clear on his intentions, he reiterated what was now his reason for existing: my elimination from the face of the earth. I ran like a guy trying to outrun a train in a bad dream. Jo-Jo blocked escape from the apartment, so I broke for the living room. *The living room's a death trap,* the survivalist on watch in my head whispered to me—*one way in, same way out.* I'm a damned bison, driven off a cliff during the big hunt.

The living room was an "A" frame with a couch, chairs, and TV downstairs, and a half-loft upstairs was Dan's bedroom. I ran up the stairs that were more of a ladder than anything, and Jo-Jo followed oh so close behind, screaming at me the whole way. Just in case I forgot, he reminded me of his intentions.

"I'll fuckin' *kill* you!"

I crossed the loft and on the other side of Dan's bed, just out of the grasp of Paws when he reached. I jumped down to the living room floor, making a perfect land and run. I guess I was wiry back then. Jo-Jo, older than me by about ten or fifteen years, stopped and thought about the jump for a second. That was the opening I needed to make for the front door, fly downstairs and out of the Bethel. Rick was just pulling up in his truck. I jumped in and barked, "Boatyard!" Rick sped off, and after another grimy day of bilge diving, I returned to the Bethel cautiously and found that Jo-Jo had indeed made his ride to New Bedford. That night I slept for the first time since the last glacial advance.

## Getting Dumped

**The owner showed** up in the boatyard in his Cadillac and told Rick he had enough of pouring money into the *Janet and Jean*. He was shutting down the whole operation. I asked to speak to him, and he deigned that I enter his Caddy. I told him just how much he was getting from me for what he was paying me. He told me he had heard about how hard I worked. He could not have thought much of me, though. What self-respecting man works that hard for $25 a day? But in the end, it did not matter. We were out of a job.

Still a greenhorn, my fishing fate was tied to Rick O'Brian, who seemed committed to investing in me as a project. The rest of the fleet had their winter crews set, so breaking in there looked bleak. I was barely making it at $25 a day, and now that dried up. Well short of the $1500 I had hoped to make apple picking (I had maybe $15), I had to quit Provincetown. When I left, Rick promised, "If I have a job, you'll have a job."

My friend Bill had a plan to return to his brand-new cabin near mine in March of '78. I would go with him, then try to get on a boat in P'town in the spring. I left Provincetown for Mom and Atlantic City in the meantime. Thus ended the first phase of my three-part commercial fishing life. I had only broken the ice.

## *Poetry and Jazz*

**I lived at** home with Mom for a few months, biding my time till we could go to Nova Scotia. Bill had a gig at "The Lighthouse" bar in Atlantic City near the actual lighthouse. The Chris Sooy Swing Band had a regular gig there too. Chris and bandmates John and Jimmy Lawler were all friends of ours. They enjoyed my poetry and asked me to read at some of their gigs. "The Lighthouse" had more of a late-night coffee house feel. They had a trumpet player, Irv Hirsch, who used to play with poets in the Village during the '50s. He offered to do interpretive trumpet licks during my recitation.

The most significant audience reaction came from a poem I had written in 1977 after the gambling referendum was voted in and well before the first casino, Resorts International (the old "Haddon Hall"), opened. The casino people promised the sky to local business people, eateries, and such. They were supposed to make out big. Everyone was going to get rich. With local business on board, the proposal passed. But something happened they could not foresee. The people (and the money) stayed in the casinos while the rest of the town continued to decay. I read this poem with Irv blowing jazz/beat-poet-type licks.

The Marlborough-Blenheim, two of Atlantic City's treasures destroyed for casinos.

## *"Goodbye, Atlantic City"*

Goodbye, Atlantic City
I remember your desolate January shores,
I've walked them with the hungry gulls lost in thought.
I've wondered at a handful of your sand with the same awe
as at a night sky filled with stars.
I remember the Swiss castles and enchanted cottages
you destroyed to make way for high-rise hell,
monolithic madness with a roulette soul.
I remember listening to your ocean
all the way from your bay
without having to strain to hear over perpetual sirens.
Goodbye, Atlantic City.
You've gambled and lost.

# The Pyre

**While at Atlantic City** in February 1978, John and Linda called from Boston to tell me a Provincetown boat had gone down with all hands. I called Rick right away, and he told me it was the *Cap'n Bill*, a well-known vessel, an icon, skippered by the good-natured Captain Ralph Andrews. Being down at the wharf, he was impossible to miss, and he struck me as a jovial sort. I remember his smiling face peering out of the wheelhouse window. I had met one of the crew, "Sully," a big man with a big beard and bigger heart. Everyone loved Sully. People still talk about him all these years later, especially women. He was kind of a protective big brother to them. Rick told me that she had gotten her nets hung up on a wreck and just flipped. Nobody had a chance—a devastating loss for a town still reeling from the loss of the *Patricia Marie*.

The news of the loss of the *Cap'n Bill* intensified my apprehension about being lost at sea. The possibility of never returning lurks in the back of every fisherman's mind on some level. When the moment came to throw the lines and head out, I would always say a little prayer, surrendering myself to whatever fate God had in mind. *Whatever it is, God, that's what I'll be having.* Then I didn't worry about it. There is no time for worry aboard the boat. Everyone just did what they needed to do. I did all my worrying when I got ashore and had a chance to think. Having a four-month break from the business allowed my fears to grow a beard. But no matter how worried or scared I got ashore, I always found myself heading for that long walk down MacMillan Wharf with a seabag on my shoulder, Long Point foghorn whispering seduction in my ear, and our boat lit up, growling, waiting to take us out to sea.

In Fall/Winter of 1976, Bill built his "pile of sticks" on a seven-acre parcel he purchased about a "holler and a half" from mine. He stayed with me while he built a cozy little nest that was 16X18 with a loft. In August of '77, just before I stumbled into commercial fishing, we had spent a few idyllic weeks going back and forth between the two cabins. There was a shallow rock well between us, so whoever was visiting the other would arrive bearing at least a bucket of water. We had a distinctive whistle that announced our arrivals and departures on the secret back trail. We were Tom Sawyer and Huck Finn. We held "High

Bill Watson at author's cabin, 1977.

Council" in those days, discussing our perfect escape from the world "back there." We envisioned our utopian existence would last forever.

When he left that August, Bill tacked a note on his door that read: "*Left for God knows where. Be back God knows when. Pray for us poor boys when the cold winds blow.*"

By March of 1978, we were more than ready to resume our reverie at the two hideaways. Bill brought two folding wooden chairs up for his abode. We caught the midnight boat again and arrived on Fraser Road about 3:30 A.M. The plan was to stop at my place first and get a fire going, for it was still winter in Nova Scotia on March 31st. We would hang out till dawn and make our way through the woods to Bill's place. We were very fatalistic about these hideaways. We would often leave them with a fire going, hoping it was all still there when we returned after a trip to town. In those days, there was no driveway, just a narrow path straight up the hill. When we pulled up just opposite the trail on the road, I told Billy that I would run up and see if the cabin was still standing so we wouldn't have to lug our gear up for nothing. When I made it to the top of the hill, I yelled down that the cabin was still there and got the fires going. At dawn, Bill picked up his chairs.

"I don't know if there's a point to bringing these over." He thought it might not be there, a possibility we always considered.

"Well, the worst that could happen is you'll have to bring them back here," I said.

On the back trail, it took about ten minutes to get to his cabin. Being in the middle of a thicket, as you neared, you could almost make out the horizontal logs of his walls through the spruce bows that encircled it. With Bill in the lead, we got to the point where we should begin to see them. Looking ahead, I saw the logs through the trees. It was my mind filling in the gaps. When we cleared the thicket and stood in the open area where the cabin stood, there was nothing but scorched earth, the remains of some burnt logs, and a woodstove that had fallen to the ground when the floor let go. Parts of that stove melted in the blaze. We stood there for some minutes, trying to make sense of the cabin's absence. The first words out of Billy's mouth were: "God bless the person who did this."

We carried those wooden folding chairs back to my place, where they remained for some 30 years. Stunned, Bill left Canada. Alone time in the forest is a treasured commodity. But my aloneness only served up the dish of grief that sat in a pile of ashes just a few paces away in the woods. Being young and taking the initiative like that and building log cabins in the north woods almost created an illusion of invincibility. We could do anything and were in the wheelhouse bound for wherever we wanted to go. Bill and I would have these retreats in the woods forever. We were set. At the break of dawn on March 31, 1978, illusions of invincibility vaporized instantly with a scorched punch in the guts. Neither of us would look at life in quite the same way again. There were three theories about how such a thing could happen. In the case of all three, proof would remain tantalizingly out of reach. We settled for knowing that we will never know. Bill said that April Fool's Day came a day early that year.

Bill Watson's cabin, 1977.

Author, 1977.

## Hitchhiker's Guide to Romance

**The love life** was non-existent during these couple of years. There were dalliances, but I yearned for something substantive. Discovering that having actual conversations meant a lot to me, I gravitated to older women. Sleeping with someone sometimes made me lonelier than avoiding it. Like everything else, I wanted the real deal. And like every time, I learned the hard way. I had too much growing up to do. But I tried.

Neighbors gave me a ride into Bear River. I needed kerosene for the lamps and some, oh yes, food. Hitchhiking back to Princedale with my gallon of kerosene and leather backpack full of groceries, an old red Ford pickup stopped for me. I put the kerosene and leather backpack in the truck bed, climbed into the cab, and greeted a beautiful woman with sky blue eyes and a warm smile. My God, I am living Jackson Brown and Glenn Frey's dream: *"It's a girl, my Lord, in a flat-bed Ford slowin' down to take a look at me."* Her name was Carol, and in just a few miles, I learned she was 37, a dancer, divorced, and living up the valley about an hour away. She was down this way to teach a dance class and was on her way home.

We were *clicking* on this speed date. I told her about the cabin, that I was a poet and fishing on the boats out of Cape Cod. She was headed up the Annapolis Valley and could only take me halfway to the Fraser Road. The ride had been much too quick for my liking, but I climbed out of the cab, went back to the truck bed, shouldered my backpack, and picked up the kerosene. Walking to the open passenger-side window, I thanked her for the ride. She surprised me with her reply.

"It's a shame we didn't get to know each other better."

I am thick in a lot of ways. I usually require the two-by-four method of learning: that is, upside the head with a two-by-four. But I needed no such schooling here. I turned and walked back to the truck bed, dropped off the kerosene and backpack, came back up front, and climbed into the cab.

"Come see the cabin."

Contemporary view of cabin.

She did. I got a fire going, and we had a small meal of wine, cheese, and apple with a dash of poetry. She had to go after a while. I took the risk and kissed her. We luxuriated in a slow, delicate, not overly long kiss. I knew if we kissed, she would be back. She said she might not. I told her she would be. We both smiled at this playful repartee. She left, and three days went by, and just when I was starting to think I was wrong, Carol came back. We began a month-long infatuating, passionate romance. Nova Scotia offered her sweetest springtime pleasures just for us, it seemed, for lovers appreciate them more.

Carol and I knew that fishing in Provincetown was coming. I had to get on a summer crew, so we clung to each moment like it was the last. When the day came for departure, she drove me down to the ferry terminal in Digby for the 5:00 A.M. crossing. We got there just in time to see the Princess of Acadia make her run at the Digby Gut for the Bay of Fundy. A beautiful sight, that boat leaving Nova Scotia, me not on it. We picked mayflowers over the next five days together.

On May 5, 1978, knowing I had traded valuable time needed to get on a boat for the summer, I tore myself away from the loving arms I had been so desperately longing for and made the 5:00 A.M. ferry, Cape Cod bound.

~ ~ ~

# PART II

~~~~~~~~~~~~~~~~~~~~~~~~

## Learning the Ropes –
## F/V *Bay of Isles*

# My "Poetry Fellowship"

**Hitchhiking down from** Nova Scotia, I stayed two days with good friends John and Linda before I set out for the trap in the drain of the world. I made it to the Boston Commons before dark. John whisked me up and took me to a Red Sox game at Fenway. We sat in the bleachers wearing trench coats with beers stuffed in the pockets, apparently a bleacher tradition. Just that morning, I was cooking a little breakfast on my woodstove before the birds were up. By 8:00 P.M. that night, I was at Fenway with 38,000 screaming maniacs.

It was late to be trying to get on a summer crew. Arriving in P'town, I headed straight for the Bethel. But there *was* no Bethel. Ralph and the crew were gone. Real people were now the rent-paying occupants of what used to be our sanctuary for misfits. Homeless again.

May was a revelation after having been in P'town only during Fall and Winter months. The sunshine richer, brighter somehow. Painters are attracted to the light there, comparing it to Italian hues. The circus that becomes P'town in the summer was not upon us yet. Down at the harbor, I visited every skipper I could find. They all told me what I had expected: every boat crewed up for the summer. No sites.

Catching up with Ralph at the Fo'c'sle, he said I should come to the "new" Bethel. This Bethel had some exciting dynamics. Ralph was staying with a great gal named Jo, and she had a roommate who might welcome my presence. He tried to sound casual when he told me all I would probably have to do was write and read poetry and be available for explorative behaviors, kind of like an enhanced poetry fellowship. (Nah. Not interested.)

Ralph brought me to a grand old house on Cook Street. There I met his gal Jo and Ronni, the one he had mentioned at the Fo'c'sle. We all sat down at the kitchen table, and there was much high talk, poetry, mysticism, laughter. I passed the interview and got the job.

Ronni, a gifted artist in her 40s, knew a lot about poetry and writing, gave me excellent feedback about my attempts at poetry, and, oh yes, our behaviors were very explorative. The house was cozy and had lots of bookshelves. I had

"Province Lands" – Cape Cod National Seashore.

a hard time giving the library the once over, slowing down to check out each title, every book begging for my time. Jo and Ronni had rooms with working fireplaces, and so, at the right time, Ralph retired with Jo. Ronni and I headed for her chambers, where we got a good fire going. More poetry by firelight but that did not last long. She smiled at me with a wistful look in her eyes. I saw it and asked why.

"I just pictured you when you are forty," she said, knowing I was but twenty-four.

That made me want her more. Maybe it was that she thought I would develop into someone better. And that being 40 would be cool. We mixed sex and poetry and came up with a lovely concoction. I must have seemed young and naïve, but that was not an issue. She was open and free-thinking and told me she had another lover who we eventually had to schedule around. But this bohemian existence was an exciting twist in my young life. She introduced me to Pablo Neruda and his poem "Horses." We read Neruda and rolled on that floor in front of the fireplace. It was a distinct improvement to have a lover that opened my mind.

I was down on the wharf every day trying to get a site, but my reluctance to leave fair Carol in Nova Scotia exacted its toll. It was way too late to get on a summer crew. But at the end of the day, I had a place to go, food to eat, and a woman to devour me. I wrote a poem describing this situation and read it to Ralph, Jo, and Ronni over breakfast in the morning.

# "The Cat"

Those ladies intellectual
With their desiccated dreams and hungry hearts
Have taken in a cat
From the street.
They're keeping it 'cause it's
Fashionable crossing the bookshelf
Desirable slithering into bedrooms
Exciting in its untamable
Animal movements.
They like my poetry. It's fortunate. It's not fashionable to keep a bad poet.

Jo and Ronni thought it a cool poem, dispelling my fear they would take offense. Older women. The best. "Those ladies intellectual" borrows from Lord Byron's masterwork, "Don Juan." He even rhymed it with, "haven't they henpecked you all?"

The sexual revolution of the sixties created unpremeditated ease during the seventies. It was before HIV. Nobody was talking about "bodily fluids." Women mainly were all on the pill. Guys never used condoms. Hopping into bed was the common parlance of the day, and in Provincetown, there were no rules. It was not just a haven for gay people. Ralph said many working women would come to P'town for the weekend to "let their hair down."

A little later in the season, after I finally did get on a boat, I was at the Fo'c'sle Bar on an unusually crowded night right in the thick of whacked-out summer in P'town. I fell in at a table with two gals, sisters, and a guy from Boston. They were fascinated with the idea of commercial fishing, so I took them down to the harbor and showed them the boat.

We wound up at their motel near Pilgrim Lake. The older-looking sister made overtures to the effect that she wanted to be alone with me, so the other two left for about an hour. Big sister and I spent a lively hour together till the return of younger sister and guy.

"Why don't you join us?" older sister said. Admittedly, I was surprised.

Whoa. Younger sister's clothes slid off before I even processed what she had asked, and she lay next to me with a nervous smile. She did not seem that experienced, so we eased our way. Then older sister interjected herself into the fun. We were giving the threesome thing proper consideration, and nobody had complaints. Except for Mr. Around Twenty. That guy was just lying there sulking on the other bed while we were in thick. I looked over at him, thinking, jeez, two gals and two guys. I was taught to share.

"Are you just going to watch?" I said.

The "watching" thing was a little creepy. But instead of joining us, he got up and stormed off into the bathroom, slamming the door. I turned to the elder sister.

"What's eating him?"

She might have thought *Not her* but said, "Oh, that's her husband."

"Oh, shit." I got up, dressed, and exited.

"You should have told me," I said on the way out, as if, even in this off-the-hook situation, some modicum of fractured morality could be applied.

I left the motel room before he could get a gun loaded and come out of the bathroom blazing with his Glock. I think this was an *I'd like to watch someone bone my wife* experiment with failed results. Did he think she was having too much fun?

It was too late to go back to Ronni's (I know. What a dog.), so I walked into the dunes and found a slight depression in the sand like a deer and slept. Some hours later, the warmth of the sun on my eyelids was my alarm clock. Brushing the sand out of my hair, I arrived at Ronni's, who sat at the table in just a bathrobe, smoking a cigarette like a pissed-off Bette Davis. She pointed to my guitar.

"See that? I almost smashed it to pieces."

*Rut-roh.* I told her I was out late, and rather than disturb her by coming in at that hour, I thought it best to sleep in the dunes. I'm thoughtful that way. Relying on my refined sense of tact, I left out the part where I was helping two young ladies let their hair down. She knew the lie but settled for morning sex to make it all better. Provincetown.

# *The* Bay of Isles

**Meanwhile, back at** the fruitless quest for a site on a scalloper, I was hanging out at the wharf when a captain gave me a lead, the only one since my arrival.

"You might want to try the *Bay of Isles*. She's up on the railway now. Skipper is George Hann."

I went down to Flyers boatyard where I had lived and died every day for weeks with the *Janet and Jean* last winter. The F/V *Bay of Isles* was up on the "ways" sitting in its cradle. This was a southern or western rigged vessel, like most shrimpers. The wheelhouse is forward, and the hull is shallow (they call it "hard-chined"), which I could see readily with her up on a cradle out of the water. I guess shrimpers fish shallower waters than do scallopers or fish draggers.

A southern rigged vessel has "outriggers" with "birds" to make up for the lack of stability afforded by a deeper hull. An outrigger is a tall boom that is nearly as tall as the mainmast. There are two: one each for the starboard and port sides. When in port, these outriggers are in an upright position. Once out to sea, the outriggers lower. I always thought a boat with its outriggers down looked like a tightrope walker with a balance pole.

At the end of the outriggers, metal "birds" are suspended on chains and lowered into the water, each steel "bird" triangular in shape. They dive straight down as the boat rolls, straightening out during the roll-back, creating resistance, and thus, slowing the roll.

The *Bay of Isles* was a newer wooden boat. She had a Cat 12 diesel engine and, with the boat at 56 feet in length, it was more than enough power. She was nice looking, painted a rich green and white. I made my way up the rickety ladder, hopped over the rail, and announced I was looking for George Hann. A stocky fellow wearing a red LL Bean chamois shirt and glasses came over to me. He was pleasant and looked more like a high school shop teacher. "That's me," he said. He informed me that he already had his summer crew fixed. *Damn. This is the last boat. I've got to get on this one.* I saw lots of activity going on, mostly painting.

"Do you have an extra paintbrush?"

He seemed surprised and stammered a little.

"Birds" suspended from raised outriggers while in port.

"Well, yeah, uh, but . . . we're all set here. I can't pay you."

"That's OK," I said and went in search of a paintbrush.

I painted all day long. George told me again he could not pay me. I told him I understood and kept painting. This made him nervous. Nothing was going on for me anyway. I might as well show someone how willing I was to work. After they shut down at night, I was back first thing in the morning, painting all the harder. George was freaking out. He came over to me again and said he was unable to pay me. I told him that was cool and kept painting. It was not my intention to make him crazy. He was collateral damage. I worked a good deal of the time next to a slender, older fellow who introduced himself as Richard. He was funny and interesting, making the day fly by. I worked ten hours till they shut it down for the night. I was back again first thing in the morning down in the fish hold painting with my new buddy, Richard, and saw George's boots coming down the ladder. Uh oh. I figured he was going to say: "OK, that's it. Get the fuck off my boat, weirdo." But he approached me with a warm smile and slapped the side of my arm with a backhand.

"I guess you'd better figure on going with us."

I got a site for the summer on the *Bay of Isles*. One of the crew, an older fellow named Snowy, could not make the trip for health reasons and needed to be replaced. George figured *I got this idiot in the fish hold willing to work his ass off for nothing. Just think what he might do if he was making some real money.*

At this point, I was getting to know some of the crew. The first mate's name was Andy. He was a grizzled-looking hard case who wore a red bandana on his head. He was no-nonsense and seemed to know his stuff. I got a distinct impression that he was not going to cut me any slack. Lacking confidence in my meager skills since I had not been out to sea much, owing to the pitiful state of the *Janet and Jean*, I knew my greenhorn apprenticeship was far from over. Andy knew it too.

Repairs and painting complete, the *Bay of Isles* came off "the ways." It felt like an inaugural boat launching; only there was no bottle of champagne to break on the hull. Someone in the boatyard loosened the brake on the winch, and the vessel rolled down the track, powered by gravity and great weight. She picked up momentum and splashed in the water, sending a small deluge up the boatyard ramp. Buoyant in the cradle, Capt. George fired up the monstrous Cat 12 diesel with a roar. No problem with power on this fishing vessel. That power saved our lives later that summer. Once untethered from the cradle, George brought her over to the wharf for gear work.

Here I met the rest of the crew, a team of Provincetown all-stars. Two older guys asked, "Where's Snowy?" when they saw me. There was Al Sousa. Tall and slender, he was affectionately called "Daddy Long Legs" or just "Legs." Al approached every watch with a silly sense of humor that never abandoned him. He was a dream shipmate who knew his stuff. He didn't subscribe to the "torture the greenhorn" school of thought. Another older local was Charlie Franks. Swarthy of complexion with a darker mood, he seemed to resent all these young longhairs breaking into fishing when they were not born to it. He rarely spoke, and when he did, it was only to the older "real" fishermen. He lived the trade and was stingy with knowledge. Why should he give one of these whelps a shortcut when he came by his knowledge the hard way? Yup, got nothing but sour looks from Charlie.

There was another young guy, Arty, who had a rocket in his pocket. Lots of energy, upbeat and talkative, I saw that he got on Charlie's last nerve. Steve, another fellow our age, was pleasant and on the quiet side. Our cook was the skipper's daughter, Jill Hann. Slim, with long reddish hair, freckles, and an engaging smile, Jill was strong-willed, made no secret that she liked women, not men, and took shit from nobody. She was accessible if you were cool with who she was and then eminently likable.

# *Dickey*

**If you spent** any significant amount of time in Provincetown, chances are, you heard something about Richard Dickey. He was a living legend; there were stories abound and tales that seemed almost mythical. After fishing most of the summer with him, I learned them all to be true.

After learning he was the best shucker in the fleet, one of the first tales I heard was that he was arrested at sea off Jamaica. Dickey, as captain, with five other crew members, got caught transferring nine tons of marijuana from one vessel to their boat. Since the boat was not registered, he was convicted of piracy and possession of nine tons of hooch. He and his mates languished in the infamous St. Catherine's Prison in Jamaica, a 17th-century dungeon. He received a death sentence, later commuted by Queen Elizabeth, and got out after two agonizing years following appeals. He often referred to this period as his "Jamaican vacation." A fisherman all his life, Dickey was an avowed drunk who stopped drinking and took up smoking pot instead. It had to be an immense improvement because the fellow I became friends with was one splendid human being.

He arrived on the *Bay of Isles* for gear work, and the respect afforded him was palpable. He had been my interesting painting buddy these past three days. George had to have asked Dickey about the possibility of giving me Snowy's site when that came up. He was slim (known in New Bedford as "Provincetown Slim") and had a full greying beard, longish hair, unruly, with a cap thrust upon it like an attempt to corral three cats. He liked the LL Bean chamois shirts like Capt. Hann, but navy blue with the sleeves cut shorter. Through repeated washings, the shortened sleeves shredded at the edges, like "The Incredible Hulk" had busted through them. He gave me one once after he cut the sleeves of a newer one. Central casting had overdone it again. This guy looked too much like an ancient mariner. When Dickey (I almost always heard him addressed by his last name) gave up booze for the herb, he also took up reading. He had a curious mind and wanted to know everything scientific, mystical, natural, unnatural, preternatural, and supernatural.

He was always talking, but unlike most people who did so and were tiresome bores, Dickey was utterly fascinating and disarmingly impish. *Good God, what is he talking about now?* And once you caught on, you'd get sucked into a kind of performance art. He was never at a loss for subject matter; his favorites were theories on constructing the pyramids, shipwrecks around Cape Cod, the lost civilization that built Machu Picchu or prehistoric alien visitation, the galaxies, or a particular plant that grows only on Nantucket Island. If we ever got blown in there, while the rest of the guys hit the bars drinking themselves stupid, Dickey would smoke a joint and hit the hills of Nantucket looking for this unusual plant he was talking about two trips ago.

This boat would do a six and six watch (six hours on, six off) and fish twenty-four hours a day with the captain's watch and the mate's watch. In addition to being engineer, Dickey was the starboard side winchman on the mate's watch, and I learned I was to be the hookup man, holy shit, for this legend.

The genuine fishermen performed most of the essential tasks on the boat, not us hippie freaks who were just along for the thrill of it all and the good beer/pot money. One such job was tying the "taggle" knot. This knot was the bitter end of the rope ending at the lower block, the business end of the taggle with the Gilson hook used to raise and lower the dredge on deck. People's lives depended

Richard Dickey circa 1978 (courtesy Susan Renehan).

on it. A knot of utmost importance, they called on Dickey to tie it. Always interested in the language of knots, I stood over him and watched each turn.

Once we completed gear work, we iced up, fueled up, grubbed up, and set out on the first trip of the summer season. For some reason, captains seemed to withhold the info about our destination. The cook could usually find out, and in this case, the cook was the captain's daughter. Bingo. Jill told us our destination was the Texas Towers. Dickey filled me in.

The Texas Towers was one of the worst maritime sinking disasters that ever occurred, though it did not involve a ship and, of course, Dickey knew every blessed detail of the wreck. The Texas Towers 4 was the last of the early warning radar stations built by the Air Force to warn of approaching Russian warplanes wanting to bomb the snot out of New York City during the Cold War. It was positioned about 70 miles off the coast of Sandy Hook, N.J., looking a lot like an oil drilling platform with massive white golf-ball-looking domes.

Perhaps never adequately braced, she was known as "Old Shaky" to her crew as she was constantly swaying around during moderate to heavy seas and would often make banging sounds. The team frequently petitioned the Air Force to evacuate them until it could be made safe, but you know how that usually goes. The whole rig went down in a nor'easter in January 1961, taking her twenty-eight crew with her. There was a destroyer, the *Bedford*, right there to help, but the tower just slipped into the sea at night, having broken off just ten feet below the surface in 185 feet of water. The *Bedford* could do nothing for the twenty-eight men lost that night, the Texas Towers now their grave.

Dickey told us the whole story while passing around a bone in the fo'c'sle, all of us hanging on his every word. The fishing was good there, he said. Instead of going around Race Point and down the backside of the Cape, the *Bay of Isles* would cut across Cape Cod Bay, down through the Cape Cod Canal into Buzzards Bay, and to the open sea.

It was a warm and sunny afternoon when we left. Jill went out and sat on the hatch cover to the fish hold with a paper bag full of fresh green beans and began snapping the ends. We were all hanging out at that point, enjoying the gentle breezes.

"I'll help you do that," I said.

"Oh, no, that's OK," she said. I could tell that she did not want to impose on a deckhand to do cook's work.

"No, really, I don't mind."

Jill finally agreed, so we sat on that hatch cover on one glorious day, crossing Cape Cod Bay, snapping the ends off green beans and talking. It was perfection.

We approached the canal entrance, and it seemed too narrow to my eye, but it could handle tankers. We were following close behind one. Though its mammoth props seemed to turn too slowly, they moved her through that canal at a good clip.

I did my first wheel watch on a boat that steered in the direction you intended. The *Bay of Isles* was light, and the Cat 12 pushed her shallow hull through the water like a surfboard with a GTO engine.

I thought she was a good boat, but Dickey had another opinion. Most fishermen were good at complaining, but Dickey was an artist. Taking a few of us on a tour, he didn't merely tell us what was screwed up; he showed us. First stop, below in the fo'c'sle, he looked up to the overhead.

"See those?" He pointed to four large bolts in the overhead, two on either side.

"Those four bolts are the only things holding the wheelhouse on deck. One or two good seas over the bow, and the wheelhouse is gone."

With the wheelhouse swept away, there goes steering, navigational aids like radar, LORAN, the radio, life raft, and, uh, the skipper. He showed me around the hull and bulkheads. Anywhere a wood screw should have been utilized, a nail instead. All Dickey could do was shake his head. Great. So I shipped out on another disaster waiting to happen. *Other than that, everything's ok, Ma. Love, Your son.*

We reached the Texas Towers and prepared to set out the gear for the first tow. It spooked me that there were guys still down there on that rig. Even though it was the mate's watch, George was there for the first tow to observe what came of the haul back.

As a hookup man, I was responsible for setting out the starboard rake. If you did not remove the pin and pound the pelican hook at the right time, that is, the roll to starboard, the rake would flip and would drag uselessly upside down on the bottom. You never want to be responsible for a wasted tow, your mistake impacting everyone aboard. I pounded the pelican hook at just the right time, and the dredge went in the water perfectly. I could feel Andy's eyes on me while I did my best to nonchalant it. *Yup. Do this all the time—nothing to scrutinize here. Move along.*

Unlike Charlie, Dickey was generous with his knowledge, and under his tutelage, I flourished. George knew where the scallops were that summer, and we had a vessel that wasn't breaking down every eight hours, so our trips were long, and it was here on the *Bay of Isles* that I grasped some idea of what these men who fish for a living go through.

Richard Dickey shucking scallops (courtesy Susan Renehan).

I had built a couple of log cabins, cut down the trees with an ax, hauled quite a few of those logs out of the woods on uneven ground, carried almost the entire building and its contents up a hill, but I learned a new level of hard work that summer of '78 on the *Bay of the Isles*.

Every 20 to 30 minutes, the deck would be full of rocks, scallops, and mud that seemed like setting cement on deck. Bend over, assholes and elbows, pick, pick, pick the scallops, bat crabs away, shovel rocks and mud, clear the deck, shuck the scallops, haul back, bend over and pick the scallops, shovel, shuck, salty sweat running down into your eyes, haul back, *Good God we've been out three days, and it seems like a week. We have eight to ten more days to go.* Haul back! It was insane. Some boats had dumping tables, hinged additions to the deck plates. Located amidships, the tables dumped all non-scallop material effortlessly over the side. No more throwing rocks or shoveling mud. It was the stuff of dreams. I was never on a boat that had one.

These trips seemed like they would never end, but they did, and, after taking out the catch at the Co-op and washing the boat down, we met in the galley of the *Bay of Isles*. A smiling George Hann placed $750 in our hands. "That's nothing," he said. "There'll be bigger paydays ahead!" George proved to be prophetic.

After living on next to nothing and ostensibly having sex for a roof over my head, this was huge. The boat fished all summer consistently, and the paychecks fatter. The dream of a year in Nova Scotia seemed attainable.

The lifestyle changed considerably after being paid 20 one-hundred-dollar bills after some trips. I tried to make my relationship more platonic with Ronni, not because of her, but it was more the idea of the setup that wore on me. She did not take this too well. There was a lot of screaming and actual throwing of furniture and some breakables. Being sensitive to such indicators, I moved/ran out. Next stop, a friend's lawn, where he allowed me to pitch a tent. Carol seemed a million miles away.

Thinking I had a severe allergy to laundromats, there was a lot of buying the same shirt, at least three times if I liked it.

## *Captain George Hann*

**Captain George and** I clicked. He was a good guy. He appreciated that I was willing to work so hard for nothing when trying to get on his boat, and I worked harder when I joined the crew. I thanked him for giving me a site. He told me I earned it, which meant a great deal to me.

I enjoyed a warm relationship with George. Mostly, we laughed and busted each other's chops. He liked the way I told jokes. One joke he particularly liked was the old saw about the guy who walks into a bar with a little ten-inch guy wearing a little tuxedo, sitting on his shoulder like a parrot. The guy orders a beer, and when the bartender puts it down in front of him, the little guy gets up, runs down the guy's shoulder, knocks the beer over, turns around, runs back up the guy's arm, and sits back down looking all mean and ornery. After the patron apologizes profusely, the bartender brings the guy another beer—same thing. The little tuxedo guy runs down the guy's arm and knocks over that beer and runs back up, sits down looking all nasty. The man apologizes again and orders a sandwich instead. When the sandwich comes, here we go again; the little guy runs down the guy's arm, throws the top piece of bread at a nearby patron, tosses the ham up in the air, jumps up and down, pulverizing the potato chips, runs back up the guy's arm, sits down looking all mean and ornery. The bartender has had quite enough of this.

"All right. You mind telling me what's going on here?"

"I can explain," says the patron. "About a year ago, I was walking along the beach and came upon this lamp, like Aladdin's lamp, you know? I decided to rub it, and out came this genie. He said he would grant me one wish. So I wished for a ten-inch prick. "*This,*" he says, pointing back at the little tuxedoed man on his shoulder, "is what I got."

Well, George loved this joke. He had me tell it to any new crew members who came aboard. He said I was his ten-inch prick because we were constantly needling each other. It eventually evolved into him measuring out about ten inches with his hands and pointing to me. *You, you little fucking 10-inch prick, you* was what he meant without saying a word. It was great.

We fished mainly off the coast of Jersey that summer, 60 to 100 miles off Atlantic City or Barnegat. Sometimes the weather was chilly and damp, and other times it was scorching hot with no breeze. I had bought a heavy navy-blue woolen sweater at the old Marine Specialties store in P'town. It was well made, warm and nice-looking, an authentic fisherman's sweater.

We had a dog watch that was foggy, damp, and cold, and I wore the sweater. The next day the weather was sunny and hot. I draped my wool sweater over the forward bit to dry in the sun. The forward bit is a post forward of the wheelhouse used for tying up. Since all our work took place aft of the wheelhouse on such a boat, I forgot about the sweater for several days. But George did not. He was looking at it for three hot sunny days from the wheelhouse. When I remembered, I went to the forward bit, picked up the sweater, and spoke to George through the open wheelhouse window.

"Ya think this is dry yet?"

"I don't know, let me see," George answered, playing along.

I brought the sweater over for him to feel, figuring he would continue the "Is this dry yet?" charade. He grabbed it and threw it right the hell overboard.

I watched it go floating by in the Atlantic, lost forever. First shocked, then pissed, I climbed up into the pilothouse and grabbed his precious red LL Bean chamois George Hann trademark shirt hanging on a hook, unused due to heat. We had a tug of war over it. When it was clear that I was not going to win this battle without ripping the shirt, I let go with the promise that this ten-inch prick was going to get his revenge. I could not bring myself to rip the shirt, weird considering I had no problem with the idea of throwing it overboard.

In the hot summer, fishing off New Jersey, sometimes the sea was flat-ass calm, an undisturbed pool. Fishermen hate this kind of weather, working beyond endurance and working through brutal heat and humidity. The goal to spend a year in Nova Scotia notwithstanding, I was in it for the storms, the excitement of them, the high adventure. That is the table a young man in his early 20s goes to feast. This stillness of the ocean, hot, humid, day after day drudgery, was not the stuff of swashbuckling. It was more a crazy marathon.

During weather like this, we would also have very unwelcome shipmates: flies. Oh, yes, we were a Carnival cruise ship for flies, the crew on the all-you-can-eat buffet menu. They looked like ordinary black house flies, but the little bastards *bit* the shit out of you. They'd bite, and you'd try to swat them to no avail. They'd land right back on you and bite you again and again for days. Later in the summer, when I was the starboard side winchman, those flies bit the hell out of my back while I was holding the dredge up in the air, trying not to kill anybody. Those maneaters somehow knew when my arms were otherwise engaged.

As a kid, I learned how to kill a fly with my hands well. If you try to swat them, they feel the air being displaced from your hand coming down, and they escape with ease. Instead, put your hands on either side of the fly and clap your hands together. They feel the air being displaced and fly up and into your clapping hands—nothing to it. You can catch them alive with one hand, a little trickier, by quickly grabbing the air from the rear to the front of the fly. If you are quick enough, they will fly right up into your clutching hand. It's all so simple, but many folks think you are some sort of Mr. Miyagi when you do this. So, George gets a load of this and pulled me off deckhand work and my sole job for a few hours was to be the official fly killer. Nobody resented this, for I was a walking death camp for flies.

We also had those sticky, spiral flypaper strips with flies stuck to them that were always so attractive hanging in the galley. I used to kid Jill and say that's where she got the raisins for her pies and oatmeal.

George would straddle the wheelhouse step and the outside rail during a haul back and look aft at the rake coming up over the side. He wanted to see how many scallops he was catching on that tow, so at that moment, he concentrated on one thing. I took down one of those sticky flypaper rolls hanging in the galley during a haul back, picking the one most loaded with Jill's raisins. I took it to George, who towered over me at the wheelhouse door while I was down on the deck. Just as the dredge was coming up over the rail, I called his name.

"George! George! Here! Here!" He only saw I was handing him something. "George! Here! Take this! Take this!"

He grabbed that long raisiny sticky bun without even looking. He knew at once that he'd been had.

"You son of a bitch!"

He tried to get it off his hand, but now it stuck to both hands, and it became more of a comedy routine. The whole deck broke out in laughter. George, well, he was swearing.

"You little fucker! I'll get you for this!"

"No, you won't. That's for my fucking sweater."

"You ten-inch prick, you," he said.

## Ordnance and Blue Sharks

**Steaming out to** the grounds on one of our trips, Dickey was telling all of us about a scalloper, the F/V *Snoopy*, dragging for scallops off the coast of North Carolina. On July 23, 1965, she had gotten an old WWII U-boat torpedo caught in her port side drag by its propeller. It was so heavy they couldn't get it up over the rail, so they tried to get it free of the dredge. The *Snoopy* took a roll to port in a swell, and when she rolled back to starboard, the dredge and the torpedo struck the boat amidships and blew her to splinters. Eight men died, including the captain. Four men survived, one of them blown a hundred feet in the air. *Great story, Dickey. Let's go fishing!*

All the boats I ever fished on adhered to a "no alcohol on board' rule. But in the '70s, everybody was smoking pot on them. When you went on a trip with Richard Dickey, you knew that bones would be smoked and weird tales told when off-watch came.

Once, he told about being shanghaied. Who gets shanghaied unless it was a hundred years ago or in a book? Dickey did. During his hopeless drunk days, he was on a bender and blacked out in a New Bedford fishermen's bar. He found himself lying up toward the bow of a strange fishing boat steaming out to sea when he woke up. There was another guy opposite him waking up to the same incomprehensible reality. They both got up and were leaning over their respective rails, trying to read the name of the boat they had found themselves aboard.

"Can you make the name out?" Dickey asked the stranger.

He told us about being in a Jamaican prison for captaining a boat full of marijuana, eating bugs, and having little to no hope of ever seeing the light of day. No matter what, Dickey was almost always telling a story. One watch as we stood shucking scallops together, he said he got married young and was drafted soon after during the Korean War. But this is how he related it: "Yeah, I got married at nineteen in 1950, and no sooner had I done that, then they drafted me and sent me to Korea." Then he turned on that Richard Dickey wry smile and said, "So I got things straightened out over there . . ."

I wrote this little poem during off-watch in the fo'c'sle after one of our always memorable sessions.

## "Off-Watch"

Clammy clothes sway
A hooded sweatshirt, green everywhere
But at its filthy brown sleeves.
It sways from the overhead with the rest,
pendulum ticking off the trip—
It's off-watch in the fo'c'sle.
Dickey lights the bone
And we float and roll like smoke
Relax and laugh away these stingy hours that starve for sleep
And deliver the no-mercy next watch.
We rest—but that snarling monster in the engine room
Never sleeps or laughs or smokes a bone.
It grinds and throttles its tune through my frame.
Soon I will be its slave on deck
And Dickey passes the bone
And tells a timeless tale
And we float on these fast few hours
Till next watch.

When we fished off Jersey, we would usually fish around the Hudson Canyon or further south, near the Baltimore Canyon. If you were to look at a topographical map of the ocean, you would see the riverbed of the Hudson becoming a full-blown canyon until it drops off the continental shelf.

When storms hit, the captain had to choose between running for a port or going out beyond the continental shelf to the deep water where the seas were less turbulent. There you could "jog out" the storm by steaming into the seas, up and down the mountains of seawater, like running on a treadmill. If you had enough fuel, it was doable.

The Jersey Coast is difficult to run to in a storm; there is no lee port. You can't go around to the other side of a stretch of land and come in on the leeward side. You always had to go straight in from the windward through treacherous inlets with wicked rips. Of course, Dickey told me all this. My hometown inlet, Absecon Inlet, is one of those. On all the old maps, it was identified as Graveyard Inlet, a well-earned title.

We would pick up all kinds of crap in the dredges. Pieces of old wrecks (they were the coolest), parts of machinery that we'd all try to identify. When a work glove or boot came up, Dickey always wanted me to make sure there was no hand or foot inside. At first, I thought he was kidding, but he was deadly serious. It may be the only way to make an identification on somebody lost at sea, he would tell me. Yeah, it was a nice line of work I found myself in. I am still grateful I never found a severed hand or foot in them, snapped bones protruding from putrefied flesh; always greatly relieved to see the usual mud and sand.

The dredge will also pick up any bottom feeders, like halibut, lobster, crab, and goosefish. What we called goosefish, the world calls monkfish. It is a kind of anglerfish. These things are butt ugly. If they were big enough, we would keep them and sell them for ourselves. The boat doesn't get a share of that. It's called "shack" and "shacking," the verb form. You could earn anywhere from $40 to $150 extra in shack at the end of trips.

A goosefish, shaped like a polliwog with a bear trap for a mouth, has top skin colored like gray/green mud, serving as camouflage. The underbellies are corpse-white. The eyes are antifreeze green, and just behind the eyes, sharp horns could cause infection if you got a puncture wound from one.

But this fish was all head and mouth. Its giant maw was lined with sharp teeth, though the jaw doesn't have much power. They would bite your boots and try to swallow your foot when working the pile, but you would barely feel this. Their mouth was more of a trap. They had a long "fishing rod" between their eyes (relating them to the angler fish family). The rod dangles a little lure at the end of this pole until a smaller fish goes for the bait. The goosefish opens its mouth so fast, the suction pulls the unfortunate fish into the oblivion of the bear-trap mouth.

The part that winds up on a restaurant plate is a slice of a tail that starts from behind the horns and tapers down to the end. This fish has no middle. Some crew aptly called them head fish. Separating the tail from its owner is a gruesome procedure. Due to their slimy skin and sharp horns, the only way to pick up a goosefish is by the eyes. Your thumb goes in one eye and your middle finger into the other, like picking up a six-pack of cans or a bowling ball. The tow cable from winch to deck block is taut and about a foot off the deck during a tow. Holding the goosefish by the eyes on that wire, you cut the thing in two just behind the ugly head, feeling it jerk as the knife cuts the spinal cord.

On this trip, the tow we were on was yielding good scallops but undersized goosefish. Many of them would come up bloody and bashed in the dredge. Since it was not worth "shacking" the smaller goosefish, we just threw them over the side, becoming so much chum for the nearby blue shark population.

Though not as monstrously big as white or bull sharks, blue sharks were big enough to cause concern, growing up to thirteen feet in length. They were built for business and traveled with other blue sharks: one big ravenous dinner theater crowd. No man would want to be in the middle of a blue shark feeding frenzy with about ten of them all taking a head-size chunk with each bite. Fishermen: betcha can't eat one.

That night during the dog watch, we threw dead goosefish overboard, and being dead, they sank slowly upside down with their pasty white bellies reflecting the deck lights, looking like ghostly lamps themselves. I stood at the rail mesmerized by their white lights when I saw a black shape knifing through the water and put the light out. And then another black form and another light snuffed out and another and another.

The blue sharks were on our dead goosefish, and they would make a run at each, swallowing them whole, putting the light out. I was standing just four feet or so from certain death if I were to fall overboard. *Man, these things are built for what they do.* They looked like flexible torpedoes with uncanny homing devices.

That night, while I was hooking up for Dickey, I noticed something long and metallic in the chain bag as he was easing it up and over the rail. I yelled for him to stop before dropping it on deck. He left the rake and chain bag suspended in the air and came over to inspect it with me.

What we saw looked like an unexploded shell from a battleship cannon. It was about ten inches in diameter and at least a yard long. Dickey said to tell Andy, the first mate. I ran up to the wheelhouse and told him what we had found in the dredge. Andy came over and sized the situation up. The three of us looked at each other. Without saying a word, we knew we all were thinking of the F/V *Snoopy* explosion.

We had to extricate this potentially live shell from the chain bag and get it overboard without blowing the boat to pieces. Andy and I stood on either side of the dredge and guided it down as Dickey expertly eased it to the deck. We were fortunate it was not blowing a gale that night. There it was, plain as day; a shell meant to puncture a hole in the side of an armored warship looking surprisingly uncorroded. We knelt on the chain bag and figured out the plan.

Cut the twine top (the nylon netting on the upper side of the chain bag that billows during a tow allowing scallops to enter), slide the shell ever so carefully out of the bag, and throw it over the side. Andy and I began cutting the twine top. Once there was a hole big enough, the tricky part was next: sliding it out without detonating the warhead.

Andy said to me, "You'd better go up forward," as in for my safety.

I took a quick assessment of the situation. I was on a piece of shit fifty-six-foot wooden boat held together with nails. The shell explodes, killing Dickey and Andy. The rest of us go into the water clinging to debris as the blue sharks pick us off for the main course after a stimulating appetizer of bashed goosefish. *No, I don't think so.*

"No fucking way," I said to Andy, "If that thing explodes, I want to be *kissing* the fucking thing." I put the back of my hand to my lips to simulate the act.

Andy laughed at that. So did Dickey. All those war films that I saw as a kid came to mind, the ones where the sweating sapper tries to disarm an unexploded bomb in WWII London. Andy and I slid that sucker out slowly, gently, like it was a newborn baby. But unlike a newborn baby, we slowly walked it to the rail and threw it over the side. Andy returned to the wheelhouse and gave the Coast Guard a bearing on it. The rest of the watch went on as usual, and we did not become another *Snoopy* story for other fishermen to talk about at some galley table. Another thing was happening too. I was becoming anesthetized to danger like everyone else.

## *The Blessing of the Fleet*

**We were making** decent money, and sometimes George elected to leave the boat in Point Pleasant, N.J., flying us all home in a small plane out of an airport in Monmouth County. It was cheaper than burning the fuel to go back and forth from our home port. As we rolled into June, Provincetown got zooier, reminding me of how we all felt about tourists in Atlantic City until Labor Day. However, the one summer event that all the townies and fishermen looked forward to was The Blessing of the Fleet.

Once a year, on the last Sunday in June and the crowning event of the days long Portuguese Festival, the bishop blessed each fishing vessel in a procession of boats steaming past him at the end of MacMillan Wharf, praying for a safe and productive year at sea. The wharf, once a workplace, was now a celebration

Author aboard F/V *Bay of Isles*, Blessing of the Fleet, 1978 (courtesy Jennifra Hann-Norton).

packed with revelers. Every boat decked out with colorful flags in the rigging and lavish spreads of food and libations; each vessel hosted its own party. Folks were everywhere: in the wheelhouse, galley, fo'c'sle, engine room, all over the deck, even in the rigging and up the mast. In the summer of '78, it was boatloads of us young freaks.

Steaming by the wharf, I stood on the wheelhouse roof with a crowd of celebrants and received our bishop's blessing, everyone hooting and hollering, ship's bells ringing, horns blasting. Then all boats went out into the bay, dropped anchor, tying up to each other in groups of three and four. You could party with us on the *Bay of Isles*, slip over the rails to the *Menco* to check out that party, and then on to the *Petrel*. We three boats anchored off Truro, others off Long Point. A lot of us were swimming. Dickey found me in the crowd.

"I keep telling everyone about my friend the poet, but you're never around. It's nice having a poet aboard, but you've lost some of it, you know. This fishing is bringing out the animal in you. You lost some of what you brought with you down from the cabin. But that's alright. Bring it up out of you. As soon as it's all out, kick it in the ass and go back to your cabin."

The whole new world of fishing enthralled me. There was only one other thing missing: Love. There were playmates at times but nothing substantive. At the stern of the *Bay of Isles*, I fell into an easy, unforced conversation with a dark-haired woman. She had a relaxed smile and a warm, unpolished beauty. Things happened quickly, and in just a few minutes, we learned we were both beat up Catholic, Irish, and from the Jersey Shore. Raised in Sea Girt, she was a photographer and a fellow freak. Each of us with parochial school nightmares in our archives, it was an effortless laughter-filled conversation. Already we were scarred soldiers sharing comradery and war stories.

Late in the afternoon, when all boats untied from one another and headed back to the wharf, the crowds hit the local bars: The Surf Club, Governor Bradford, Old Colony, and Fo'c'sle. Being a Fo'c'sle guy, that's where I ended up. My photographer from Sea Girt was there too. I offered to buy her a beer. She invited me home, where we kicked off our hard fall into real love, the aching, intoxicating, can't think of anyone or anything else variety.

Susan Renehan was thirty-one, well known in town, and worked at the Café Edwige, right next door to the Fo'c'sle. Owned by John Yingling (Jingles), the Edwige was a very hip eatery. Once I threw my lot in with Susan (most people called her Susie, but I liked Susan), my base of friends and acquaintances expanded to include some very creative folks: Artists Jackson Lambert, Gene Sampson, Frank Milby, Susan Baker, poet Keith Althous, potter and musician

Debbie Kahn, poet Alan Dugan and on and on. Susan was also friends with Richard Dickey. They had shucked scallops together the previous winter when the F/V *Little Infant* was shell stocking. There was a Provincetown/Bear River, Nova Scotia connection that I learned of after falling in with Susan. Gene Sampson and Charles Couper both moved from P'town to Bear River and carpenter Don Frothinger. I met all these great folks up there when I brought Susan back with me.

The beauty of Provincetown seemed enhanced by love, the air sweeter, the sunshine more golden, everything seemed staged for our benefit. Even ice cream we shared was elevated to orgasmic levels, love changing the chemicals in our brains as dramatically as any drug.

Putting to sea now had a whole new flavor. Whereas before, I would be raring to go because of boredom and loneliness, I now had to tear myself away from loving arms. Susan would walk that long slow walk with me down the pier at midnight with Long Point foghorn bellowing. We would take our time with a long kiss. I could see the wet sparkle of smiling eyes in the dark that told me she loved me. We'd throw the lines, and we'd watch each other get smaller as the boat pushed further out into the blackness. All fishing couples know that the goodbye on the wharf could be the last. And then it was ten to fourteen days of insane drudgery until I could see her again. My love-altered brain perceived it as months.

One night during a mid-summer trip, I was standing with Dickey at the shucking box. "Susan is the kind of gal I'd like to marry," I said.

He stopped shucking and looked at me like I should know this.

"Don't come to Provincetown looking for a wife. You're at the wrong end of the earth. That's like going to Sodom and Gomorrah looking for a straight fuck."

With fair weather, work was hard and monotonous. Shucking alongside Richard made that more tolerable. I only really liked fishing when the weather got rough, but during the summer, storms were fewer, and every day became indistinguishable from the next, feeling like a cruel endless loop.

There are those images that burn themselves into your hard drive for your entire life, some by reason of horror or loss, others by joy or warmth. An example of the latter came at the end of a long trip and when our love was young. Returning to port via the backside of the Cape, the first thing you see is the highlands of Truro and further up in P'town, Pilgrim Monument. It means "home' is at hand.

In the few years I fished, I saw many ports but none as beautiful as our Provincetown. When coming around the point, that last hard curl to the Cape

Low tide, Provincetown.

and head into the harbor, the town itself is your welcoming committee. 19th-century buildings forming a perfect amphitheater around the harbor and built on dunes that increase in elevation as the town gets deeper, capped by the monument; I never tired of seeing her this way. I had been aching to see Susan for what seemed like a month on a chain gang.

We came around the point on a brilliant summer morning, sun skittering on the water, Dickey and I taking it all in by the rail. The *Bay of Isles* was cruising at a good clip cutting through the calm harbor. And I saw her, the object of my obsession through grueling watches for days on end. Susan liked to windsurf, and here she was out in the harbor in a dark blue one-piece on a windsurfing board. She was pretty good at it, too. The *Bay of Isles* came within thirty feet of her as we headed for the inner harbor. She looked up, and that she recognized the *Bay of Isles* registered on her face. Then she saw me waving to her, no, climbing out of my skin for her. She beamed that "Susie" Renehan smile at me, and, distracted, she fell off the board into the water. She came up smiling and pushing her hair back so she could see. We headed to the Co-op to take out our catch, wash down the boat, get paid about fifteen $100 bills, and begin four days of the best that life has to offer. Yeah, Susan seeing me while on that windsurf board, falling in the water and coming up smiling, still see it.

## Manasquan Inlet, July 3, 1978

**By mid-June,** I lost track of the times I could have lost a finger, hand, arm, or anything else I might miss if it were gone. It made me appreciate my older shipmates, who had survived a lifetime of pushing their luck.

We were fishing the "westard," meaning off the Jersey coast again, southwest of Cape Cod. It became so unbearably hot and humid one trip, George shut it all down for about an hour so we could go for a swim. He sent one guy, the only guy with any sense, to climb the mast and spot for sharks while the rest of us stripped and jumped over the side and went for a refreshing swim.

The water was crystal clear about ninety miles out. I opened my eyes as I always did in the ocean at Chelsea Avenue beach in Atlantic City. There you could see little because of the particulate the crashing waves stirred up. Out here, there was none of that, and it seemed I was looking through goggles. I could see the hull of the *Bay of Isles* and its prop, and I remember thinking how shallow she was in the water. I thought how that would be bad in storms. She certainly would not make many long trips in winter. I thought of my friends and Maguire cousins who were, in all likelihood, swimming at Chelsea beach at this very moment, not knowing I was swimming with them, only a bit further out.

Hygiene on the *Isles* was a foreign concept. She did not have a shower or even a head (toilet, for you landlubbers). We had to crap into a five-gallon plastic bucket and dump it over the side. Not much in the way of privacy there, as you would sit on the bucket right on deck. If the weather was so bad that you might get washed overboard, you could take the bucket down into the noisy engine room. At least if you fell over there, you were still inside and not lost to the sea. We pissed right over the rail into the ocean. That Jim Croce lyric, "Don't pee in the wind," always played for me then. Sometimes the winds could be deceiving, and you'd get piss on you anyway. Dickey told me, "Spit before you piss or puke." Ah, Dickey. Was there anything this man did not know? Yes, given the choices, I'd rather get hit in the face by spit.

We younger fellers did not like the idea of working in the heat and humidity with scallops, fish, mud, and sand for ten days or more without showering. I hated climbing into my stinky bunk with gritty, smelly hair.

Since there was no shower, the only alternative was the deck hose, which always pumped fresh seawater. We used it to clean the deck between tows so the footing would not be slippery and to wash the scallops before bagging. The only problem with the idea of bathing with the deck hose was that soap does not produce bubbles in salt water. I didn't know that before the summer of '78, but sure enough, I tried and couldn't produce a single bubble.

We had stopped in New Bedford a few times on the way to the westard for gear or repair. Arty and I went into a marine supply store there and found what I thought was a myth: salt water soap. It came in a good-sized squeeze bottle and was supposed to produce luxurious bubbles even in the Dead Sea. We bought some.

About three days into one of these humid, disgusting trips, Arty and I had had enough of smelling like a rhinoceros, so we stripped naked and brought out our new panacea: salt water soap. Using the deck hose, we produced such a lather we were unrecognizable under the suds. It was a joyous affair. It felt so good, we whooped and hollered through the whole thing. Dickey, George, and Daddy Long Legs laughed. Charlie scowled. It was supposed to be bad luck to shower or shave before you put into port. Bad luck or no, Arty and I were squeaky clean, and we could tolerate ourselves once more.

Fishermen are a superstitious lot. Once I was whistling (while I worked). That drew a reprimand from Dickey.

"My boy, you never whistle on a boat. It brings the wind."

Dickey often prefaced his Dickeyisms with "My boy." One that sticks in my mind was when we were in a storm, and Arty was awestruck by the ocean and its might.

"Man! Look at those waves!" Arty said.

Dickey set him straight with a grin.

"My boy," he said, "Them's ain't waves. Them's *seas.*"

He was an articulate, well-read man. His use of slang here was purposeful and somehow put a finer point on his correction.

You never leave a hatch cover upside down. Yep. Bad luck. If someone were going down the hole and laid the hatch cover upsidedown, the captain would scream bloody murder at him. Bad luck to stick a knife in the mast, too. And the most egregious offense is to say the word "pig" on a boat. That brings the worst luck of all. I asked Dickey why. He explained it this way: "The boat is a Lady. She'll be insulted if you use this word because she'll think you are calling her one. And her wrath will be great." (I think I heard a thunderclap when he said that.)

I noticed he never used the word "pig" in his explanation. I even heard some of my mates say "those little animals with the curly tails" rather than use the "P" word. In any case, no more whistling for me. (Porky Pig whistled a lot, didn't he? Wow. Double-whammy.)

On the morning of July 3rd, the VHF, a radio in the wheelhouse constantly updating the marine weather, was spewing warnings about a major blow headed our way. Things like this are usually classified as "summer squalls," storms that kick ass and develop quickly. The captain hit the bunk after his watch (6:00 A.M. to noon) and seemed unconcerned about the warnings. All through the mate's watch, the weather got worse. The seas were building, and bringing the dredges over the rail was becoming an adventure. I wrote in my journal that I could hardly see what I was doing because of wind-driven rain and seas stinging my eyes and face. I did not like the feel of this western rigged shrimper with its outriggers and diving birds. If they had built the thing right, to begin with, they would not need all this crap. It didn't feel natural.

By the time George woke up for his next watch, around 5:30 pm, it was a real rodeo on deck. He listened to the weather update again and gave the order to leave the rakes aboard. We were headed for Manasquan Inlet. Dickey, often the contrarian, thought that it was too late to make a run for a port. We should be running, he thought, for deeper water off the Continental Shelf, not one of these Jersey Coast lee-less ports.

The little fifty-six-foot boat would disappear between mountains of water and then find itself on a crest. You'd get that feeling you get on a roller coaster when you reach a peak and are about to head down the other side; this accompanied by the chorus of demons wailing as the winds cut through the rigging and the outriggers banging and rattling.

The galley and wheelhouse are attached on a southern rigged boat. You could stand in the galley and look out the door or a window, so that's where I parked myself watching this spectacle, "birds" diving at the end of outriggers, trying in vain to compensate for the great seas thrown at us. I wondered which was worse, the storm or the boat? Andy usually did not say much, and when he did, it usually wasn't to me. He came up behind me as I was watching the crisis unfold. He almost whispered in my ear like it was a secret, and my greenness would prevent me from recognizing the obvious.

"You know we're in trouble, right?"

"Yeah. I know," I answered flatly.

I had been fishing long enough to know this did not look good at all. Complicating the scenario, it was near dark, and we would be trying to make

Manasquan Inlet some hours later in the pitch black. George had never been through this inlet before but had a chart for it. I had never been *through* that inlet, but I had *been* there. Manasquan Inlet is a narrow channel bounded by long rock "jetties" on either side. I had walked out to the end of the north jetty with a gal and made out in summer 1976 when I was playing rock and roll for a living: another world, another life ago. The jetties sat high above the waterline, and to gain entrance to the inlet, you had to thread the needle between the two. In the dark. In a storm. Yeah.

Once darkness covered all, we just hung out at the galley table in our oil gear while the *Bay of Isles* got the shit beat out of it. The overhead leaked, so you had to do some creative sitting to avoid drips. Nobody was down in the fo'c'sle, perhaps an indicator of the level of confidence everyone had in the *Bay of Isles*. If this boat flipped, you did not want to be down there. Though subtle, I could see the worry even on our old-timer mates who had seen everything. The Isles was getting pounded and making scary noises. I thought of the wheelhouse bolted down with four bolts and nails holding the rest together. Dickey, the author of my misgivings, sat opposite me at the galley table with a whimsical look on his face. If anyone knew the gravity of our situation, it was Dickey. He extended his hand to me.

"Well, mate, if we meet again, I hope it's ashore," he said with his impish grin.

"Either way, Dickey, I'm sure it will be a pleasure," I smiled and shook his hand warmly. He liked that.

We poured outside on deck in full oil gear, sou'westers on or hoods up as we came closer to this windward port. The rain was driving in sheets sideways, and the seas broke on our faces; you could taste the difference between the fresh water rain and the slaps of salt seawater. Approaching the inlet, we were driven forward by high, rolling seas. George ordered the outriggers up. Each outrigger had a small winch that raised or lowered it. Raising this gear in a gale proved challenging and scary. Once they are high enough, they swayed back and forth, crashing into the boat and rigging. They had to be secured.

At the end of the starboard side outrigger, one of the birds was not secure, flying around at the end of its cable like a blue jay protecting a nest, attacking everything. The Cap sent me, the ten-inch prick, about a third of the way up the outrigger with some nine-line to secure it. Made of hard steel, the birds weighed about eighty pounds.

I did NOT want to get hit by that thing, hanging onto an outrigger. After ducking a few times when it made wild passes, I pounced, lashing it to the outrigger when I got a spin that went my way. No blunt force trauma or lost fingers. Didn't fall off or overboard in the dark. Nice.

There were four men in the wheelhouse, Capt. George, Al "Legs" Sousa, Mike Andrews, whose dad Ralph was skipper of the *Cap'n Bill* (lost the previous February), and Charlie. The rest of us were standing on deck, the idea being if this thing went south, at least we could jump ship and hope not to get tangled up in the rigging when she went down or pounded into the rocks by the seas. These converted shrimpers had a flat back stern. While some had flat backs but were narrower, Eastern rigged boats often had elliptical sterns, so a following sea tended to break around them. A big wide flat-back stern, like the one on the *Isles*, provided a maximum surface for a following sea to push the boat forward.

The deck awash, the dredges shifted and slid over the deck; we nimbly jumped around, avoiding so much sliding steel. You wouldn't want to get yourself a broken leg or ankle at a time like this. Many a scalloper has experienced the rite of riding a sliding dredge in a storm.

There was shouting from the wheelhouse. Arty staggered back from the bow with an update. Yelling over the wailing wind, he said that instead of threading the needle *between* the two jetties, where George thought we were, we were instead bearing down north side jetty from *outside* the inlet. Twenty to thirty foot following seas drove the *Bay of Isles* right towards it.

Dickey and I were on deck just aft of the winches. I was trying to spot the jetty coming up, but all I saw was crazy water ahead, but then, when the water went down, a valley between seas, the black rocks of the jetty appeared with white water breaking all around, like some monster bearing its teeth, framing them for a moment. Then the water came back up, another mountain between the valleys, and this considerable jetty that seemed so high up out of the water that summer day where I was kissing a pretty girl—totally disappeared under the water. It's funny the kind of stuff that runs through your mind in an instant during a crisis: *Wouldn't that be weird if I got killed in the same place?* Definitely.

It was far too late to turn to port or even starboard. The only thing to do was try to put her in reverse and fight the following seas. This piece of shit boat might be a floating sheet of plywood, but they didn't skimp when they put the engine in her. George had three guys hold the wheel straight while he gave her the power in reverse. The idea of the three guys on the wheel is the rudder is not built to withstand so much water pressure in reverse. Too much power and the rudder could swing too quickly to port or starboard and snap right off, and then there would be bouquets at a memorial service on a wharf.

George was "giving it to her" in bursts with belches of black smoke and fierce roaring from the muffler pipes, but the *Bay of Isles* kept heading straight for these big black rocks that would alternately appear and disappear. The entire vessel vibrated violently during these reverse bursts from the Cat 12. This beast railed against going to the slaughter.

"Mickey!" Dickey hollered to me over the vortex of wind and roaring diesel, wearing an odd smile. I couldn't imagine what he would think was funny at a time like this. He nodded aft as if to say, "Get a load of this."

I looked aft in time to see a towering thirty-foot sea break into the flat stern, shoving us toward the disappearing rocks. Yeah, that's pretty funny, Dickey. I smiled back at him anyway.

George, desperate now, tried to back her up, the shaft shuddering, the entire vessel from keel up shaking. The old term, "shiver me timbers," revealed its significance to me at that moment. Arty thought it was time to make a move. About twenty feet from the jetty now, it was the moment of truth. In seconds the *Bay of Isles* would be smashed to pieces by the jetty in the full force of the following seas. Arty yelled to the wheelhouse.

"Which way should I jump?"

Charlie, that font of knowledge and willingness to share it with younger mates, shouted back, "Jump *down*."

Thanks, Charlie. What a douche. But there is another way to look at this. Facing almost certain death, this Provincetown fisherman found room to break somebody's balls. Impressive.

George had no choice but to go full throttle in reverse and risk losing the rudder. It was the only move left. Three guys held the wheel to save the rudder. The battle between the Cat 12 and the following seas was full bore now. George punched the throttle. The dragon in the engine room roared, and thicker black smoke belched from the exhaust pipe. If we wrecked on the rocks, I was ready to make a jump for it, clear the rigging, avoid being smashed on the rocks, kick off my size thirteen boots (thank you, Chris Scanlan) and try like hell to make the beach. Improbable, but you've got to have some kind of plan. George risked full throttle again. The shaft vibrated hard, but our advance toward the jetty seemed to slow, just a little at first, till we were jogging in place. The Cat 12 exhaled flames from the muffler pipes with such velocity I thought she might explode.

The boat finally stopped advancing into the rocks, then, almost imperceptibly, she seemed to back away a little from the black teeth of the jetty. We heard shouts from the pilothouse, cheers of triumph. The *Bay of Isles* was backing up. Now that we were backing away, the following seas battered us even harder, but we could feel we were slowly making headway. *Come on, baby! Back up! Back up!*

Once she was clear enough of the rocks, George put her in forward and turned to port, attempting to clear the north jetty. As we were doing that, we took the seas broadside. Since she sat so shallow and the outriggers secured and not in use, it was rock and roll time, the dredges sliding everywhere on deck. *Hey everybody! Let's play "Don't Snap Your Foot Off At The Ankle."* Now, the idea was to get out far enough and make another run at threading the needle, this time *between* the jetties, thank you very much. But even there, it was a cauldron, the seas pushing over the top of the north side jetty. George made a run for it.

The Point Pleasant side, or south side, was lit up by the boardwalk. People gathered there watching this drama unfold. We were going to be "The Wreck of the Week." The *Bay of Isles* came through the Manasquan Inlet that night *sideways* driven by the seas. Then I learned what Dickey was talking about there being no lee port on the Jersey coast. We were a good way into that terrible inlet before George could get complete control of the boat, straighten her out and head somewhere to tie up. I do not think many of us believed we would make it in that night.

There was a payphone on the docks where I made an adrenaline-filled call home. We were only an hour north of Atlantic City. My oldest sister, Ree (short for "Marie"), answered.

"Ree! Ree! Do you believe this storm?"

"What storm?" she said. "It's raining."

Wow. Two worlds. These days, when it rains, I think of the boys out there. Our rain is their storm. God bless you men struggling to survive while I happen to notice that it's raining.

The next day, I received a visit from Tom Lynch, a lifetime friend. He had been at Mom's when I called. Being only an hour away, he said he'd run up and see me. Tom was my right-hand man building the cabin. Walking down the pier, he looked like he had just gotten out of prep school compared to us *scruffians*. I took him aboard the *Bay of Isles* and introduced him around.

Below in the fo'c'sle, I introduced him to Mr. Congeniality, Charlie, who greeted him with an indifferent shrug. After his visit, he told my mother he didn't know how I worked with such scary-looking people. Funny what you can get used to.

(Note: The *Bay of Isles* met her fate in May of 2020, about nine miles south of Manasquan Inlet near Barnegat Light. She ran aground on a submerged jetty and was ripped to pieces by the rocks. The U.S. Coast Guard rescued the crew.)

## Almost Killed Taking a Dump

**For a while,** being almost killed is a novelty. It is a big deal at first, but when you are in a business where the slightest thing that goes wrong can easily lead to a loss of life or limb, you get a little complacent. You go from, "Holy shit! I almost got killed!" to "Can you turn up the music a little more?"

Sometimes you give out a war-whoop after a narrow escape. Most times, everyone just laughs. Sometimes they laugh *at* you as in, "Ha! Ha! You almost got killed, you stupid fuck!" If they gave out awards each season for the most ridiculous way a crewmember almost got killed, I would have walked away with it in the summer of '78.

The luxurious toilet facility on the *Bay of Isles* was a five-gallon plastic bucket with a line tied to the handle. Get some sea water from over the side (this makes solid waste removal a lot easier), then try to find a "private spot" on deck so you can sit and get some thinking done. When you have thought all you are going to think, you then dump the raw sewage overboard in the most environmentally conscious way possible.

The spot most of us favored was between the stern shucking box and the stainless-steel washer. There, as you sat on the cozy five-gallon plastic can behind the washer, you almost disappeared. Shucking boxes are long wooden rectangular boxes that are nailed, screwed, or bolted to the top of the rail so you could dump scallops for shucking. The *Bay of Isles* had three: one each port and starboard (in Cape Cod speak that's: "stahbid") just forward of amidships and a third long one, about eight to ten feet long, nailed to the top rail of the flat-backed stern.

On a southern rigged vessel, the galluses are aft of amidships, making it more susceptible to entanglement of the tow cables; this happened on one trip, and George went ballistic. When we returned to port, he had steel stops welded on both sides of the stern. When we went onto a turn, the cable, sliding along the stern rail, was blocked by the steel stop.

So, sitting on my comfy five-gallon can, thinking deep thoughts, staring vacantly at the aft shucking box opposite, I leaned back against the stainless-steel washer. I noticed a little daylight between the bottom of the shucking box and the top of the stern rail.

Then the daylight was gone; the shucking box was now flush with the rail where it belonged. Weird. Then, there it was again, daylight between the bottom of the box and the rail, only this time there was more of it. Then there was none. What in hell? I looked to the right of the shucking box and saw the tow cable had jumped over the metal stop, its chief purpose thwarted.

The cable was now lying on the side of the shucking box. My little pea brain started to whir and click. This piece of crap shucking box nailed to the rail was taking the full weight of the dredge, the cable, and the torque of the engine. The nails could not hold that kind of pressure and were letting go. The guy at the PA system in my head made an announcement: *Get out of here. NOW!*

I jumped up high off the bucket and to the starboard side just as the shucking box let go. It smashed into the stainless-steel washer full force, shattering to pieces. The steel washer got bent and dented but held. I landed on deck just out of harm's way with my pants down at my ankles. This earned a lot of "Ha! Ha! You almost got killed, you stupid fuck with your ass hanging out!" kind of laughter. If I had stayed where I was and managed to survive, any steak and potatoes meals going forward would be drinking straw-only affairs. I was fortunate this did not occur at night. I would not have had the daylight under the shucking box as a warning. I would have indeed been killed taking a dump. What a stupid fuck.

# "Bluebirds"

**Sometimes we left** the wharf short a man or two. If that happened, we could not do the six and six watch. When we deviated from that schedule, it was known as "breaking watch," which always meant more hours on deck, less in the rack. We would do the six and three, that is, six hours on deck, three off. That could be hard on a crew after so many days. The worst is the nine and three, but the skipper knew you couldn't keep up that kind of pace. If we could hire a guy or two in a different port, we would. We hired a guy named Chipper in Point Pleasant. He was a young, good-natured, and very experienced fisherman. He wound up making a few trips with us. After his addition, I noted in my journal about our "very poetic" mate's watch: Andy, Dickey, Mickey, Chipper, and Ripper.

There was always a competition between watches, each trying to put down more bags of scallops than the last. You strived to cut more buckets than the guy next to you at the shucking box. Well, my shucking mate was Richard Dickey, arguably the best cutter that ever graced the fleet, so I knew I was not going to beat him. I competed with myself. My journal says, "cut three buckets and a piece" last watch and "I will try for four next watch." Sure enough, the journal says, "Cut four buckets. Hands sore." I worked on my shucking, like studying an instrument, and improved a good deal from greenhorn gawkiness.

I had a slow blooming relationship with Andy, our mate. He was knowledgeable and an excellent first mate. Level-headed and somber, he was not very talkative, but when he did speak, you listened. Despite my evident heart and soul commitment to the work, he liked it better if he could keep me dwelling in the cellar. A lot of guys in the fleet are like that. Dickey, however, thought I was doing great.

The three of us were sitting at the galley table during a mug-up. Andy, feeling the pressure to beat the captain's watch, insinuated that we would be putting more bags down in the hold but for my shucking. I knew I had improved, not just at shucking, but with the deck work. I pointed my finger at him.

"If you don't think I am pulling my weight on this boat, I want you to say it to my face right fucking now."

I had been doing this long enough to know when a deckhand was pulling his weight. This was bullshit. His ordinarily stoic, set face showed a spontaneous reaction. He was surprised and set back on his heels a spec. Dickey jumped on it.

"Ya know, when I first met you, you were the young poet with bluebirds flying all around your head. Now you're a hard-nosed motherfucker." Dickey said.

As much as he could, Andy smiled due mostly to Dickey's tacit approval of my response. He backed off, pretty much for good. A lot of these guys came at you hard. I am of a gentler disposition, and this was perceived as weakness. When they sensed that, the next step was to drive you into the deck. If you summoned a false bravado, they would see through it. You had to find what inspired a vigorous and equal counterattack, something that dredged up an unmistakable genuine intensity. Injustice is the thing that burns me. It pissed me off, them being dickheads and playing a game out there in the middle of it all, where staying alive and getting home is the priority. You had to stand up and call them on it and not back off, no matter what they threw at you. Only then could you get on.

## Transitions:
## Richard Dickey Out/Joe Lisbon In

**As engineer of** the *Bay of Isles*, Richard Dickey knew every inch of the boat. It was no secret that he thought the only thing worth a damn on it was the engine. As far as he was concerned, they should have torn the whole boat apart around the engine and started over and maybe put a HEAD on the damn thing this time. What were they thinking? Nobody's gonna have to poop for twelve days? By the middle of July, Dickey was done. He "got through" on the *Bay of Isles*. Our mate, Andy, and cook, Jill, left with him.

It was shocking news for Susan and me. What made it worse was Dickey coming over to our place and going on about what an unsafe horror the boat was. It was hard for us to listen. I wasn't going anywhere. Money had to be made to finance a year in the North. There were no other sites open in the fleet in mid-July. He told us about his plans to get his own boat in September and asked me to go crew. I had planned on leaving by September, but if Dickey got a boat, his offer would have tempted me. He never got it.

When I arrived at the boat for gear work, the first thing to greet me was a black beard, barking orders, and obscenities. Eyes dark as his beard, he was urging us "fuckin' maggots" to get to work. He was the new mate, Joe Lisbon, himself a legend in P'town. George came down out of the wheelhouse and introduced us. I could see him eyeing me up and down like all these real fishermen of Provincetown did with wash-ashores.

George, reading the situation, said to Joe, "He's a good man . . . even if he is a ten-inch prick."

Joe Lisbon looked at George with that WTF? look on his face. George made me tell him the joke about the little man with the tuxedo sitting on the bar patron's shoulder. So that is how I met Joe Lisbon, telling him a dick joke while we were supposed to be doing gear work before the next trip. I could tell Joe wanted work, not dick jokes from me. He laughed politely, only because George had requested the dumb-ass joke, and got back to business.

Joe, a Viet Nam vet, was known in town for his no-nonsense gruff response
to everything. He was intimidating, but those who knew him loved him, for he
was sentimental, loyal, and compassionate beneath his course ways. There were
other changes. Layne was the new cook. Most boats had male cooks, so George
was progressive. Layne was attractive and had a buoyant personality; some
might say "spunky." Even though we were all used to Jill, Layne was not hard
to like. She cooked well, and like most ship's cooks, she was a strong advocate
for the crew. Another new shipmate was Roger Diaz. Roger was a teacher and
was trying his hand at this fishing business for the summer. Pleasant, cultured,
well-read, amiable, and easily given to laughter, Roger and I were tight during
our time on the *Bay of Isles*.

Then George dropped the bomb on me: I was the new starboard side winchman, and Roger was my hookup man. Huh? The winch is a skill position. If you
screwed up, you could hurt or kill a hookup man. What, was George bored?
I had been learning to run the winch under Richard Dickey's instruction and
was developing some proficiency. Dropping the rakes on the deck safely in foul
weather was a real challenge, and Dickey never put me on the winch in anything
over 25 mph winds. Now I was the guy in all weather, a sobering prospect.
Usually, we stopped fishing and started surviving when it reached winds reached
45 to 50 mph. In the higher winds and rough seas, the dredge could come over
the rail with such momentum that the rail would not stop the dredge during
the rollback. It would crash into the rail and spill up and over to outboard and
spin out of control. That's when you saw the hookup men dance. I once had the
dredge swing straight for my head, but I was the winchman holding the drag up
in the air. If I let go of the taggle rope, the dredge would drop on me. All I could
do was lean way back. The dredge came within a foot of my head.

I thought they were out of their minds, but George and Joe were dead set
on this. Despite my worry, it worked out fine. Joe Lisbon, who could do anything on a boat, generously helped me learn to manage the gear in foul weather.
(Roger Diaz survived being my hookup man.)

Things were different after Dickey, Andy and Jill left. I went to see Andy
before we left. He said they should have made me mate. I said I didn't know
enough to do that job. I knew nothing of navigation and tons of other vital
stuff.

"You know more than you think," he answered. This from the guy who
seemed to prefer keeping me at greenhorn status. There is no way I could have
been mate with my current skill set, but I was surprised I was to hear this from
Andy.

The balance of the summer brought us a few more emergencies. The Gilson hook, the hook on the lower taggle block, got loose and started swinging around on deck, with all of us trying to avoid it and corral it at the same time. It hit one of our guys, Steve, in the head. He was dazed and got a nasty, bleeding head cut. We had to steam into Montauk, New York, and get him checked out at a hospital. He was alright though he did require about twenty stitches to put his scalp together. When something like that happened (and you didn't die), everyone broke your balls about it. They had shaved his head around the wound and the visible stitches invited "Frankenstein" references.

The worst was what happened to Mike Andrews, who had just lost his dad, Capt. Ralph, on the *Cap'n Bill* the previous February. Running the portside winch, Mike was good-natured and even-tempered. We were fishing an area off Long Island, New York, and Sandy Hook, New Jersey, called "The Ruins," owing to all the shipwrecks there. The starboard taggle "two blocked": the lower block with the Gilson hook was raised too high, and it jammed into the upper block at the top of the boom. The heavy dredge was stuck way aloft. We had to pull them apart somehow.

We got what is known as a snatch block, a portable metal block that can be used anywhere. We hooked it onto the dredge, ran a line through it, and took a few turns on the portside niggerhead. Mike pulled hard on the snatch block rope with the winch, trying to separate the two blocks. I stood next to him, not more than two feet away. We heard a metallic snap. A weld on the snatch block failed, and the torque pulled the block back at us at blinding speed. There was no time to react.

It hit Mike Andrews on the side of his head, cutting his ear in half, and he went down like a sack of cement on the deck right next to me. He got up almost immediately, but we had to lay him down for wooziness, like a prizefighter who didn't know the fight was over.

It was a bloody mess. Mike's ear was hanging off his head by just a strip of skin. If that block had been two inches to the right, it would have cleaved his head in two. If it had been two *feet* to the left, it would have done the same to me. We were used to seeing blood on deck, but fish blood, not human. George called the Coast Guard, who sped out to our coordinates and evacuated Mike off the *Bay of Isles*. The Coast Guard was very efficient getting him aboard, considering a very choppy sea and the two vessels rising and falling alarmingly out of sync. Equipment failures. This business was dangerous enough without shit like this happening. George steamed into Montauk, and most of us went to the hospital in South Hampton to be with our mate.

They got a specialist to sew Mike's ear back together, but he was finished on the *Bay of Isles*, George sent him back to P'town. I heard years later that he had trouble with that ear. I do hope that was not the case. I never saw Mike again, but he was a great guy and a good mate.

# *Mutiny*

**Since our near** demise in that narrow Manasquan Inlet, we made several trips out of Pt. Pleasant, New Jersey. Fishermen need a watering hole near the fleet, and Point Pleasant's hole was Jack Ford's. A fishermen's bar must be tolerant. Bartenders understand these men who go to sea, what they go through, and what it's like to get a break from it. You can get away with a lot of shit in a fisherman's bar. You rarely see a guy get flagged in one.

Our crew gave Jack Ford frequent business in 1978. Whenever we were in and had a little time to kill, most of the crew would be there, including Captain George, who liked a beer just as well as the next guy. George was a lot of fun, and he was even more fun with a few drinks in him.

Steaming orders were for 4:00 P.M. George left the bar earlier than we did, being the captain. We headed out around 3:45, about six of us heading down to the boat. Ahead, we saw a form, a body, lying on the sidewalk. We approached cautiously, and there was Capt. George sound asleep, curled up like a baby, looking comfy, snoring away, his head resting serenely on folded hands like a pillow. He had not fallen; he had tucked himself in on the street in Point Pleasant in broad daylight.

Yeah. In fifteen minutes, we'd be steaming out into the open sea with a skipper who drank so much he decided to take a little nappy-poo on a sidewalk. Forming a ring around him, we held an impromptu council. Do we wake him and help him back to the boat so he can steam us out of that crazy-ass inlet in a delirium? It would have been Joe Lisbon bringing us out, and we all knew that but the collective wisdom, and I believe it was unanimous, was, "Nah, leave him here. This will sort itself out." We broke our circle and headed back to the boat sans skipper. Joe Lisbon was back at the boat, having gotten the Cat 12 roaring and ready to go.

"Where's George?" he asked.

"Sleeping."

"Sleeping?" said Joe, "What? Where?"

"About a block and a half in that direction."

"What the fuck?" Joe said, none of it making sense to him.

He climbed over the rail and headed for George. So now the captain and the mate were off the boat, and we crew hung out and considered our options. We decided to tell Joe that we should wait until midnight before we throw the lines. And that this was non-negotiable.

About fifteen minutes later, we saw Joe laboring with George, who had his arm over Joe's shoulder. We helped Joe get him over the rail and tucked him in his bunk below, where he was asleep almost immediately. Joe then gave the order to throw the lines.

We stood there, none of us moving for the lines. We told him about our idea of waiting till midnight. Joe was having none of that, saying the orders were to steam at 4:00 P.M. We said we were not going to sea until midnight, time enough for the cap to sleep it off. *Oh yes, you are,* Joe insisted. What happened next surprised the hell out of him. One by one, we stepped over the rail and walked off the boat. I was one of the last in the procession. I put one leg over the rail, and Joe yelled my name. I believe he thought, *"You're pretty new to this business, and you'd better think before you walk off this boat."*

"Mickey! Don't you leave this boat!" he ordered.

I hesitated, hearing my name called like that burned a hole between my shoulder blades. After pausing for a second while he spoke, I walked off the boat without looking at him. We left Joe Lisbon on the boat, cursing a blue streak, and headed back to Jack Ford's. Where else would we go? Libraries were closed. At about 11:30 P.M., we came back to the Isles en masse. Joe spoke first, sarcasm dripping from every word.

"So, are you ready to go fishing, *now?*"

Nonchalant responses in reply: "Yeah, sure." "Let's go." And that Cape Cod vernacular favorite, "Finest kind."

We threw the lines at midnight, and George, after a refreshing nap, took us out through Manasquan Inlet to go fishing.

## *Mr. Bluster*

**Fishing on Joe** Lisbon's watch required a thicker skin. He would bark from the wheelhouse window, telling us fucking maggots to get to work or work harder.

"That's what you look like to me down there crawling around on deck, fuckin' maggots," he'd yell as we were all asses and elbows.

As I got to know him more, I realized this was Joe's form of humor. We all knew, including Joe, we were working as hard as we could. Guys like Todd with self-esteem problems would have had some difficulty with that. I was on the starboard winch, Joe on the port. He was yelling at Roger on deck. Roger was almost green, older, and a little awkward; his work pace slower. Joe barked at him, pressing him to pick up the pace. For some reason, maybe that fishing loosened me up some, I pushed back on it.

"Is that all you know how to do? Yell, yell, yell?" I hollered. "You can't even say 'Please pass the fucking salt' without fucking yelling!"

Oh, I had his attention now since nobody *ever* yelled at Joe Lisbon. He looked at me in a strange way, like he was observing an odd specimen, a freak of nature. I went on and gave him some good obscenity-laced critical feedback. I guess I can put some words together when I need to. The crew on deck stopped working, curious, watching this idiot with a blow torch in the gun-powder room, waiting for the inevitable. When I had played myself out, and it was now Joe's move, he said *nothing*. He laughed, turned, shaking his head, straining to suppress his smile all the way back to the wheelhouse. I decided I liked Joe Lisbon.

## Charlie and Me and the Buoy Knot

**Point Pleasant was** getting to be a habit for the *Bay of Isles* that summer. On a balmy August night, we were heading out from Manasquan Inlet at sunset. There was little wind, but there was still a big fat slow rolling swell from a blow we had a few days before. These swells could continue for days unless we got wind coming from the opposite direction to knock them down some. In the dwindling light of early evening, George, always calling on me to do the hairy stuff, noticed the mainmast light was out and told me to go aloft and change it out. Okay, Cap.

Armed with friction tape, a bulb, and a knife between my teeth, I climbed the mainmast like an extra in a cheap pirate movie. The top of the mast was about three stories above the deck. You don't want to fall here. The boat rolled from starboard to port and back on this running swell, so you are hanging over the ocean from one side to the other, swaying back and forth on an inverted pendulum. The higher up the mast you are, the more dramatic the swing. Then cut the friction tape around the globe with the knife, hold the new bulb in the mouth (I thought of Uncle Fester), remove the globe without dropping it, unscrew the old bulb, replace it with the new, tape the globe in place, all with one hand. The other hand clings to the mast to avoid the falling three stories thing, all while swaying high over the water—piece of cake, Cap.

Sometimes the captain would decide to head for a different spot but would mark the current tow with a buoy. Or he used a buoy on a tow as a turning point marker. These buoys had metal reflectors on top to be seen in the sun and on the radar screen. So, George wanted a buoy on a tow and asked me to tie a buoy knot to the float and set it out. Let's see, buoy knot, buoy knot, didn't cover that one in the Boy Scouts. Rather than go back to the captain and say, "Gee, George, I haven't a freaking clue how to tie a buoy knot," I went to that font of knowledge standing nearby, Charlie.

"Charlie, help me out here. How do you tie a buoy knot?"

My tone suggested that I was requesting a temporary truce in this "I'm the real fisherman, and you're a total horse's ass" scenario he had going. Charlie just shrugged as if to say, "I dunno." I did not even rate an auditory response. I had been fishing with this guy for two months, and he was still a prick.

"Thanks a lot, MATE," I said. "Thanks for helping out a fellow MATE."

I guess I was trying to appeal to a basic tenet all fishermen honor, if however grudgingly, that recognizes all parties on the same ship as mates, and we, if you will, sink or swim together. Let's hear it for shame-based interventions. Charlie grabbed the buoy from me, annoyed, tied the knot, and showed me how to do it with an attitude: "There, see, you little fuck-head?" was implied. We threw the buoy over the side together. I thanked him. I'm not saying he was ready to smooch me. He probably disliked me even more for it. But I learned how to tie a buoy knot (also known as an anchor hitch) from a guy who knew his craft. I can still tie one all these years later. Thanks, Charlie.

## Greenhorn No More

**We put into** New Bedford whenever we needed specialized repair or equipage. Once George was in such a hurry to be bound, we backed over a stern line before the crew could safely pull it onboard. The line got sucked up by the prop, the shaft thumping all the way from Provincetown to New Bedford (which irked the crap out of George), where we had to hire a diver to go down and undo the mess.

As summer wore on, changes on the boat continued. Charlie left, and I can't say that I missed his personality.

We certainly missed his expertise. Being older now, I understand his attitude better. He just wished things were the way they were "back in the day" before us young freaks and adventure junkies infiltrated the fleet, interlopers all. The crew was less experienced in his absence.

One afternoon in New Bedford, this was glaringly apparent. We were "end for ending" the tackle lines. Since they lift the dredges onto the deck, the rope had to be healthy. As rope ages, it gets brittle; no doubt helped along by continuous exposure to salt water, sun, and tremendous stress. Boats with hydraulic block and tackle use metal cable, so replacement is less of an issue. Rope tackle has a more immediate expiration date; it had to hold, or someone could get killed.

George got the new line in a New Bedford boatyard, and everyone was in on the act of end-for-ending the tackle. After cutting the old taggle knot, the new line is taped to the end of the old line, pulled through the various turns of the blocks until the entire circuit of tackle is new. Now came the all-important, almost mystical, taggle knot. There was some difference of opinion as to how to tie it. George had one idea, Joe Lisbon and Legs another. I'll bet Charlie would have known.

George: "How did Dickey tie it?"

Dickey was the apparent last word in all things gear-wise and had tied the knots we had just cut to pieces. No one seemed to know, but I remembered very well how he had tied it. Being interested in the language of rope, I had paid rapt attention to every turn of the process.

"I know. I watched him," I said from the back of the crowd.

Surprised, everyone turned and looked at me. The blocks lay on the hatch cover like patients on an operating table. The circle of men surrounding it opened to allow the young whelp access. Everyone was quiet, evincing images of the moment adolescent Arthur approached Excalibur to remove it from the stone. I perfectly reproduced the knot that I had seen Richard Dickey tie. Joe Lisbon was the first to speak.

"That's it. Good," he said, recognizing its correctness, turning instantly for the wheelhouse.

High praise indeed from Joe.

I duplicated the effort on the other block. Those knots did not let go, and a trusting crew worked around the dredges the rest of the summer. These Provincetown fishermen allowed a skinny kid from New Jersey with bluebirds flying around his head to tie the taggle knots. Walking away from the hatch cover, I knew I crossed a line: I wasn't green anymore.

## *The Triangle*

**Roger Diaz was** my hookup man. That I did not kill him with a dredge, I hope he appreciates. He was older than me and greying, and, like me, he was not your typical fisherman. Educated and a teacher by profession, Roger and I talked our way through each watch much like I had with Dickey, making long trips more tolerable. We could talk about literature, poetry, anything. The more experienced guys were a little hard on him. Like Dickey, he was an excellent complainer, very articulate, and an avid subscriber to common sense. He disdained stupidity and could respond to it with bitter sarcasm.

We made a trip that was a study in frustration from start to finish. Everywhere we went, George could not find scallops. He was very reactionary at times and could strike out in a different direction because he was pissed off. The decision was to head out way east, where we had never been all summer.

Someone had been in the wheelhouse and got a peek at the chart and claimed we were bound for the northern edge of the Bermuda Triangle. That made for unusual fo'c'sle talk or "scuttlebutt." We had already been out about ten days when George made this "far east" decision. Man, we were ready to "head for the barn" and say goodbye to this hot, humid, scallopless waste of time. After the last tow, instead of the typical 24-hour steam back to port, it would be far longer and cost us more fuel. Whether or not we were on the edge of the Triangle, I do not know. It seemed to me it would have been a lot of further south. But peculiar things occurred once we arrived at the grounds.

First, the dredges got crossed, which enraged George. Stomping his way aft, he grabbed the portside cable where it went down to the water out of the gallous and downright throttled it with both hands. He had a few off-color words to say here as well. Then things started to break; welds began to fail, stuff that never snaps or breaks. The compass seemed possessed, spinning more than staying on bearing. Everyone was blaming it on The Triangle. George said even the LORAN numbers were off, and he was not sure where we were exactly. But the trip dragged on. George was determined to bring a good catch to the wharf, but the dredges kept coming up empty.

There were sliding windows in the aft part of the galley, which you could open and speak to the winchman standing at his post. Our spirited cook, Layne, slid open the window by the starboard winch during a tow.

"Mickey!" she said in an excited whisper. "We're out of water!"

It took me a few moments to realize the importance of what she was saying. This was good news. No, it was great news. You can't stay out to sea without fresh water for too long. Maybe now George would put an end to this busted trip. Roger came over.

"What's up?"

Layne could hardly contain her joy. "We're out of fresh water."

It was hard to believe. The water tanks on these boats were big, and since there was no shower and *certainly* no head, that tank should have lasted forever. Its only use on this boat was for drinking, cooking, and washing dishes. *The Triangle!*

I spread the word on deck. It swept through us all like a cool fresh breeze in the fetid humidity. Everyone was excited, all of us wanting to go home. Then an awful thought occurred to me. The *Bay of Isles* had an emergency five-gallon plastic container of fresh water lashed outside the wheelhouse. Maybe George would ration that water like Captain Bligh and try to squeeze out another day or two of fishing. I voiced my fear to Layne and Roger.

The thought of this infuriated Layne. She swelled up before me, and I instinctively got out of her path. She stormed out of the galley in her apron and onto the deck, headed straight for the emergency fresh water with a kitchen knife. She slashed the line securing it to the bulkhead, and tossed the can right the hell overboard. Roger and I watched it sink in our wake as the boat passed by, surrendering our last drop of fresh water to The Triangle. We were astonished.

"There! Now we can go home!" Layne said in triumph.

We all spontaneously cheered our modern-day Fletcher Christian. It was a great moment. When George got up for his watch, Layne informed him that we were out of fresh water. He was pissed, "How could this happen?" written on his face.

He turned to us and said, "That's it. We're bound."

"I understand," I said. "700 strikes and you're out."

We hauled back and left the gear onboard and set a course for Provincetown, Cape Cod, thank God. Layne was the hero of the trip, and I will never forget her spirit that day.

# "Getting Through"

**I had made** no secret of my plan to spend a year in Canada. George had been expecting it. My last trip aboard the *Bay of Isles* began on August 15, 1978. This time we had as crew the famous fast-cutting Jo Jo, he of the infamous, obnoxious drunk act. The last time I had seen Jo Jo, I was on the wrong end of his murderous intentions and jumped from a loft to escape him. But this was a completely different person.

Scalloping Jo Jo absolutely rocked. I suspect people put up with him when he was drunk because he was a great guy and a born fisherman. Always talkative and personable, he had a great sense of fun and a kindly way. Apologizing for giving me a hard time (murdering me would be a more apt description), I was surprised he even remembered it. He was something to watch work, too. He was short, stocky, and all muscle; one of those hard workers who made it look effortless and always made the gear behave as he wished. His shucking was like watching an accomplished professional athlete, like a major league pitcher hitting his spots. We should have had a shucking contest that summer with just two participants: Jo Jo and Dickey. There would have been much wagering, fortunes won and lost, drinking of beer. Sea Biscuit vs. War Admiral. It would have been the classic battle of furious speed vs. patient accuracy. Lost opportunity there.

George fancied himself a good chess player. I used to play with some regularity in my younger years and played the game like I do anything else: relentlessly. I told him that I played too, so he challenged me to a high stakes game in the galley as we were steaming out to the grounds on an earlier trip: his two shares plus 10% of the catch versus my share. A bunch of guys hung out and watched this essentially theatrical exercise. I defeated him and made him sweat it out. I blathered for days about how I would spend those two shares plus 10%. He seemed worried I intended to collect. My reward was the fun of needling him and making him think I might be serious.

This last trip turned out to be a broker, with not much scallop and plenty enough lousy weather. We had to put one of the crew off in Point Pleasant, so we were seven-handed. The plan was the six and three watch for ten days. Ouch.

The journal: "Monday, August 21 7:08 on (wheel) watch. It's blowing. Too sloppy to fish. Laying-to on portside rake (the rake used as an anchor with the boat tethered). Presently in the wheelhouse listening to rock and roll. I'm the only one awake at present, minding the ship, having a good time. Sea is beautiful—swells and white water. It's only rock and roll, but I like it."

During my first ever wheel watch, I was steaming in the dark to the Nantucket Shoals. This time was very different. We were laying-to, which meant that the boat was without power and dealing with high seas. Laying on a rake was the same as being anchored. The vessel will naturally face the oncoming seas. My responsibility was keeping an eye on the radar for unannounced guests and scan visually out the wheelhouse window for anything out of the ordinary. It was a pretty nasty storm, and I was enjoying every bit of it.

Joe Lisbon had an abscessed tooth. A man's man, he put up with it for a while, but it swelled, and it could not be ignored. I also noted that we were having trouble with the gear. As I was bagging up, the captain said we were bound. We arrived in P'town on the night of August 22nd at around 11:20. I was in the wheelhouse hanging out with George during the last hour of steaming. Whenever George Hann and I hung out, we laughed a lot. He let me take the *Bay of Isles* through The Race and around The Point in the dark, a function usually reserved for the captain. It was an incredible thrill for me and wondrous to behold that curve of lights around the harbor of our home port. It was the last time I would stand on the deck of this boat.

After this last trip, I told George I'd be getting through. We shook hands amiably, and I took my gear off the boat. He called me a ten-inch prick for old time's sake. George was a good man, and it was on his boat I became a fisherman. We parted on the best of terms, and he told me to look him up next spring when I returned. Already feeling nostalgic about it, I left the *Bay of Isles*, but now I had a lover to take to my nest in September and—wait! Carol. What was I going to do about her? I was so busy being in love and trying not to get killed that I hadn't given that part much thought.

Susan was committed to Café Edwige for another week, so I enjoyed a week of leisure in P'town in late summer. My journal went from chronicling fishing trips to entries like: "Reading Keats. Having banana pancakes ala Renehan at the Edwige." I ran into Dickey a lot and spent time in his home with his Portuguese earth-mother wife, Betty. Betty was an absolute doll and was a perfect complement to Dickey. That she loved him so was apparent. She shared his no-nonsense life view and loved a good laugh. The journal: "Spend the morning at Dickey's. We talked all morning of ancient ruins and mysteries: Egypt, the Andes, England, Mesopotamia, etc." Ah, Dickey, I miss you.

I stopped by to see our grizzled former mate, Andy. He said he was headed north or west and hadn't entirely made up his mind. That was the last time I saw Andy, and I wonder what became of him. Lobster had gotten on a tuna boat during this hiatus and asked if I wanted to pilot the boat.

I made my way to the harbor the next day and found a speed boat of about 25 feet in length. On the bow was a long "pulpit," an extension of the bow like a narrow catwalk with a waist-high cage around it to keep a person from falling overboard. I was wondering how you catch tuna with this rig. I had seen yellowfin tuna taken out at the Co-op. Some of the larger ones could approach 1000 lbs.

Lobster explained it to me. This was a harpoon operation. Being a small craft, it wouldn't do to take it sixty miles offshore. One to five miles was more like it. Far enough, though, to not want to have to swim back to P'town. One guy's job is to be the spotter. He scans the waters with binoculars, horizon, looking for tuna breaking surface. If he thinks he sees something, he sends the pilot in the direction of the sighting. Then the harpooner takes his gear out to the very end of the pulpit, hanging out over the water on the narrowest of platforms, rocking and rolling to the seas. Once the harpooner spots his target, he will point the harpoon in the direction of the fish. The pilot's job is to steer the boat in the direction of the harpoon. It is a chase, and when the pulpit man sees the opportunity for a shot, he will "from the depths of Hell stab at thee." At least that was the theory.

We never got close to a tuna. All day long, we just scudded around out there and never saw a damn thing. It was a great day for a speed boat ride and a few beers, though. I know this is an "over the long haul" kind of operation, like, if you get a big enough fish, days of searching would be worth it, but I was coming from the constant action of scalloping. Every twenty to thirty minutes, you had a haul-back to deal with and shucking. The only thing we did that held my interest here was that we "longlined" for bluefish while looking for tuna. A long-line is just that: a long line with a series of baited hooks towed behind the boat. Bluefish, for their size, are good fighters, especially hauling back by hand. You'd think you had a shark at the end of the line, but it wasn't enough to overcome my scallop boat-acquired ADHD. I quit when we reached the wharf.

One morning, I walked on Commercial Street with Boston, Susan's black lab, who became a close buddy. I ran into Dickey, who was out driving around. He liked to smoke a bone and drive, so he shanghaied Boston and me, and we went down to Wellfleet. He showed me many enchanted hollows and hideaways that Joe Tourist never sees. Richard was the perennial tour guide to anything cool on this green earth, and he relished the role.

He took me to the Herring River, which was now boiling with flopping herring. Dickey said they were staying there, waiting for the tide to change, so they could continue their inexorable trip upstream to spawn. Many were mangled and had chunks missing but were still alive. They moved in swirls in the water. He told me the seagulls were having their way with them until the tide changed. Gulls were diving like Stukas and taking pieces out of the squirming herring. It would be like walking down a crowded street, and suddenly a baseball-sized chunk of your arm is ripped out. Geez, and I thought I had it hard.

We went to Cape Cod or Highland Light. The Highlands of Truro was the highest part of the Cape where the last glacial advance piled the pulverized rock. Here the land drops off to the beach, a hundred feet down. At such a sharp angle, you could get killed if you went over the edge. At this highest point, they put a lighthouse. I had seen this lighthouse many times but from a different perspective. The journal:

> M: "I've seen this from sea, but I've never been right here."
> RD: (amused) "You old salt, you."
> When we made it back to Provincetown, a black cat darted across the front of the truck's path and skittered into an alley. Dickey cursed and muttered, obviously disturbed. From the journal:
> RD: "Thanks. Just what I needed."
> Further on down Commercial Street, a light-colored cat crossed our path in the opposite direction.
> RD: "See that? That cat just erased the bad luck."
> M: "You're a superstitious old bastard, aren't you?"
> RD: (grin) "I'm alive, ain't I? (pause) Hey, I've been on a lot of shaky boats."

Yeah. I wrote it in the journal like that. But Dickey made me do it. He was so damned theatrical.

We planned to leave as soon as Susan finished at the Edwige. Hitching with a dog straps you with a distinct handicap, so she talked to friends Frank and Karen Milby. Frank is a well-known watercolor artist in P'town. They were

interested in going up and staying with us for about a week, wanting to see
Nova Scotia and Bear River artist friends.

In early September, Frank, Karen, their children Shaila and Brandon, Susan, Boston, and I piled into the Milby's station wagon and headed north. I
had a one-hundred-year-old valise that I used to carry. It contained nothing but
poetry and five thousand dollars of hard-earned fishing cash in one-hundred-
dollar bills. A year on a hill in the woods was now becoming a reality.

~ ~ ~

# PART III

## The Cabin

# *Beginnings*

**Asked many times** what possessed a 19-year-old kid to buy six acres of land in Nova Scotia to build a log cabin, I realized the answer is in the question: Possessed. So how did I become possessed?

Things could have been a lot worse than growing up in Atlantic City, and I do not know anyone who complains about it. It had the beach, ocean, back bay, and marshlands, seven miles of boardwalk, all for the townies in the offseason. Our house was the last house on Chelsea Avenue, right on the bay, four blocks from the ocean.

Dad had the Irish Disease. During the '50s and '60s, the way people dealt with addiction and its collateral effects was underdeveloped at best, compared to the armory-full of resources at our disposal today. We behaved in the textbook codependent ways, our interactions sickened by living side by side with disease. My role, as per ACOA (Adult Children of Alcoholics), was "Mascot." He is the one who entertains, making everyone laugh to distract from the pain circus. If the mascot gets serious and displays an honest reaction to the craziness, well, you do not have to take him seriously, do you? He's just the comedian. Such displays were often dismissed with the judgment that I was "over-emotional," the content of what I was saying was therefore never addressed. But that's the idea.

Dad was a police officer in Atlantic City and well-respected in the outside world. Everyone raved about what a great man "Mack" was. I wondered who this great man was and why he did not bring some of that greatness home with him. He was not a loud, obnoxious, beat the wife kind of drunk. He was withdrawn and disinterested. He worked and slept. When he was not doing that, he drank and gambled away any extra money that might have increased our comfort level. Any joys he found in life were clearly found outside our home.

Our lives revolved around his shift work. When he was on the midnight to eight shift, Mom put a sign on the front door that said, "Father Sleeping" so people wouldn't bang on the door. We could make no noise at all, Mom being hall monitor, shushing us when our voices edged above conversation tone.

He would not come home right away from shift work, the bar his first stop. Mom was always trying to make sure he would get home with enough time to sleep it off and rest some so he could make the next shift; the family's survival depending on this. Sometimes she would drive to the bar, and, not being afraid to play the shame card, she would send one of my sisters in after him.

Most people could not tell Dad was drinking. We could tell just by looking at his face (the blunted, a little bit stupid *Who, Me? I haven't been drinking* face), by the sound and cadence of his footsteps coming up the back steps (too much thinking, too mechanical: *Here's a step, now another*) and even by the way he closed the car door when he arrived home. He'd shut it with a delicacy not in evidence when he was sober. (*Man, I'm so fucked up, gotta be careful with this door!*) He drank to feel normal and drank on the job. A friend of his told my mom that Dad would have to have a quart of liquor in him before he would even stagger a little.

If his shift work allowed, he would join us for dinner. "Drinking Dad" would pick on us. He would not pick on Mom, a losing battle if there ever was one. Anyone talking at the table became a target. I was talkative, outgoing, and inquisitive, leaving myself wide open to criticism. Okay, I was a chatterbox. The Maguire men were men of few words. I was more like Mom, which I assume annoyed the crap out of him. Mom would see me launch into a topic and would try to save me by subtly shaking her head "No" so only I could see, but by then, it was too late. The world was so full of cool stuff and possibilities; I just wanted to talk about it all. Mistake.

My friend Tom Lynch had a dad who did things with him. Captain on the same police force, Mr. Lynch, when his shift work allowed, would play ball with Tom, go places, do cool stuff like archery. Man, that killed me. *Archery.* Mom saw the glaring difference and would yell at Dad to get up from the couch where he was drinking beer and go out and "have a catch with your son, dammit!" Yeah, those were a lot of fun.

In my teens, I finally mustered the courage to share with Tom that Dad was a drunk, the dark family secret. Until then, I had no one to talk to, and it was all bottled up inside me, so much so that I had to go on the bland ulcer diet because of acid reflux. Dad took me to the doctor because stomach acid was eating holes in my mouth. The doctor, family friend Eddie McKnight, knew about Dad's alcoholism.

"Is he under any kind of stress?" he asked Dad right in front of me, trawling for a nibble of insight.

"No. Just his music . . ." Dad answered.

My music? I played in a rock and roll band, and music was one of the few respites I had from this insane tug of war between my parents. How freaking out of touch can you get? Can I have another Rolaids?

I once saw the desperation of his addiction. We were watching TV when he got up to go to the kitchen for a beer. I walked in on him and saw his trick. He liked to drink Rolling Rock, the green devil. He was standing at the fridge with the door open, and I saw him drain a 12-ounce bottle in three seconds like it was a frat party contest. I had never seen anyone drink a beer, or even a Coke for that matter, with such urgent need. I surprised him, and when he looked at me, I could tell I had caught him at something, seen his dependency. The exposed expression that had made it past the checkpoint of his secrets was quickly veiled, and "Nobody Home Dad" returned to his face in a flash. He cracked open another Rolling Rock and went back to his couch in the living room, where I guess every night was "Two-for-One" night.

Having had so many Boy Scout camping trips under our belts, Tom and I were allowed to go camping by ourselves. We had an old Army pup tent and camped on Babcock Creek near Mays Landing. It was January or February, frost forming on the inside canvas. In the middle of our adolescent all-nighter with the flashlight on, I swore Tom to secrecy and unveiled my shame at last in that frozen tent. When I finished telling him, I was not prepared for his devastating response. He said, "I know." My God, so everyone *knows*? Did they sit around the dinner table discussing it like: "Please pass the dinner rolls . . . where was I? Oh, yes, we were talking about Mickey's dad being a hopeless drunk. . . ."

Dad even went away to rehab. Twice. The ACPD forced him to, or he would lose his job. He remained on the police force thanks to Tom's father, Captain Lynch, who had grown up with Dad. Before the first stint in rehab, Mr. Lynch said to Mom, "Of course, Marie, you know he's an alcoholic?"

Mom was thunderstruck. The daily struggle over drinking was one thing. The life sentence of the stigmatized label and all its baggage was quite another. "Of course," she replied without missing much more than half a beat, but she told me later that her world crashed down on her head in those few seconds. I don't know how Mom did it, raising three kids without much from her husband or even the rest of the family.

Dad's mother was of little help. We were renting half of the duplex my grandparents owned. Mom gathered her strength and told my grandmother, who we called "Mom-Mom," the heartbreaking news that Dad was going to rehab for alcoholism. The first thing Mom-Mom said was, "How will the rent get paid?" No help there. Mom told her off. Annoyed to remind her that this was her son's life they were talking about, she told her she would get her rent because Dad would still draw a paycheck thanks to Capt. Lynch.

Well, Dad went away for over a month. When he got home, clean and sober, he seemed like the Harold Maguire as he was meant to be. He had color in his face, not that familiar bloated, pasty look. Svelte and sharp, aware and present, he looked like a movie star. New Dad was nothing like Drinking Dad. He took us in when he looked at us and even asked questions that required an answer. We allowed ourselves to hope things were going to be quite different. But as the weeks stretched to months, Mom noticed little things, familiar patterns, sounds, looks. Not wanting to believe it at first, she came to suspect that he was sneaking around, stealing nips here and there. So we all participated in a bottle hunt. Yay, a bottle hunt!

Being a part of this sad reconnaissance had a strange effect on us. Until then, it felt like we kids were innocents to be protected at all cost, a neutral country between two hostiles. But Mom had been fighting this losing battle alone for years and needed allies. There was a new connection to her now. I had grown up and made the team somehow, had turned pro, was a confidante. It felt like we were all now old enough to talk plainly about what was wrong with this family. The battle lines were evident now. There was a new intimacy that we all shared on those hunts. But man, the cost. We all wanted to be the one who discovered the prize, hit the walk-off homer. It was fun and challenging until we found it: a bottle of vodka. Congratulations, you have won . . . what did we win? Something worse than nothing. I learned later that vodka is the choice of alcoholics because it is more difficult to smell on the breath. My mother was a mixture of rage and defeat when we found it, and our fantasy of a better life evaporated away with the vodka fumes wafting up from the sink where she dumped it.

He eventually went to an ACPD mandated second rehab. But we had been trained in the lowered expectations department, and "hope" was relegated to "myth" status. Dad blamed Mom for both rehabs and made an even bigger deposit in the resentment account, so it was all a big waste. But not entirely, I guess. Some of us learned something.

# Trouble

**Before Scouting, I** explored trouble as a potential career option. Typical of that time, a classmate and I broke into a house in Chelsea Heights. I went to the china cabinet and initiated the systematic destruction of the dishes ritual, which led to other improvisations when I ran out of teacups. I was literally swinging from the chandelier over the dining room table when a retired cop happened to be passing by and, on hearing the ruckus, came in and nabbed us both. He asked my friend's name, and he dutifully told him his name and where he lived. Me, I didn't give my real name. But instead of making one up, I gave the name of another kid I knew. Well, that came back to bite me in the ass, and soon enough, the patsy's parents called my parents. I was in real trouble over this. Mom was livid.

"Why did you give them Bobby Martin's name?"

"It's the only name I could think of."

Good God, how she screamed at me. "What the hell is wrong with your own name?"

Mom's brother, Uncle Joe, thought that was great. Mom was outraged by his point of view, but he stuck to his guns.

"The kid's a survivor," said Uncle Joe.

Being raised in an orphanage in the 1920s along with his brother and sister, being a survivor was a highly valued quality. Mom couldn't buy into it and went with moral indignation with a side of shame.

As a police officer, Dad never wanted to suffer the humiliation of getting sent on a call and having one of his kids be the reason. He didn't say much to us usually, but he made an exception here.

"Don't you EVER be the reason I'm sent out on a call."

OK, Dad. Sure thing. And there's never been a limit that's above testing. Chuckie Scott and I were in an abandoned industrial building next to the rail-road tracks not far from home. We thought it was cool to throw bottles and bricks at this big-ass empty sheet metal cabinet, mainly because it made so much noise. And since we felt it needed an assist, we screamed as we smashed.

It was amazing to us that two young fellows could make that much noise. I guess the nearby residents thought it was amazing too, and they figured the cops would be equally amazed. In time we heard the crunching dry gravel of a vehicle pulling up in front of the building.

We ran upstairs for a better look. It was a police car—a police car with *my dad* getting out of it. Dad's warning and implied death threat hit me like a brick on a sheet metal cabinet. We heard my father open the sliding barn-type door to gain entrance and then his footsteps coming up the stairs. There were only seconds to act. And I froze. Chuckie made for a back window for a hang jump from the second story. I was usually the first guy to impulsively suggest we jump off a roof or out of a building, but the thought of being obliterated by my father seized me up. Realizing at last that this was my only hope to settle down and have a family someday, I ran for one of the other back windows. Chuckie and I looked at each other for a surreal moment, hanging together from the outside of a building, letting go simultaneously. We landed in weeds unscathed and ran like hell. I had cheated father-induced death by mere seconds and avoided breaking a leg in the fall. Dad never found out I was the reason for the call. Spoiler alert: I was able to settle down eventually and have a family.

# Scouting

**It was a** critical time in a young life; you know, when the die is cast, determining whether you will become a serial killer or a productive member of society. One of my friends had joined the Boy Scouts, and he was doing all kinds of cool things like winter camping trips and learning how to survive in the wild. He had a paper route, and his troop was going on a trip to Canada. He asked me to take his route for about ten days. When he returned, he told about all the cool stuff he did there: hiking, canoeing, and working with rope. The closest I had ever been to Canada was its map on the Canada Dry ginger ale bottle. Seeing I was intrigued, he invited me to a meeting. I went, joined the troop, and soon we went on our first trip.

We were going to "The Cabin" on a lake in Oceanville, New Jersey. The Lily Lake cabin looked to have been built during the Depression, possibly a Civilian Conservation Core project. The cabin was about 20 by 40, made of logs with a stone fireplace. A shed-like room adjoined one end with an old potbelly stove that served as a kitchen. The windows were shuttered, no glass, the cabin unfurnished. The troop slept on the floor along both sides of the long walls, barracks-style. We built a fire, setting up an evening of songs, skits, ghost stories, jokes, and camaraderie.

That there could be an alternative to the exhausting battle between my parents was a radical thought, but here it was: a winter trip to a log cabin—no angst, arguments, blame-shifting, or guilt. No being picked on. It was like living with the constant buzz of a bad fluorescent light and being surprised by the silence when someone finally turns it off. We worked on projects as a unit, exploration and hikes, moments of hilarity, times of instruction, and solemnity. There was responsibility and accountability and quite a lot of staring at the fire. It was an environment where the right thing always happened, and if it did not, it was made right. There was order to the universe. There was respect for one another. There was brotherhood. I was enthralled.

In the quiet of the first night, except for the measured breathing of a troop of sleeping scouts and the occasional snap of a coal, I got up in the soft orange light of a hearth full of embers. The log cabin, in the warmth of low firelight, sanctified by the incense of a bit of woodsmoke, was more beautiful and compelling than any machination of my imagination thus far. It was impossibly magnificent. As if driven by that night's Spirit Guide and mindful not to wake anyone, I opened a shutter to a snowy night. Scrub pines were loaded, arms bent. Gauzy bands of snow sifted in the wind across frozen Lily Lake. As I gazed back and forth from the formidable coals in the fireplace and log walls bathed in their glow, to the winter scene outside, I surprised myself when spoken words escaped my throat.

"I want this."

The boy-mind thought "this" was a log cabin in the snow, but I was really talking about peace. My higher self nailed it. *So, this is peace. Yeah, I'll be having more of that.* It was an image I brought into my troubled home like a life jacket after that short but epic trip to the Lily Lake cabin. From then on, the vision of that cabin became a shelter because I knew someday I would grow up and build my own peace construct. Possessed now with how I felt at that open window during a December night, this cabin yet to be made became my primary preoccupation for the next nine years.

The energy and waywardness that found expression in breaking and entering, vandalism, and starting little fires here and there was now entirely redirected

Oceanville, New Jersey log cabin after it burned.

toward earthy pursuits and high-minded ideals and campfires. We learned how to build a fire even when all your wood is wet, how to use flint and steel to start it, how to cook complicated meals on an open fire, how to use a map and compass, where to find edible plants found in the wild, how to stalk deer, tell direction from the stars, how to use and sharpen an ax and a knife. We learned a lot about rope, knots, and their many purposes.

Our scoutmaster was inspiring, and his standards high. Nothing short of excellence in anything we attempted was acceptable, from washing dishes to pitching camp. Our troop almost always, okay, *always* won the coveted best camping skill trophy at the camporee competitions with other scout troops. One year we slept in lean-tos lashed together with rope topped with moss and lichen rooves. The next camporee, we repeated building lean-tos, but rather than lash them, we used a bucksaw and joined them together with dovetail notches. Another camporee was in a field at the edge of the marshland. The other troops camped in the dry field while our troop went right into the marsh and built what we called muskrat huts on stilts that we entered from underneath. Once, we lashed treehouses into the tree. During a winter competition, we made igloos and slept in them for two nights.

We made a working drawbridge out of poles and rope lashing. I learned lifesaving techniques and first aid protocol. I learned to think calmly and clearly in an emergency, to find water, and make a solar water still. We learned to signal for help in various ways, memorize the semaphore flag alphabet, make water rescues, resuscitation techniques, and safety applied to everything we did.

Not "cool" like being on the football or basketball team, many kids considered you a sissy if you were a Boy Scout. But I persisted undeterred. And while I was absorbing all this sissy stuff, the Scout Laws profoundly affected me: A Scout is Trustworthy, Loyal, Helpful, Courteous, Kind, Obedient, Cheerful, Thrifty, Brave, Clean and Reverent. Our scoutmaster motivated us to aspire to each of these ideals. His great gift was sensing what might be missing from a youngster's character puzzle. A big missing chunk of my puzzle was the self-confidence piece.

After about a year, I was made a patrol leader, which gave me some responsibility and a little leeway in decision-making. During our second or third summer camp in the Pine Barrens, we camped along the Wading River near the ruins of 19th century Harrisville at Bodine Field. That year the plan was to have the troop canoe a few miles downriver to the next campsite called Beaver Branch. We had a map of the river, but no one from the troop had canoed it before. There are some twists and turns but, let's be clear: this was not white-water rapids. It was smooth, easy cedar water in flat New Jersey. But our scoutmaster made a big deal of the "uncharted waters" and that we had to send an "explorer" ahead to chart the river first. Cool. I knew it would not be me.

It was me. On an inflatable canvas raft, I paddled the run alone. I could not figure out why it was me instead of my comrade and friend, Peanut Lloyd, who seemed far more capable. But I needed this more, and our scoutmaster knew it. The troop would await me at Beaver Branch. In the mid to late '60s, the heroes of the day were the astronauts. The race to the moon was going on, and they were the Lewis and Clarks of the day. They were all naval commanders. The scoutmaster surrounded my exploratory journey with so much pomp and circumstance; it was the final touch when he addressed me as "Commander Maguire" to the rest of the troop. They came down to the river's edge to see me off into the unknown.

During the run, I tried to make mental notes: "Submerged log here. Bad current near turn there" and so on. I was alone on this river in the middle of a wilderness with no one to lean on but myself. It was the first time in my life that anyone had faith in me to succeed on my own. When I arrived at Beaver Branch, the whole troop stood at water's edge cheering and clapping as I made shore: the splash-down of an Apollo mission. We all hiked back to Bodine Field with much excitement, where I was escorted to the headquarters tent for debriefing. Inside a chart of the river waited, and there, Commander Maguire imparted his knowledge of the hazards of the mighty Wading River. I think it was a stroke of pure genius to put this task on a mixed-up kid with tons of passion and no self-confidence to back it up. It was a fresh start.

I made Eagle Scout at age 15 in 1969. Dad had a habit of being drunk when you needed him most (Thanksgiving, Christmas) and made no exception for my Eagle Court of Honor, though I had hoped. State Assemblyman Smith was there to lend his officious title to the import of the event. Dad shook my hand and said he was proud of me. He was shitfaced. There it was: the *drinking but trying to look like I haven't been* face. And the tacit admission that *I just can't make it through my son's Eagle Court of Honor without a few pick-me-ups* obliterated the "I'm proud of you" message. I would not hear that part of the message until I understood addiction a little better.

There were a couple of instances when I broke through whatever wall he put up and impressed him. When we were 13 and 14, Tom and I began camping on our own. Dad drove us the first time and hung out for a while as we went into the woods, cut dead standing timber with hatchets, and made one of those lashed lean-tos with the moss and lichen roofs that I had learned to build in the scouts.

"Kid knows what he's doing," he told Mom after he left us.

Tom, the elder, got his license before me. We drove out to the middle of the Pine Barrens on those sugar-sand dirt roads to nowhere in winter. We had dressed lightly in a classic January thaw and hung the car up hopelessly, trying to turn around. After sunset, the temperature dove to night-time in January. Forced to hike twelve miles out to Batsto, we would have to call home for a ride, about an hour's drive.

"Historic Batsto" was closed and dark. But there was a payphone. We searched our pockets and found cash but no coin, except for a penny. So what do you know, I had learned from a ruffian I had worked with on the beach how to make a dime phone call on a penny. In the sixties, payphones had slots that you put the coin in flat, not vertically. If you put a little foamy spit on the penny and gently let it go in the nickel slot, after several tries, you would hear "ding-ding," and the payphone treated the penny as if it were a dime (in the nickel slot. Go figure. Who thinks of this shit?).

I got the "ding-ding" first try and called home collect (you had to "ding-ding" before you made a collect call). Mom was not happy. Dad even less so. The source of his unhappiness was the drive out there before his midnight to eight shift. So, we hung out in the cold and waited. Dad described going in the blackness through a series of marginal roads. He found us waiting at the park. I know he wasn't thrilled but overall, he was good about it. What he said to Mom surprised me, though I heard it from her later.

"Don't you EVER worry about that kid in the woods again!" That had a nice ring to it.

Harold Maguire was talented athletically and artistically. That these talents were rarely given the attention they deserved, I think, is why he drank. If your innermost yearnings are ignored, you must then anesthetize.

Around 1967, our scoutmaster decided to have summer camp somewhere other than the Pine Barrens. At our weekly troop meeting, he told us we were going on a trip for summer camp. He closed his eyes and instructed us to open an atlas of North America randomly, after which he would put his thumb down. Whatever lay beneath the thumb, that is where we would go for a month in the summer.

Staring at us from under his thumb was Canada's Province of Nova Scotia. To a thirteen-year-old boy, it sounded far off and magical. I thought it a country unto itself. We went the long way, up into Vermont for an overnight, across New Hampshire, Maine, and New Brunswick, Canada. It was an enthralling idea, being in a different *country*. We camped for several days at Fundy National

Park on the cliffs overlooking the Bay of Fundy, famed for the highest tides in the world (56 feet). I wondered what all the non-sissies were doing. After several days at this park, we drove around and into Nova Scotia, down the Annapolis Valley, and out Rt. 8, where we camped for a few weeks at Kejimkujik National Park, locally known simply as "Keji."

When the month-long trip neared its end, we headed down across the old Bear River Bridge, through Smith's Cove, and into Digby, where we took a three-hour ferry ride across the Bay of Fundy to St. John, New Brunswick.

Two things made a bold impression on my young mind: The stunning combination of sea and forest and the people of Nova Scotia. A more generous and amiable people cannot be found.

# Father Joe

**Preoccupied for eight** years with the serenity I discovered that winter night at the Lily Lake cabin, I made drawings and floor plans. I bought *The Foxfire Book*, that era's bible for young folks exploring a simpler life. Foxfire was a rich compilation of Appalachian wisdom, lore, and methodology, all related to living off the grid 19th Century style. There were chapters on log hewing, shingle making, animal husbandry, and the like, but I wanted more hands-on knowledge. A freshman in community college now, I had heard that one of the teachers from our Catholic high school, Father Joe Wagenhoffer, was building a log cabin on a piece of land in Dorothy, New Jersey, near Mays Landing. He had a new gig as chaplain at the college.

Father Joe was about as close to being called a "hippie" that a Catholic priest could be. He and his colleague, Father Vince DiPasquale, had hijacked the high school's religion classes, a compulsory subject in Catholic schools, and made them platforms for cultural and human awareness. Fr. Vince was friends with radical activist priests Phil and Dan Berrigan, who were arrested for breaking into Selective Service offices to burn draft records during the Viet Nam War.

Fr. Joe and Fr. Vince requisitioned a school bus and took the religion classes on a field trip. Yay! A field trip! It was a light-hearted jaunt to the migrant farm workers' quarters in Vineland, New Jersey. The whole class snaked their way through chicken coops where hardworking families from Mexico lived on dirt floors in squalor, their children silent, reacting wide-eyed to this squeaky-clean invasion of entitlement. They, like zoo animals to us, were a shock to our white middle-class sensibilities. *Keep moving. Please do not touch any of the exhibits.* The ride to the farm was raucous, as you would expect from a busload of teenagers. The ride back was eerily quiet. Now that's a religion class.

Fr. Joe was a gentle and fanciful soul. After being schooled for years by the likes of Sister Mary Danny Trejo and Sister Mary Charles Bronson, he was a welcome surprise to us and, I think, a fine example of what it looks like when someone has God in their life. In the fall of '72, I asked him if I could help him in exchange for know-how. His building was already two logs high when I joined him. We worked long hours every weekend for several months.

I was finally working logs with my hands, not just in my imagination. Joe's lodge was hand-made, as in not a kit. The kits have perfectly shaped logs turned on a lathe, so each one looks like the other. A hand-made cabin has one-of-a-kind logs. They are more natural, with all their irregular bends, bows, and knots. While I'm trashing kits here, I've got to add that you get to cut your own notches with a handmade structure, an essential rite in log cabin building. It is just giant Lincoln Logs, one of my go-to toys as a child and an excellent blueprint for putting together a log cabin. Now the next Lincoln Log cabin I would build would be my own, and, after having produced one with Fr. Joe, I had a good idea how to go about it.

# The Open Road

**In January of** 1973, I went with my girlfriend Sue to the Atlantic coast of Nova Scotia to look at a piece of land we discovered flooded. On the way back, we took the *Bluenose* ferry from Yarmouth, Nova Scotia to Bar Harbor, Maine, a six-hour steam through a winter gale. I struck up a conversation with another young guy on the boat. We managed somehow to smoke a joint out on deck in the storm. He was Andy Fleishman, and he had bought an old farmhouse in Bear River, Nova Scotia, homesteading there with his gal and another couple.

"Come to Bear River and look me up," he said as we parted.

At 19, I sold my 1968 Plymouth Satellite to my parents for $400, creating some funds to buy land. In April of that year, I went out on the road with a high school friend, John Aleo. It was spring break at Atlantic Community College, and we hitchhiked to Nova Scotia on a quest, the destination: Andy Fleishman in Bear River.

We got a ride to Boston with some friends who took us on a day trip to Walden Pond in Concord. Having just read and been inspired by *Walden,* I procured a stone from the site of Thoreau's cabin, which I planned to incorporate into the foundation of my soon-to-be log cabin.

From Boston, we started our hike north. Once we were on the highway and got some rides, the feeling came over us for the very first time, alive and free, almost airborne. We had the world by the short ones. Oh, hell, Robert Service said it way better:

> When, though my pockets lacked a coin, and though my coat was old
> The largess of the stars was mine and all the sunset gold;
> When time was only made for fools and free as air was I,
> And hard I hit and hard I lived beneath the open sky;
> When all the roads were one to me, and each had its allure . . .
> Ye Gods! These were the happy days, the days when I was poor.

(from "The Joy of Being Poor," Robert Service)

We got a few rides as far as southern Maine and got picked up by fellow freak Gary Lawson. He was driving a little Saab, and we somehow both fit into the back seat, packs and all. Hitching in that era was cake. Freaks picked up other freaks. Gary was a freak who had to do weekend stints with the National Guard. He would stuff his long hair under a short hair wig, put on his military duds, and become unrecognizable. He brought us to his place, one of Bangor's great old 19th century wooden houses. Kind and most generous with a well-developed sense of the absurd, Gary and I became friends, and over the years, I would usually stop there on the way up or back from Nova Scotia. He came over the next year and helped with the building project for a time.

We started the next day on one of the more challenging legs of the Nova Scotia hitch: Route 9 in Maine. It was a twisting, winding, at times precipitous two-lane logger's highway. For a hitchhiker, it could be the doldrums. If you didn't get a ride all the way across, you might languish somewhere along the way. We got good rides, however, and made it across the border without incident. It was coming dusk as we left the town of St. Stephen, New Brunswick, Canada. We were out of the country, on the loose, and nineteen years old.

Walking about a mile outside of town, we made a sharp right into some woods and pitched my old Army surplus two-man pup tent. This was an old-style WWII-era canvas tent with no floor. Trespassing on someone's land, we had to be low key: no campfire, no undue noise. Just lay down quietly in the dark and sleep unnoticed in the thicket. I had decided that there would be no hitchhiking after dark for this and any subsequent hitchhiking trips. The pup tent went every trip, so I could just walk into the woods and pitch a camp. A hitcher at night is difficult to see, and it is more difficult to size up the driver. I liked a moment to decide if the guy offering me a ride looked like he would use my fingers for pizza toppings.

It was damned exciting laying there in the woods in Canada with a ferry ride across the Bay of Fundy waiting for us in the morning. I had slipped the corral at last and was running free. To be in the wind and away from the angst at home was intoxicating. We got up early to catch the 9:00 A.M. ferry. Breaking camp went swiftly. We made it to St. John with one ride, where we boarded the *Princess of Acadia*.

She was about the size of a small cruise ship. The bow yawned open, and she swallowed up tractor-trailers whole, cars as appetizers. We went up on deck as close to the bow as we could, and after a three-hour steam, we watched the *Princess* approach the Digby Gap. It is commonly referred to as Digby Gut, but I have heard both, and it was the former that I heard first. That afternoon on the sparkling Bay of Fundy, the *Princess* approached that break in the North Mountain,

Approaching the Digby Gut from the Bay of Fundy aboard the *Princess of Acadia*.

opening to the Annapolis Basin. It was April, and the North Mountain was wearing its fresh spring green cloak, lighter than summer green. Waterfalls here and there plummeted over forested cliffs down to the rocky beach below.

We got a ride to Bear River, a picture-postcard town known as the Switzerland of Nova Scotia. Situated around the hills where the tide meets the fresh water on the Bear River, this former schooner building town looked much the way it did in the 19th century. We went over to a gas station and asked if anyone knew where Andy Fleishman lived. A fellow getting gas overheard and gave us a ride to the farmhouse. Welcome to Nova Scotia.

We hopped into this nice fellow's 4-wheel drive vehicle and headed up Brook Road, following one of the branches of the Bear River that flowed down from a freshwater lake miles away. The road hugged the river, which was roaring with white water around the rocks and boulders at this time in April. Only in dreams or poetry could such a place exist. Our kind chauffeur pointed out "Indian Hill" road on the left, entrance to the Mi'kmaq reservation.

We turned left onto Thomas Road, little more than a one-lane woods road cutting through the forest until, after a mile, it put you at the dooryard of Andy Fleishman's place, an old gray farmhouse with bright blue shingles on the roof. Andy came out, and I reintroduced myself.

Andy and Vicky and another couple, Don Levin and Nancy, were farmsteading at the old farmhouse on the Thomas Road—growing crops, raising chickens, goats, keeping bees, making butter and candles. In other words, the two couples occupied the pinnacle of the counterculture movement. There was

Bear River, Nova Scotia, from the one-lane bridge in town, 1973.

an old-fashioned wood-burning cookstove with oven and the warming ovens up top, a hand pump in the kitchen for water, and at dusk, they lit the place with the warm glow of kerosene lamps. That night we sat around the kitchen table after a wholesome meal.

"Let's go visit Joe Leblanc," Don suggested.

John and I joined Andy and Don for a nighttime hike through the woods to Morganville, a few miles away. Our hosts lit two old-style kerosene hurricane lanterns, and we headed out on a trail through the blackness of the forest. These guys were so serious about doing it up right, they wouldn't deign to use a battery-operated flashlight. The boulder-strewn trail was winding and uneven, the lamps carving a narrow tunnel through the dark.

We arrived at Joe LeBlanc's house at last. He was a personable, soft-spoken man. And he was our entertainment for the evening. I was getting my first taste of what folks do in the country. People "called" on each other. You visited and sat down and talked until the visit was over. Back in the rat race, we always must have something going on, but in Nova Scotia, the world changes, and you are content to read quietly, talk with visitors, or, my personal favorite, sit and stare at my log walls. We headed back when the conversation thinned, and we repeated our trek threading through the dark woods back to the farmhouse.

After a day of checking out their farming operation, John and I set out on foot from the center of town in Bear River. The idea was to get off the blacktop, onto dirt roads, and knock on every farmhouse door we saw.

"Hello, I'm Mickey Maguire, and I am looking for land for sale. I plan to build a log cabin," became my standard greeting when someone answered the door. Almost everyone invited us in and offered us tea, cookies, or pie. They would invariably suggest someone who lived down the road from them. It helped break the ice if we could say that so and so up the road said we should stop there.

We hiked up the big hill, the start of the Clementsvale Road, and headed out toward Clementsvale. Past that hamlet, the Virginia Road takes you up to Rt. 8, one of the few roads that cut across the entire interior of Nova Scotia. We walked up to Rt. 8 and then headed toward Liverpool on the Atlantic Coast.

In all, we hiked about 25 miles from Bear River and walked the same distance back. Before we left Nova Scotia, our hosts at the farmhouse showed us a waterfall on Brook Road that they said was great for bathing in the summer. Though we hitch-hiked back to the states with no definitive land deal, it seemed I was onto something. Everywhere we went, we ran into young people pursuing the simple life. I had found a hub of counterculture activity. The Bear River area then became the focus of the land search.

We chose to take the Bluenose, the ferry from Yarmouth, Nova Scotia, to Bar Harbor, Maine. On arrival in Yarmouth, it was too late to catch the boat; that would have to wait till morning. Our attention then turned to where we were going to lay our heads. We asked around about a hostel. Someone suggested we ask at the RCMP station. The Yarmouth Mounties said the hostel was not open this early in the season, but they kindly offered to let us sleep in a room adjacent to the sergeant's desk. We laid our sleeping bags under the cafeteria-style tables.

I've always had to find the very edge of the precipice or the thinnest ice and do a spirited tap dance there. Not wanting to go through U.S. Customs carrying hashish, I told John I would smoke the hash in a police station in full view of the sergeant's desk. John told me I was out of my fucking mind.

"No, man! It will work!"

I knew it would. In those days, everyone who smoked tobacco did so unencumbered by laws banning the practice in public places. The desk sergeant was smoking, and so was I. In the darkened room, we saw through the open door, watching the desk sergeant smoke his cigarette. If I broke off a piece of hash and stuffed it into the end of a cigarette and took a huge hit, the hash is consumed in one hit, and the stench of tobacco smoke would mask the odor. In this manner, I got high in a police station in view of the sergeant's desk. Though, I think John was probably right.

## *June 1973*

**In June, I** returned to Nova Scotia with my girlfriend, Sue, who had a VW bug. Man, that was a lot easier than hiking 50 miles of dirt roads. I had a torrid romance with her for quite a while until she finally realized she was in deep with a self-absorbed child. She told me off in a note that said I had "the mind of a three-year-old and the penis of a twenty-four-year-old." At age nineteen, I took this as a compliment. I couldn't give a rat's ass about the three-year-old mentality insult, but man, she said I had the penis of a twenty-four-year-old. You could accuse me of missing the point. But how, if you were a guy, would you have felt if your girlfriend told you had the mind of a twenty-four-year-old and the penis of a three-year-old? Yeah, I thought so.

Sue and I brought an excellent array of chemical enhancement. We had returned to Andy Fleishman's again and made forays seeking land. We had dropped hits of Mister Natural blotter acid and headed out in the bug on the Thomas Road. As we came around a tight curve, we were head-on with a vehicle coming the opposite way. Both cars swerved and left the road, and I got the VW hung up on a boulder. The VW bugs had steel plate bottoms, so the car just sat there wobbling on the rock. Out of the vehicle came Brian Harris, Greg McEwan, and Alan Harlow. We didn't know it at the time, but they were doing "Frog" blotter acid. Good-natured, amiable Brian was bearded and wore a ready smile. Greg and Alan were Mi'kmaq and lived on Indian Hill. Alan was swarthy and built like a big bear. Greg was fairer and of a smaller, wiry build. In the middle of "What the fuck do we do now?" Greg presented the solution.

"We'll pick it up and put it back on the road."

I looked at him. No, man, this thing will have to be hauled out of here with a winch. We watched everyone grab onto the vehicle in preparation for lifting. I was thinking, *no way*. But I took a spot and grabbed a bumper.

"OK. On three," said Greg. We lifted the car, walked it over to the road, set it down, and went back to the farmhouse where Greg and I played guitars, the first of many such jams and the beginning of a long friendship.

# Two Characters of Frasertown

**Several people told** us to see George Goodin and Richard Milner on the Fraser Road as we went from farmhouse to farmhouse. Frasertown was settled in the early nineteenth century beginning with the first Fraser, a Scot, who stowed away on the Atlantic crossing with a goat. It might just be me, but I think a goat would make that difficult. *Pay no attention to the bleating emanating from under my trench coat.* He built the first habitable building on what would become known as Fraser Road. It was a log cabin. While it was not a full-blown town, it was more of a spread-out affair and thrived for a time. What fed this community, in addition to logging and farming, was the stave mill. At the head of the Moose River, which lay in the valley between the ridges of Power Lot and Fraser Roads, was situated a mill that made barrel staves. The operation employed men from Princedale, which included Frasertown. After many years, the mill shut down, and homesteads began to disappear over time, many of them just yawning cellar pits today. Part of the mill stands yet, hidden in a thicket of pine trees. Frasertown as a town slipped into oblivion until after the Summer of Love. Young people, freaks, flowed in waves to the area, some to the Fraser Road, searching for cheap land. When Frasertown had faded, people just called it Fraser Road. Now the "hippies" resettled the road, and it was referred to as Frasertown once again.

One of the first was George Goodin. George was homegrown. He grew up in the watchman's house that overlooked the stave mill. His father, Lenny, was watchman and worked in the mill. George went to the one-room schoolhouse on the back road to Annapolis in Princedale. When the New Age dawned, he went to Vancouver Island and lived in a treehouse on the beach. When he returned from British Columbia in 1970, he was turned on and had long hair. He bought 40 acres "more or less" (as the deed language goes) for $75 from Murray Milner. Murray felt guilty about the deal and threw in an overcoat.

In a hollow, George set out to build a log cabin. It was 16x24 with a front porch overlooking a swiftly running brook. Audio therapy, anyone? Check. Our instructions were to go down the Fraser Road and stop just past the log cabin on the hill that belonging to Jerry Rogers. It was also16x24 and sat in the open on a cleared hill. Built only a year before my arrival, but owing to being exposed to the elements, the logs bleached silver-gray, and with Jerry not caring much if things were square when he built it, this place looked 100 years old.

We parked just past Jerry and Wendy's and located the downward trail on the opposite side of the road. It was just a little footpath descending into the hollow about 300 yards down. We heard the springtime cacophony of the brook long before we reached the long wooden footbridge that crossed it. The bridge led to the small clearing where George Goodin's camp sat. I stood transfixed. Long had I fantasized about how my dream home would look. But this was real. It was proof that, yes, you can do this.

George's woman, Rhonda, was serving a meal on the porch to the background music of the wild brook. We introduced ourselves, and George said he had seen us on the ferry crossing the Bay of Fundy, a fellow long-haired freak. He did not know of any land for sale but suggested I speak to Richard Milner. George was now the second person to mention that name.

George Gooden's log cabin.

He invited me to look around inside, where the delicious smell of burning hardwood accented the palpable sense of peace and comfort. Seeing my dream realized raised anticipation to a fever pitch. We left George and Rhonda to their paradise by the stream and set out for Richard Milner's, where we found him atop his old farmhouse roof with three helpers shingling.

"Mr. Milner?" I called up.

A wiry fellow, with dark, piercing eyes, bristled about being addressed as *Mister*. I introduced myself and told him about my quest for land and my intention to build a cabin.

"Well, I think I know of a piece of land that might be for sale. I'll show it to you," he said and started down the ladder from the roof.

"Oh, no. You're busy. And you have helpers here. You shouldn't leave them."

"Won't take a minute," he said and was now standing next to me on the ground where we shook hands. Thus began an enduring friendship.

We piled into his pickup truck and headed back down the Fraser Road past Jerry Rogers and George Goodin's places. About a mile down, we parked and headed uphill into the woods. The land was a hillside and foliated with maple, golden and white birch, beech, ash, spruce, fir, and pine. It was lush with ferns and boulders covered with emerald moss. We wound up at a site dominated by tall pines. At this spot, you could look through the trees and see across the valley to the ridge at Power Lot.

"What do you think of this?" Richard asked.

I told him it was gorgeous (after I found my voice) and would love to buy it. Back at the house, Richard called Sam Berry, who owned the parcel. He was willing to sell six acres for $50 an acre. That night we went over to Sam's, where I gave him $300 for the land. He signed a deed and said he would be over the next day to cut the lines with me. The dream was a huge step closer to fruition.

We met him at the land the next day and, armed with the sharpest ax on the planet. Sam Berry proceeded to cut the lines for the parcel. In those days, there was never a thought of a surveyor. People just eyed it up and did the best they could. The line that bordered the Fraser Road was curvy, so he went about it thus: 416 feet straight back on either end of the tract and 624 feet across the back end connecting the two. The line on the road took care of itself. With the lines complete, I assessed the six acres. In addition to good hardwood stands, there were concentrations of spruce and fir. I would not have to outsource for cabin logs.

Sue and I had to get back to the states shortly after that. One task remained: Getting the deed registered in Bridgetown, about 40 miles away. Richard insisted on doing this for us. I gave him the required $35 fee, and we headed back to the states. About three weeks later, I received the registered deed in the mail. The language of the deed was musical; at least to my ears, it was. It read, "Beginning at a spruce tree situate on the East side line of the Fraser Road in the area known as Princedale, just south of the Birch Brook, so-called . . ."

Richard Milner was in his early thirties when he came down off that roof to show me that piece of land. I was mortified that he would leave the guys helping him shingle his roof to show some scrawny long-haired kid from New Jersey a piece of land. If it had been me, and I am sometimes accused of being a nice guy, I would have said, "Sure. I might know of a piece of land. Let me just finish up here on the roof, and we'll go take a look." Not Richard. Down off the roof in a flash and down the road in his truck we went. Not only does that give you a glimpse of who Richard was, but it also shows a lot about the people of Nova Scotia, for there are many who would have done the same.

He lived in that old homey farmhouse with his wife, Liz. Possessed of great rural wisdom, sweetness, and generosity, Liz had a whimsical sense of humor. Sue and I spent a lot of time there, staying in the house or camping in their field. We took many meals at their table, and I gleefully embraced everything about Nova Scotia living. Feeling it my bones, this was life the way it should be. I observed the workings of the wood-burning kitchen stove, how to make it behave with the manipulation of three different dampers. We toasted our bread on the surface of the cast iron using a spatula to flip it. Richard carved slices of home-cured bacon cut right off the slab, and eggs were from the hen house with their deep orange yolks. We picked wild strawberries in their fields. They were small, about the size of a thimble, but sweeter than anything that had the gall to call itself a strawberry. Richard took me out into the field and set me loose with a .22 caliber single-shot rifle and beer bottles. Their hospitality boundless, Richard liked to say, "If you go hungry in this house, it's your own damned fault."

Richard's parents, Myers and Jean Milner, often visited. I wound up addressing them as Mom and Dad, for they had become my defacto Nova Scotia parents. Myers and Jean were legendary in the area. They had an abiding love for each other but had notorious arguments that sometimes culminated in them shooting at each other with firearms. During one such incident, Myers fired a couple of shots at her as she ran across a field.

"You never even hit me," Jean said, gloating, as Myers told it.

"Hell, I've shot deer on the run in the neck. I just wanted to see how fast you could go," said Myers.

Jean threw a hatchet at Myers during one argument and drove it right into the wall beside his head. One of the best wood splitters I ever saw was Jean Milner. I went over one day for a visit, and Jean stood atop a big pile of firewood with an ax. She systematically devoured the entire pile, reducing it to halves, quarters, and kindling while speaking to me conversationally. She did so without a chopping block. I don't know how I could even balance atop a randomly piled heap of firewood. She could have made toothpicks out of the whole pile if she had wanted.

Myers and Jean both grew up in the area. One of the twenty-one siblings of two different mothers, Myers' homestead is now one of the yawning cellar pits in Princedale. The consummate woodsman, Myers was a hunting, tracking, and survival guru. During World War II, he was part of a special unit of freelance assassins who dropped behind enemy lines. Their job was to kill as many Germans as possible. When it was plain that he was a crack shot and could handle himself in the wild, his commanding officer recruited him for this special outfit. Myers shot with his sniper rifle, knifed and garroted untold numbers of German soldiers. He had, on some level, kept count. It was those numbers, he admitted, that woke him up at night in a sweat.

Everyone brought their chain saws to Myers when they went on the fritz. He could fix anything, and when he sharpened your chain saw, it felt like getting a new one. I think he did it for the company as well as something to keep him busy. While he was sharpening the chain in his workshop, he would talk to you and tell you stories in a slow drawl. He had a dry wit and was very keen. When he referred to Jean, he would call her the "the ol' woman."

Jean was the local bootlegger. Not bootlegging in the usual sense, she was not distilling spirits. She bought large quantities of beer and sold it after hours at a substantial mark-up on weekends when you could not buy a thimbleful at the provincial liquor store. There were many bootleggers of this type throughout the province. You know, the boys are half-loaded on a Friday night in some backwoods camp. They realize the beer is getting low. The least drunk of the crew was the designated driver to make a run over to Jean's. Nobody minded paying the mark-up. They were in the beer after store hours, and the party could continue.

# Busted

**The most important** part of the quest achieved: I now had a place to *put* the cabin. Some dismissed my obsessive ramblings as a childhood pipe dream. I was just a nineteen-year-old talking like I was ten. (Still an issue.) That I had a deed with my name on it changed that perception considerably. Even then, there was judgment about the path I had taken. But here, the thickness of this skull worked in my favor. Unable to see anything else, I pushed toward the goal.

I made plans to return later that summer in August. My best friend from childhood, Tom Lynch, and Steve and Tom Noonan, were all interested in making the trip. Steve had a small repair business and had a pickup truck, would drive. We left Atlantic City on an August morning and headed up the Garden State Parkway. All was well until we encountered a sign: "ALL TRUCKS MUST EXIT." Steve figured that meant pickups too. It did not, but he insisted we exit. That put us on State Route 34 in Colts Neck Township. I was driving, my shoulder-length hair blowing in the wind. It might have been that blowing hair that got us stopped.

A New Jersey State Trooper was following us, and after a few hundred yards, he put on his lights and pulled us over. He asked me to step out of the truck and produce my license. Steve proceeded to get the registration out of the glove compartment. Then the trooper went to the back of the truck grabbing a bag that belonged to me and examined the contents. He found a few metal 35-mm film canisters with screw-on tops, the official weed containers of the sixties and seventies. He picked one up and shook it back and forth: *nothing in that one.* He made a big show of this process, clearly enjoying himself. He picked up the next canister and shook: chicka-chicka. His eyes lit up.

"Ah, what do we have here?"

He was toying with me. He opened the canister and found it near filled with pot and a nice chunk of brown Lebanese hash.

"Whose bag is this?"

I owned it as my bag. With my hands pulled behind my back, the trooper cuffed me tight enough to feel uncomfortable and shoved me over to the patrol car. There he pushed my face down over the hood, frisked me, and said I was under arrest. After suffering the indignity of a good old-fashioned frisking, he stuck my license to a clipboard and had me stand before him answering questions. I don't much remember what he was asking me. My inner voices were all I heard. You know, the ones that say, "Oh, shit. You got your ass arrested, and your dad's a cop." "I guess we're not going to Nova Scotia now." And then, the worst voice of all, "You have ten hits of Mr. Natural acid in your wallet."

Yep. Ten hits of blotter LSD with that cartoon figure of Mr. Natural in his "Keep On Truckin" pose right inside one of the see-through sleeves meant for family pictures. There were no photos in the sleeves to help poor Mr. Natural blend into the scenery. Open the wallet, that's what you see first, Mr. Natural. *He's family, man.* The laws for cannabis were one thing. The laws for possession of LSD were another. It was the big leagues. I had to get that wallet out of my back pocket and off my person. When they brought me back to the tank, the cops would search everything, and Mr. Natural would be outed.

Standing there answering questions for Officer Clipboard, my hands, cuffed behind my back, went to work. I got into the rear jeans pocket with one hand and pinched the wallet in the "scissors" of my index and middle finger, slid the wallet up out of the pocket, and waved it back and forth for Steve, standing behind me, to see. I was hoping he understood what I wanted. The wallet waved at Steve, whispering in anxious wallet-speak, "Take me! Take me! Take me!" I was still looking directly at our trooper, answering his questions while he jotted things down on the clipboard. It had to be now. Then I felt the wallet leave my scissored fingers. Steve was a smart cookie. As bad as this situation was, I thought we just made it a little better. As the trooper was preparing to move the whole show back to the station, Steve had a chance to aside to me.

"What was in the wallet?"

"Ten hits of acid."

I just got the *look.* The "You are out of your fucking mind" look. (I get that a lot.) The trooper walked around to the front of the truck and returned with a plastic bag of pot. Whatever I was carrying was in the film canister. Steve, who owned the vehicle, did not get high, nor did his brother Tom. The trooper said he found it under the front driver's seat and claimed he had spotted it when looking in the passenger side window. I get it. The fix is on. He had to have probable cause to search, so there it was. I had just enrolled in "Having Your Rights Violated 101" and attended my first class. The tuition is steep.

They processed me back at the station house: mug shot, fingerprints, more questions, and then to a holding cell where they shackled me to a bench by the wrist. The anchor point for the shackle was too low, so you could not sit up straight, which, I am sure, was by design. Can't let them perps get too comfortable, right? In the next room, the troopers began to weigh up my contraband. They put the grass on the scale and called out the number of grams as they accumulated. They informed me possession of 25 grams or over was a felony, and under was a misdemeanor. For hash, it was 5 grams. They made a big show of it, cheering as the grams went up and booing in disappointment when both measurements fell just short. They really wanted that felony arrest on a nineteen-year-old long-hair. My comrades left for a few hours and returned to bail me out. I was given paperwork with the heading, *The State of New Jersey vs. Mickey Maguire*. Only nineteen and officially at war with an entire state.

"Don't leave the state," the arresting officer said to me on the way out.

"Yes, sir."

The next day we left the country. He never mentioned leaving the country.

# Uncle Cliff and the "Pig and Whistle"

**Despite our run-in** with the law, we made it to Nova Scotia that August and returned in December. I met the Freaks of Frasertown, great folks who would become my friends and neighbors. We were one of many enclaves of young people, communities that sprang up on dirt roads well beyond the power lines. We all felt that something fresh and unique was going down; we were a part of the movement and, perhaps, in the vanguard.

My lifelong love affair with Nova Scotia, punctuated by a series of heart-breaking departures and rapturous reunions, was acknowledged by Richard Milner in what I considered a most intuitive and even generous way. He was an intensely passionate man who, not fitting in either, inhabited the fringe area of social acceptability, living life on his terms. He would always say to me upon arrival, "How long you home for?" or at the beginning of a project he was helping me with, "When you come back home, this will be taken care of."

He knew the depth of my love for Nova Scotia and the Maritime way of life, for he loved it himself and recognized without much discussion that it was a passion we shared. I always considered it generous of him, a native-born Nova Scotian, to allow me, an outsider from New Jersey, to call this paradise "home," not that I was from there but that my soul found comfort in its hills and recesses and its simple, earthy ways.

"We'll have to bring you over to Uncle Cliff's, to the Pig and Whistle," Richard said during the December trip.

He saw the question on my face and explained that his Uncle Cliff, one of Myer's many brothers, was a bootlegger, and his joint was known locally as the Pig and Whistle. We hopped into Richard's car and drove way too fast through windswept snow to Uncle Cliff's place. I thought of a Christmas card scene when I laid eyes on it: a grayed wooden structure from the 19th century that had once been a schoolhouse, its window of multi-panes with snow sticking in the left corners of each pane of century-old distorted glass.

We opened the door to this dream and stomped the snow from our boots, the first thing to hit us—kickass in your face, woodstove heat. The old potbelly stove sat in the center of the room so that, back when it was a school, all students could benefit from its warmth. The tobacco and wood smoke mixed, a kind of North Woods incense. Snow swept down outside, almost a white-out, broken up and framed by those many panes of glass. The stove was cranking, and I felt like I landed in the palm of the god of Yeah, This is What I Had in Mind.

Uncle Cliff presided over this illegal tavern in the woods. Richard introduced me to his kin, and Uncle Cliff warmly shook my hand. I did not get much of what he said, but he didn't have to speak for me to understand his intentions. He wanted us to have a good time. White hair and a long white beard, his eyes were wrinkled by laughter. You can tell what kind of road a person has chosen by the map of their wrinkles. When you're old, you are stuck with how you wore your face for life. Uncle Cliff had a road map to bliss written around his eyes.

"He might drool a bit, but he means well," said Richard.

Uncle Cliff was our backwoods Buddha. He presided over the main table with a grin, rotund and looking like a red-neck Santa about two days before a scheduled rehab. The place was one big room, and it didn't look much like living quarters, more like a make-shift tavern in the Yukon in 1902. The hot product being sold here illegally on the weekend was quart bottles of Moosehead for $1.00. The folks here were not part of the hippie infusion; these were the older generation of Nova Scotian woodsmen. It was an honor to be welcomed so to their secret saloon. I think these men afforded us freaks grudging respect, for many of us went to them for their invaluable knowledge about how to do things the old way, the *right way*. Right out of the gate, we respected them and their lore. We were interested in how their parents and grandparents lived. We were willing to work.

Everyone smoked cigarettes. They flicked ashes onto their pant legs and rubbed them in, the Nova Scotia ashtray. Seated in a chair near the stove was a fellow with a guitar, Jerry Gabriel. He was a friend of Richard's who loved a good time and his country music, the real stuff. He knew many of the best heart and soul songs by some greats like the Hanks: Williams and Snow (Hank Snow was a native Bluenoser). He knew his chords, kept good time, and was a decent singer. I had my guitar with me and backed him up. Though I was later to play country, swing, and bluegrass music professionally, up to this point, I had been playing rock and roll, so I brought that sensibility to it, and Jerry loved it. It leaned toward rockabilly, for country and rock are first cousins. At the end of each song, he would smile and laugh and say, "You're good. You're good." Another couple of swigs of Moosehead and into the next tune we'd go.

We passed a glorious December afternoon there at Uncle Cliff's with the snow coming down all around us and the Moosehead flowing. It *could* have been the Yukon in 1902. I was in love.

# We Cut the Logs With an Ax

**I graduated from** the two-year Atlantic Community College in December and transferred to Glassboro State College in January 1974. A billionaire industrialist named Rowan donated millions of dollars to the school, so it is now called Rowan University. Childhood friend, John Anderson, had transferred in from the University of Dayton, and we decided to get a place together. Like Frank and Jesse James decided to go for a train ride.

Both our dads were Atlantic City policemen. John and I have been friends since the ripe age of five. Doing our best to create anarchy through twelve years of Catholic schooling, we now found ourselves renting a house in college. Come spring break, John and I drove up to Nova Scotia to cut the logs. It was March and cold in New Jersey, but Nova Scotia felt like the Arctic Circle.

We stayed with Richard and Liz for a few days and then on to the land to make camp. Temperatures reached the mid-teens during the day and went down as low as 20 below zero Fahrenheit at night. Our army surplus down sleeping bags were adequately warm. The challenge was when we were up and about and not swinging axes. We built a fire high but had to turn ourselves around like a roast on a spit to distribute the warmth. You could singe your eyelashes, but your back would have the heat sucked right out of it in seconds. Keep turning!

Greg, Brian, and Allan, our Bear River friends, came over to help us cut trees. Before the work began, I told them of the caveat: all trees had to be felled with an ax. This condition was not popular with my helpers (Brian Harris, you know who you are). My love affair with history and respect for the old ways as my only justification, we cut the trees the very way Mr. Fraser had in the 1830s when he built a log cabin on the road that bears his name.

Me (L) and John Anderson, first Holy Communion.

John Anderson (L) and me resting during the cutting of logs for the cabin, March, 1974.

## Blood Brothers and Picking the Spot

**Temperatures rarely broke** the 20s by day, but labor was vigorous, so we usually worked up a sweat. Greg stayed with us during one of those night-time human-rotisserie campfire sessions. He said he thought we should become blood brothers. I thought that was too cool for words, for his father was chief and, though it was an elected position, folks considered Greg a Mi'kmaq prince. Cool, that is, until I realized what had to happen. Standing opposite each other, the campfire between us, light snow dusting our camp, Grey Cloud, his native name, unsheathed his hunting knife and sliced the palm of his hand in a quick, effortless stroke.

My turn. Holding my Buck knife over my palm, I had to come to terms with something more potent than my whims about coolness: the self-preservation instinct. *Whoa! Let's hold on here for a sec, mister.* I had been cut, bashed, and slashed through the years without too much concern but to take a knife to my hand purposely was unnatural. Not able to go for the broad stroke Greg had just pulled off, I worried it back and forth in a small way, hoping I would break the surface and make a little blood. It wasn't working. Greg, bleeding, asked me to hurry up. Queue up the Final Jeopardy theme music. Greg looked pale. Finally, I broke through with the most acceptable amount of damage I was willing to absorb, having to squeeze for just a few drops. We joined hands over the fire and became brothers of the blood for life.

John and I walked the property with an eye toward where this cabin would sit during its time. That it is a hillside and very uneven made walking slow and difficult. It is a beautiful piece of land with a good evergreen to hardwood ratio. We went high up to the back line. The Annapolis Valley in Nova Scotia is bounded by the North Mountain and South Mountain, Fraser Road traversing the backbone of the South Mountain. As we descended from the back line, the forest gave way to a copse of short beech trees and was fairly open in this area. From this perspective, we saw about two miles across to a field on the next ridge. I decided this is the view I wanted to spend my days enjoying.

Greg McEwan (Grey Cloud) and Steppenwolf, Brian Harris and friend, March 1974.

Greg was building a cabin on the reserve that summer, his logs already cut. John and I went over to help him and Harlow haul logs to the construction site. As with the cutting of the trees, we got outclassed by Greg and Allan. I marveled that they carried two logs at a time to John and my one.

"I think we could carry four," said Greg.

They stacked four logs, two on either side of them, and walked them about ten yards.

Before we left Nova Scotia that spring break from college, we had cut sixty-three trees by ax. (It would be fair to say Greg cut half of them.) We felled and limbed the logs and left them for hauling out in the summer. Since the sap was not running in March, sap peeling, the easy method of removing the bark, could not be utilized. It would have to be shaved off with a drawknife, another ancient lore, later in the summer when I returned. So instead of going to Florida for spring break and partying till we puked, we cut sixty-three trees for a log cabin. Good for nothing, lazy hippies.

# *Mom*

**There was this** sense that Marie Maguire belonged to everyone. She took people at face value and evaluated everyone by what was in their hearts. It didn't matter to her if you were white, black, straight, gay, Jew, gentile, whatever; she had cherished friends of all these persuasions. If you had a good heart, you were in, baby. People gravitated to her, a champion for the downtrodden, outcasts, misfits. She understood. She made friends easily and instantly, as her advice was always sound and straightforward, her support unwavering. People who experienced her warmth knew there was something special going on here, despite a lifetime of tragedy and hardship.

Born in Philadelphia on September 21, 1921, Marie's mother died when she was five years old. Her father put her and her two brothers in Catholic orphanages in Philadelphia run by the Sisters of Perpetual Misery (actually, Sisters of Charity, but that's a stretch), where children, due to the tattered condition of their donated garments, had their clothes literally beaten off them regularly.

When she was twelve, she left the orphanage to live with her paternal grandmother from Ireland. You'd figure that had to be an improvement, but she was cruel and sadistic. Mom told me her grandmother would tell her to be home by 9:00 P.M. Though she was home on time, her grandmother had moved the clock to 10:00 P.M. and would beat the daylights out of her. At age sixteen, Marie ran away and got a job as a mother's helper in Atlantic City.

In 1971, Mom fell down a flight of stairs and broke her neck. She entered the hospital paralyzed from the neck down. Though recovery seemed a longshot, she recovered much of her mobility except for a withered left hand, which, she would be quick to tell you in later years, she used to hook onto the top of her ladder when painting or scrubbing walls. In 1984 she was diagnosed with cancer and had a double mastectomy with a year of chemo. But still, this tough old Irish broad persevered. And she had somehow made her life about celebrating the finer qualities she found in others. She told me she decided to give back as an homage to a few kind hearts who looked out for her when she was young. She became, with her everyday kind acts and thoughtful gestures, a prototypical social worker. As she approached ninety, people would ask her to reveal her secret to long life.

"Keep moving and take a teaspoon of WD-40 every day," she'd say.

For her ninetieth Christmas, she asked for (and received) new knee pads and a six-foot ladder because the four-foot was not high enough for her.

After Mom passed in her 94th year, Cousin Kevin Maguire called from Australia. Through a deluge of tears, he offered this gem which says as much about her as anything. In Atlantic City for a visit, he was worried to find her atop a ladder (hooked on with her paralyzed left hand), painting the outside of the house.

"Aunt Marie, what are you doing?"

"Painting the house."

"But Aunt Marie, you're 86 years old."

"The house doesn't know that," she said.

Mom (Marie Maguire), age 90 with her Christmas ladder and new knee pads.

# "I Was a Young Man Once . . ."

**During the years** following Mom's broken neck, she got stronger, and Dad got sicker. He smoked four to five packs of Kools a day and drank. When I was seventeen, he took me for my driving test around 9:00 A.M. On the way, Dad asked me if I wanted a glass of orange juice. I went along with it, so we had to stop at Angelo's Fairmount Tavern, a neighborhood taproom that reinvented itself into a nice Italian restaurant in more recent years. I swear, it was a good portion of our money that brought about that place's renaissance. We sat in a booth, and they brought him a tall high ball glass a little over half full of vodka neat. I figured it was his usual pick-me-up because he never specified what he wanted. He tossed that back like a glass of orange juice. I drank mine knowing I'd been had. That he was a cop, drinking, and taking me for my driver's test was an irony not lost on me.

The beginning of the end was when he had an ingrown toenail on his big toe that got infected. He went to a podiatrist who operated. He gave Dad a shot of local anesthesia, but the needle hit the bone and started an infection. It turned into osteomyelitis, and they eventually amputated his toe. He had no circulation to enable healing. The pain was deep-rooted and unrelenting. Dr. McKnight told Mom and Dad he had the body of a seventy-year-old (he was only fifty-three when he died) and the circulation of a person with diabetes.

When the toe area would not heal, they had to take his right leg, just below the knee. The pain persisted. Neurosurgeons performed a cordotomy, a procedure where they put a needle into the spinal cord, burning out sections to try to deaden his pain. It failed. He had what Dr. McKnight described as a "wall to wall" heart, meaning he had congestive heart failure; his heart filled his entire chest side to side. He was a wreck of a man. Through it all, he smoked, drank, and ate pain killers like Skittles. What little connection we ever had as father and son occurred during his last few months of life. With his amputation, he needed me to help him into and out of the bathtub. That put our relationship on a different plane. Dad could not drive anymore, so I drove him to Angelo's with some regularity. I sat at the bar with him, and he actually bragged me up to his barfly friends.

"Tell them what you are doing," he would say.

I told his buddies about the land I bought for $300 in Nova Scotia and that I had cut sixty-three trees with an ax and was returning that summer to build a log cabin. I had made him proud, and I can't say that it did not feel satisfying.

Dad's existence during this time was a sad one. He was failing, in pain, and doped up with pain killers. I had the pressing issue of trees lying in the woods that had to have the bark shaved before woodworms got into them. I had to get up there to deal with them and build the place.

I departed Atlantic City around 9:00 P.M. on June 18, 1974. Having called a cab to take me to the bus depot, I went up to the front bedroom.

"Dad, I feel bad about leaving you like this," I said, "I've got logs laying in the woods."

"No, you go build that cabin," he said. "Don't stay here and wait for me (to die, was implied). I understand. I was a young man once." I guess he believed in me enough to know I was going to build it. I kissed and hugged him and went down to the waiting cab. It was the last time I saw him alive. We always kissed, just like him and Pop-Pop. All the Maguire brothers kissed their father, and so we did. Somehow it never felt forced. It was real. So, it's something.

## Putting It All Together

**A bus trip** from Atlantic City, New Jersey to St. John, New Brunswick, Canada—you can check that one off as "torturous." A trip like that would be grueling enough with just a suitcase. The pile of shit I had was unthinkable. A small hill of tent poles, canvas, sleeping bag, clothing, ax, tools, cookware, guitar, and untold miscellanea, elicited many an evil eye from bus drivers. They had to help transfer this construction project from one bus to another in AC, New York, Boston, Bangor, and St. John. Arriving at the ferry terminal in St. John after they had closed for the night, I took advantage of shelter under the front door canopy and slept atop the pile till the crew woke me up on their arrival at dawn.

Coming through the Digby Gut this time felt quite different. This obsession, beginning when I was eleven, well, it all amounted to this trip, this moment, didn't it? *Here to build the cabin.* Yeah, that had a nice ring to it.

Arriving in Digby, Nova Scotia, Jack's father, Dad Salsman, picked me up and transferred me and my small mountain of equipage to the six acres in Princedale. I would never, today, that is, as an older feller, attempt a building project of this magnitude without a vehicle. Youth.

After making camp at the pine tree site, I walked down the Fraser to say hey to my new neighbors. Mike and Sharon were back now, and Jack and Faye were putting the finishing touches on a rustic frame cottage with slab wood facing. Big Wally Kelly had a shack right on Fraser Road.

Mike Phillips. How to describe him? If limited to a single word description, this comes to mind: dynamo, firebrand, mad scientist (sorry, two words), wunderkind. Mike hailed from Nantucket and graduated from Goddard with a degree in "Wood." Yep. He showed me the diploma. During the Viet Nam War, he was one of many young men who fled the country and the Selective Service System. He bought 70 acres of land back about a quarter-mile off the Fraser Road and built a 20x30 log cabin.

It became the model home for the Freaks of Frasertown. It even had an upstairs bedroom. Tending to the taller side and trim, Mike had the long, dark hair and beard of a hippie Jesus. Wearing a perpetual, almost impish grin, he was always scheming to build something better or make living in the woods off-grid easier or come up with many interesting ways to get intoxicated. Mike Phillips was the chief mixologist on the HMS *Frasertown Freak Show*.

Mike had built his cabin on stilts made of tamarack (known locally as hackmatack). Hackmatack is a conifer that loses its needles in the winter. It has a spiral grain and is valued for its resistance to rot, even when buried in the ground. Farmers had long used it for fence posts, and many of the stilted buildings at the head of the tide in Bear River were sitting on hackmatack posts. Since my land was mainly a hillside, the front of the place would have to be up off the ground. Jack Salsman had a hackmatack on his property next to mine and kindly offered it to me.

After talking with everyone who had done the building with logs immersion, particularly Jerry Rogers and George Goodin, because their places were 16x24, it became clear that I was going to need about forty more trees. Mike lent me his chain saw, and I learned on the spot how to use one. The operation was much easier than using an ax, and I could fully appreciate why Brian Harris had complained to me the previous March. The other big difference here was cutting trees when the sap was running, which meant that you could "sap peel" the logs. After limbing the tree and removing all knots with the chain saw, the saw cuts a single line in the bark, running the length of the log. Using an old tool called a "spudding iron," you pried the bark down on either side of the line. You could grab a wide section of bark and peel it off in one long ribbon.

During this period, the tasks at hand were to cut and peel more trees, find a way to get them to the building site, for they were scattered all over the six acres, and start digging the holes for the hackmatack posts. "Digging" is a term used in the most liberal sense. It was more like bone-jarringly brutal battles between your pick or mattock and the rocks of the last ice age. Much of Nova Scotia is glacial rubble; rocks and boulders are the province's chief bumper crop. The holes had to be a little over two feet deep to go below the frost line and about a foot and a half wide.

After squaring up the building site with string, excavation began on the post holes. Every stroke of the pick or mattock found a rock. The shock would travel from the handle of the pick and right up the bones of the arm like a jolt of electricity, and there was no way to tell if you had struck the top inch of a boulder the size of a Volkswagen. I think that of all the tasks involved in this project, excavating those holes was the hardest.

# "Sasquatch"

**I was camping** at the "Pine Tree Site" in a much bigger tent than my hitch-hiking shelter. Nights were long sitting by the fire, though I found solitude comfortable despite being such a social creature. Jack and Faye lived a little way the other side of me. If they were out, I could hear their old 1940s-era Chevy truck lumber by on the Fraser on their way home. It had its own unique rattle-trap signature sound. Jack would always toot the horn as he went by.

One night while tending my fire, I heard Jack's truck go by, Jack tooting his horn as always. Some minutes later, I heard a scream come from the Fraser Road right adjacent to my property. It sounded like a man in excruciating pain. My instant reaction was that it might be Jack who had gotten hurt. I loped down the path without a flashlight. Greg McEwan, Grey Cloud, taught me how to follow a path at night with no light. Look up at the night sky and follow the break in the trees.

Barreling down the path toward the road and whoever had screamed, my body slowed down, imperceptibly at first, but then it slowed to a walk and then a complete stop. But it wasn't me who ordered the halt. It was that preternatural guy at the controls in my head that handles all the instinctual, gut-level stuff. Then, as if he had flipped a switch, there was that crawling feeling in the scalp. The revelation hit me as that guy at the controls announced over the PA: "May I have your attention, please? *That* was *not* human."

*Holy shit.* With this to drive me, I made it back to the camp quicker than it had taken me to get halfway down the path. Back at the campsite, I zipped my "bear-proof screen" on the tent and sat inside with an ax in my lap.

The next day, Jack told me he was on his way home in his truck when he saw something cross the road and duck in the woods, my side. Stopping his vehicle, he heard something slow and lumbering, plodding through the woods. He figured it was a bear.

We were not the only ones who had seen or heard something. Four miles away, a woman in Clementsvale reported she had seen something big behind her house but could not identify it. So, I got accused of spotting a Sasquatch and everyone had a good laugh. I laughed along too. And I bought a 12-gauge shotgun. That was the creepiest sound I ever heard in the woods.

# Mickey vs. Mouse

**Between the time** of the ax as my only weapon and the 12-gauge shotgun, Jack had lent me his hunting bow with razor-sharp arrows. Archery would have been useless at night, but at least it was something. When you are camping in a forest in the middle of nowhere alone, an equalizer instills a little more confidence. I was living on a shoestring budget, and food was the most valuable possession, given the energy output the building effort required. The tent had a floor and a zippered door, but when I came back from the construction site, I found something had invaded my coffers and consumed or carried off a portion of the food. This was most distressing, and as each attempt to secure the larder was thwarted by my adversary, my concern grew to hatred. It was a matter of survival.

One afternoon, on a break from digging holes, I headed back to the Pine Tree site to get a snack from my meager pantry and entered the tent. There, in the corner, surprised and cowering, was the beast competing with me for survival: a little gray field mouse. He was trapped in one of the far corners of the tent and staring at me, what D.H. Lawrence would describe as "a many-fingered horror." I grabbed the closest thing I could find, a hammer, and moved in, raising it about a foot above this vermin that would compete with my very existence. *You son of a bitch, I've got you at last.* All I had to do was bring that hammer down, and this competition would be over. He looked back at me right in the face with his ink drop eyes and quivering whiskers. *Shit.* I couldn't do it. It did not seem a fair matchup: mouse vs. hammer.

I figured I had to give him a sporting chance. I would want the same opportunity. I scooped him up in a boot and stuffed a sock in the top, sealing him off. I brought the boot outside, strung the bow, popped the sock out of the boot, ran back about five yards, and zeroed in on the boot with one of the hunting arrows.

At first, nothing happened, and I was praying it would because I could not maintain the draw on the bow forever. My foe popped his head up out of the boot, looking around for his adversary. He spotted me, jumped out of the boot, and ran the other way. My hand was steady, and I released the arrow, sticking in the ground between his flailing legs, lifting him about an inch for just a moment while in stride. I had removed a speck of hair from his underbelly, but that was all, and he scampered faster than anything I had ever seen move and was gone. Though I had failed to kill my enemy, he had gotten the message to shop at a place with a more liberal shoplifting policy. He never returned, a tactical draw but strategic victory.

## Hippies Jump On People's Cars:
## Details at 11:00

**In response to** my need to have all the logs gathered at the building site, Jerry Rogers offered to help. Jerry had built what looked like a relic from the 1880s up on a hill overlooking the Fraser Road. He was able to haul twenty-five logs with his tractor before one of his tires began to leak. It was an excellent start.

Jack and Faye's cottage was the furthermost out on the Fraser Road going toward Guinea. During the hot summer of '74, they would sometimes get the notion that a swim or bath in Beeler's Lake, about three miles away, was just the thing. Their old blue, late 1940s Chevy pickup would rattle down the Fraser, and they'd shout out into the woods when adjacent to each of the camps.

"Beeler's!"

After a few moments, any interested parties would run down out of the woods and jump on the truck. By the time they reached the end of our enclave on the Fraser, the vehicle would be full of the Frasertown gang, and off we would go for our much-needed bath and cooling swim. All of us rabble piled into the bed of that old pickup could have been the inspiration something R. Crumb would have drawn. *Truckload of freaks, man.* We used the lakeside by leave of Art and Alice White, who owned the lakefront property. Art and Alice had left Ohio in '72 and were working a farm in Princedale. This method of gathering up interested bathers did not go unnoticed by the locals.

An older woman in Clementsvale warned anyone who would listen at a church gathering, "Don't drive slow on the Fraser Road. The hippies will come running out of the woods and jump on your vehicle!"

## *July 14, 1974*

**On July 13th,** Mary Lou, my lover I had met at college, arrived from the states. We had fallen hard for each other and got engaged but had not told our families yet. That we were too young would eventually be borne out. But, despite my dalliances, I was always looking for real love, whether I was capable of it or not. It was enthralling to share the beauty of Nova Scotia.

Mike Phillips had lent me a more spacious tent that I pitched at the building site in a move up from the Pine Tree Camp. That shortened my commute to work considerably. I had bought an antique rope bed at an auction, setting it up in the tent. We had a joyous reunion.

We were awakened the following day by a voice calling my name up the trail from the road. It was Dad Salsman. This had to be bad news. My mother had called, and I was to call her right away. We drove into Clementsvale with a sense of dread and used the Salsman's phone. Dad had died at the Veterans' Hospital in Wilmington, Delaware. We caught the afternoon ferry and made it to New Jersey in 22 hours. Mary Lou had not even spent 24 hours on the land.

At Harold Maguire's wake, the double line to get in the door stretched well down the block. He had a police honor guard standing by him, and as a WWII vet, he had the flag-draped casket. At the church, the Knights of Columbus stood by the casket with swords crossed above as he passed beneath. There was a full ACPD motorcycle escort for the half-hour drive to Holy Cross Cemetery in Mays Landing. Dead at 53, he would never see the cabin that he was so proud his son was building. I thought if I could have gotten him up there, we would have connected over that, playing with our woodstoves up on the hill. He wouldn't have wanted to leave. Someday, Dad, you, and I will sit together, our missing pieces filled.

# Gerald Oickle and Lion and Bright

**A week later,** Mary Lou, my friend Tom Lynch and I left for Nova Scotia with the task of turning a pile of logs scattered over six acres into a cabin. We set out to find someone who could haul the remaining logs to the building site and got a lead on Gerald Oickle in Bear River. Gerald had oxen, and he agreed to haul the logs. We set a date, and he arrived at 9:00 A.M. with his two oxen, Lion and Bright. They were just getting back from an exhibition in Lawrencetown, so we were treated with seeing them in their show regalia, bejeweled headdresses, and brass knobs on their horns. I went ahead of the oxen with a chainsaw and cleared wide paths for them to get to the logs. It was hard work, but it was a joy to watch Gerald work those oxen, their every move punctuated by their brass bells jangling. I learned that day the literal meaning of the phrase "strong as an ox." Gerald would hitch up three or four logs if he could, and they would uproot boulders, roots, and anything else they ran encountered. They hauled logs across the length of the property and then about 100 yards up the hill to the construction site. It was quite a job just clearing the way for the oxen to get at their quarry. Gerald mentioned to Mary Lou that I worked very hard all day, a genuine compliment from an old-timer who practically invented hard work. There were a few logs that were impossible to get to with the animals. Tom and I would have to carry those out ourselves, over broken ground and through dense thickets. Gerald, Lion, and Bright completed their work at 3:00 P.M. I thanked him for his help and asked what the charge would be.

"Would $10 be too much?" he asked.

During the next few weeks, Tom and I hauled the balance of the logs on our shoulders over rough terrain. I thought this could be how they trained Green Berets. We cut the hackmatack tree from Jack and Faye's property and hauled it up the hill. There was no driveway, so everything, a cast-iron cookstove, 100 lb. bags of gravel we shoveled ourselves, bags of cement, bundles of shingles, the entire cabin had to be carried up that hill.

We got the holes excavated, having discovered three-quarters of all the rocks in Nova Scotia. There were a few "Now what?" moments at this time. But

Gerald Oikel with Lion and Bright the day we hauled the logs out of the woods, August 1974.

God is good. Father Joe Wagenhoffer, the log cabin building priest, had arrived for a visit to Nova Scotia. He had written a letter to the judge who sentenced me after the pot bust, asking for leniency and offered to act as my probation officer. The judge agreed, and after said probation, my record was expunged.

Father Joe's cabin was about two logs high when I helped him, resulting in zero experience in the foundation department for me, but he was now here to compensate for my late enrollment in Cabin Building 101. Getting settled, he pitched a silk parachute as a teepee. Fr. Joe brought a certain jovialness to the work camp. He soon set about building a camp table with attached benches that made the campsite a little homier. Most of all, Joe brought his foundation knowledge at the right time. He helped mobilize me, and soon we were mixing concrete for the footings that encased the hackmatack posts. It was here that I tossed in the stone I had liberated from Thoreau's cabin site at Walden Pond.

On August 5, 1974, we put in the foundation posts. Water for cement was carried by bucket from Birch Brook at one end of the property and up the hill. We all put our initials in the concrete on one of the low posts.

Next came the sill logs. At 26 feet in length, these logs supported the rest of the building. They were thick and had to be carried by hand to their resting places on the posts. Here and with every notch, the logs were spiked with 8 to

10-inch spikes. I used the blunt part of the ax-head (the poll) opposite the blade to drive the spikes like a sledgehammer. There is no room for errant ax swings. A ten-inch spike that gets bent about halfway in is a total butt pain. There is no straightening it out and no pulling it out. If it goes wrong, the best you can do is flatten it out and try another.

Gary Lawson came over from Maine to help when we were putting in the floor joists. Instead of milled lumber, I used logs for joists, though I spaced them too far apart. The floor was a tad springy till the application of the second flooring. Once the subflooring was complete, we had a platform in the woods and a place to have the cabin's first party. Folks came up from Bear River, and most of the Fraser Roaders were there. There was music in the dark till the wee hours on our little concert platform in the forest.

## The Cabin Goes Up, Nixon Goes Down

**I was a** crazed construction fiend once we had a foundation and floor. With the logs where we needed them, we started on the walls log by log. That it would get dark was frustrating, and we often worked into the night by kerosene lamp. I discovered the strange, grounding elixir made of sweat, dirt, and sawdust. The gritty feel of it on the skin, the smell of it seemed to affirm that what I was doing was simple, pure, and honest. My incessant, goal-driven behavior must have driven Tom a little crazy. He came to help, but I don't think he planned on what amounted to slavery, waking every morning to the sound of the chain saw.

We had a little AM/FM battery-operated radio. On August 8th, 1974, we were tuned in. Word had it that something big was about to go down. With the U.S. embroiled in the Viet Nam War and then Watergate, President Richard Nixon became a symbol of all that was wrong with the country. It would be hard to find a more fitting enemy of the counterculture. We broke for a bite to eat at the building site and listened to the static-punctuated resignation speech of Richard M. Nixon and rejoiced. There was shouting and even dancing. Somehow it felt like the promise of the '60s could be fulfilled. After all, the evil king had been dethroned.

# The Four-Log High Party

**Once the building** reached four logs high, we needed windows, as they would dictate how the rest of the project would proceed. This was construction on the fly, to be sure, planning a building based on windows you might find. In Nova Scotia, the word got out that Mickey needed windows, and three days later, I had seven old windows. I paid $5 for the large window in the kitchen area and the two that became the swinging windows in the front. The other windows were given to me by Dad Salsman out of his barn.

While this window procurement phase was going on, work stopped, and we had visitors from the states: John, who had cut the logs with me, Linda, Dan Pittaro from Atlantic City, and Gary Lawson from Bangor. It was an opportune time to have a big party. I had no chairs, but the log walls were the perfect bench-size height at four logs high. Aptly billed as "The Four-Log High Party," many who were there still remember it by this moniker. The whole crew from Frasertown and Bear River came. During this raucous affair, my friend Dan from Atlantic City approached me in a state of distress.

"Your friend Greg, the Indian. He told me he could make one cut in my belly with his knife, and I would be scooping up my guts from the floor."

"Oh, that's just Greg. Don't worry about it."

Dan found no comfort in this. Greg liked to shock people with the scary talk. I somehow understood this and would give it back to him in kind, the idea being that it was a challenge to reply with something even more outrageous. Then we'd both laugh about it. Dan did his best to avoid Greg the rest of the evening within the confines of a 16x24 area.

Anyone at the Four-Log High Party remembers the meteor that exploded in the sky over us. With no roof, this platform was an observatory in the woods. We were all involved in our revelry, singing, playing guitars, and threatening guests from New Jersey with disembowelment when a meteor streaked overhead. But this was not a distant over-in-a-second streak. This celestial body had entered the atmosphere low, and it seemed slower than most. It was bright because of its proximity to us, lighting up our entire platform in the woods like an enormous streetlight. But for the brightness, I think we would have missed it. Everyone turned and watched this thing burning up in our atmosphere. We had a perfect hilltop view as it streaked from north to south and went out over the southern sky, where it exploded and broke up. We heard it. It sounded like a muffled "puh." The cabin's second party smoked the first and set the tone for what would become many musical and joy-filled evenings within those log walls.

# Roof Raising Party

**Work went on** at a fever pitch throughout August and September. It was exciting and satisfying to observe the growing project from the campsite, each day bringing noticeable progress. By the time the project neared completion, I had lived in a tent for almost four months. Tom and I were close to finishing the walls toward the end of September. We ran out of logs during the topmost course and had to cut down a few more trees, putting them up green. That meant carrying the green water-laden heavy logs out of the woods over broken, uneven ground from some distance away on our shoulders. *These kids today.* The sap was no longer running well, necessitating shaving the logs with a drawknife.

During quiet moments, it became clear that woodworms had gotten into the logs. This infestation was the result of leaving the bark on too long before shaving. The worms, when young, will feed off the white substance between the bark and the wood for some time before they are strong enough to bore into the wood. Once they do that, they tunnel their way into the softwood. You know they are there—the gnawing and gnashing being quite audible, sounding like a creaking floorboard. I pictured my future self, sitting with a book on a quiet night, trying to ignore the woodworm glee as they tore through the all-you-can-eat buffet of my walls. *Didn't anyone teach you not to chew with your mouth open?* They had to go.

I engaged Mr. Hagan from Clementsvale to treat the logs and get rid of my woodworms. He arrived with his equipment and asked if I had a ladder. It never occurred to me to have one. We just climbed up the walls if we needed to go higher. I put my finger up to signify: *One moment.*

Running down to the log pile with the chain saw, a hammer, nails, and, using all the thin ends of waste logs, I constructed a ladder with all its imperfections in ten minutes flat. I ran the finished product up the hill to Mr. Hagen, and he was the first to use what is still the ladder for the loft to this day.

We set a date for an old-fashioned roof-raising party and sent word out to all the fabulous furry freaks living in the area. One thing remained for us to do: the plate. The plate is a layer of lumber (I used 2X4) that goes on the top logs all the way around. It provides a flat, uniform surface for the roof rafters to rest. The top logs needed flattening to accept the plate, accomplished with a chainsaw and hatchet. A day before the party, Tom and I finished the plate in a cold, driving rain. Nothing like a deadline.

The morning of October 1, 1974, dawned chilly and clear. The sky was that illegal Nova Scotia blue: *Sorry, that's just too blue. You know that's illegal, right? I'm gonna have to issue you a summons.* Freaks showed up from all over with tools, food, beer, dogs, and guitars. The party set up inside the roofless box, and beer started flowing immediately. Gee, we were having a good time until friend Phillip Harvey walked down to the woodpile. He had also built a cabin in Deep Brook during what seemed to be The Summer of Log Cabins.

"If we are going to put this roof up, we better get started."

Thank you, Phillip, for being the catalyst. Work started in earnest, and six of us went aloft to erect the ridge beam and rafters. We had gotten the lumber from the now-vanished Bear River lumber mill. While we were working and banging away above, many were down below eating, drinking, and playing guitars. Sometimes a hammer would drop to the floor with a loud bang, eliciting the warning from above, "Watch out for that hammer!"

On that October afternoon, under an illegal blue sky, standing high on the roof of an eleven-year-old boy's fantasy, I felt something that all too often proves elusive in alcoholic families:

Satisfaction. *Glad to make your acquaintance. I've waited half my life to meet you.*

Gary Lawson during the floor joist phase, August, 1974.

Mission impossible: leveling log floor joists.

Laying the first floor (L to R: Gary Lawson, Mary Lou Brodek, the author).

Up on the hill, 1974.

Almost halfway there, 1974.

Halfway mark.

My hair had to go into a braid, like here, or a bandana to prevent getting caught in the chainsaw.

Tom Lynch, my right-hand man throughout the project.

Tom Lynch holding a window in place for the photo.

Author cutting a notch. Start with a chainsaw, finish with a hatchet.

Before collar beams.

Cabin ready for collar beams, top logs and plate.

The collar beams prevent the cabin walls from spreading.

Ready for the roof!

My ten-minute ladder, still the way to the loft today.

First rafter at the roof-raising party, October 1, 1974.

Aloft during roof-raising day.

Standing on the new roof, I took this picture, October 1, 1974.

Drilling holes for the wooden-pegged front porch.

Summer of 1977.

Contemporary view: Beth reading.

Finished cabin.

# Finishing Touches

**We had to** get back for the fall semester at college, and on October 1st, it was getting late, but the roof was not complete, and the doors and windows remained uninstalled. There was a fellow who offered to finish it off in exchange for a rent-free winter. We accepted the offer and left for school, but when we arrived at Glassboro, we discovered it was too late to begin classes, setting up a debaucherous semester of parties.

In January, we heard that the fellow did not finish off the place and move in, leaving it open to the elements. The thought of snow lying inside drove me crazy, so Mary Lou and I went up to finish it off before the start of the spring semester. If we finished the roof, put a layer of tar paper on it, and boarded up the windows and doors, it would wait till June when we would come back and make it livable. While there, a neighbor showed me how to rabbit hunt without a dog chasing them up, which would come in handy over the next couple of years while living on $50 a month.

Coming from Atlantic City, where most snow storms turned to rain (yeah, we're talking a lot of childhood disappointment), it was righteous to have the almost daily occurrence of snow in Nova Scotia. However, we did have a classic January thaw, and I could be up on the roof with no shirt on January 12th. Friends helped me put the tar paper on the roof, and it was back to Glassboro for the spring semester.

As an English major, I took a course that spring called Environmental Ethics taught by Professor Ed Wolf. We had to do a paper for two-thirds of our grade at the end of the semester. It seemed silly to write an essay for an environmental class without touching on the scene happening in Nova Scotia. So I wrote about the building project and Nova Scotia back-to-basics experience and titled it: "Where I'm Living and What I'm Living For: An Environmental Ethic (with apologies to Henry David Thoreau)." Thoreau had subtitled his *Walden* with "Where I Lived and What I Lived For."

When I got it back, Dr. Wolf had written on the face sheet: "I don't see how I could possibly put a grade on this." And he did not. I got an "A" for the course, and he was so taken by the paper, he visited us for a week that summer in Nova Scotia with his son, Chris.

When we returned in June of '75, we found the tar paper had ripped up in places, but the cabin was in excellent shape. We un-boarded the windows and doors and shingled the roof. That done, next was framing in the windows. Gary Lawson from Maine came over again to help. Once we had her all closed in, we made the place livable. The back-breaking stuff was behind us now. Putting in windows and doors was damned exciting. We bought a tapestry of a sylvan scene with deer that stills graces the wall.

That summer, Bill Watson began another one of his North American jaunts, a trip he calls "The Circle." He had previously crossed Canada to British Columbia via rail and hitchhiked down to California, south into Mexico to the Yucatan Peninsula, and back up to New Jersey. Embarking on a similar tour, he decided to check out my Nova Scotia project first.

Arriving in the evening on Fraser Road and not finding the trail to my place, Bill found his way to Jack and Faye's driveway. We were at a party with Jack in Upper Clements, but Faye was home with new baby Jana. She entertained Bill till we got back and walked him over through the darkened woods path between the two cabins. Faye entered the back door first. "Look what the wind blew in from New Jersey," she said.

Stepping in from the darkness to the warm oil lamp glow of the log cabin, his eyes darted here and there like nervous birds landing everywhere at once. He was enthralled. I knew what he was thinking, having done the same thing when I walked into George Goodin's place. He had a "You can actually *do* this!" moment. We had an idyllic visit with Bill that made quite an impression on him. Richard Milner had helped Tom Lynch buy seven acres just a little further down the Fraser Road from my place. Bill and his brother Martin went in with him on the land. Bill Watson decided there would be a log cabin to build the following year.

# The Salsman and Maguire Expedition

**Jack and I** went on a three-day canoeing trip into "The Interior" that summer. A route perfectly fit our time frame: five lakes and two rivers with several portages linking them all. They were Weyland Lake, Oak Lake, and the two Northeast Lakes, ending at Mulgrave (or Big) Lake. Mary Lou drove us out to Rt. 8 and dropped us off at the first lake. We had a little food, backpacks with sleeping gear, and a shotgun. After we left the first lake, we were miles from the nearest woods road. Our places on the Fraser Road seemed like civilization compared to this.

Portages over rocky and broken ground, uphill and down, with full gear backpacks and a canoe covering our heads, signaled that this would be a working vacation. Once we were in the interior, we saw a few trees marked with blue paint. Jack told me that meant it was "Crown Land," meaning government land. Here were the only virgin forests I had ever seen. Massive original growth that had never seen an ax or chainsaw. These were the true North Woods.

We camped on an island the second night. As we beached the canoe, the dark sand seemed to move back toward the island, leaving white sand behind. *That's weird.* We took a few steps onto the island, and the dark sand seemed again to move back and away from us. On closer inspection, we saw that the dark sand was thousands of tiny frogs, some no more than half an inch in size, that moved away from us with each step.

Having been captivated by "Huckleberry Finn" as a boy, the idea of camping on an island like Huck and Jim delighted me. We made a fire and reveled into the night, the only human souls for miles.

The North-East Lakes were rugged and a haven for many majestic sea birds. Imposing boulders poked through the surface, making small islands. We "beached" our canoe on one such boulder and swam from it.

On the next to the last day, Jack and I made it to Mulgrave or Big Lake, the last and only lake of the five with an access road. There were coves and islands here, and we spent a substantial part of the day exploring. Toward day's end, we made for a camp belonging to the Mersey Paper Company. This ramshackle two-story building had been built in the '20s or '30s and had been in disuse for many years. A dilapidated structure now, it had a great room and fireplace. Although a wreck of a place with no windows or doors, we decided it would make an adequate camp for the night.

After cooking up some dinner in the still functional brick fireplace, we sat on the front porch on a bench to watch the sun go down over the lake. Sitting about three feet from each other, I saw a blur between us as we talked.

I doubted that I had seen something, maybe a big "floater" inside the eye. But there it was again.

"Did you see something?" Jack asked me.

"Yeah. There's another one!" And another, and, wait, the blurs were bats. Bats, little gargoyles, scratching out from under greyed shingles, unfurling all around us, puffs of air felt on our cheeks as they poured out by the score, the hundreds and then thousands, blocking out half the sky creating their own dusk.

Darting out uncomfortably close to our faces, within an inch or two, I'd say, our nocturnal companions rendered sitting on the bench for the evening impossible. This Mersey Paper Company camp was a mega bat hotel. We were the intruders; the bats, surprised by new obstructions, made on-the-spot adjustments to their flight patterns to avoid smacking into our heads. Thinking if we moved too quickly, we'd get a bat in the face, we inched our way to the great room. A blazing fire in the fireplace seemed to keep the swirls of them at bay until we bedded down. The fire reduced to glowing coals. Pulling sleeping bags closed over our heads, we listened as bats filled the room until the air around us was boiling with them.

Somehow we managed to sleep with these ". . . *children of the night. What music they make.*"—Count Dracula (*Dracula*, 1931 Universal Studios)

The following day broke warm and sunny, and we had, by default, reclaimed the great room from the bats. After breaking camp, we launched our canoe and headed for a party, a summer's end affair that drew freaks near and far. It seemed a perfect conclusion to our adventure, two mountain men coming in from the wild to an annual rendezvous.

Paddling around the final bend and into a cove, it was a strange sight to see so many people when we had not encountered a soul for three days. We paddled harder, and they cheered, many wading out with beers and other celebratory beverages. We were the return of the Lewis and Clark Expedition. Folks helped us beach the canoe, greeting us with hugs and kisses.

"Yep," we said, hamming it up, "We heard there was a party, so we left three days ago. . . ."

It was a perfect summer at the new log cabin. We went up on the roof frequently to lay on our backs and watch the stars. Being raised in the light pollution of the Jersey coast, we had never seen stars like this, diamonds encrusted on black velvet. The Milky Way was visible every night from that hill; the grand painting signed periodically with the sweeping script of a meteor.

# The "Curriculum" Hits the Wall

**I graduated college** during the spring of 1976, a year late but with good reason. That it happened at all was a near miracle. I had been in the English Secondary Education track and was doing the final phase called "practicum," or student teaching at Williamstown High School. I had to tie up my mid-back length hair in a ponytail and wear a straitjacket suit that felt so wrong on me it almost burned my skin like the elven rope to Gollum's neck. *It burns us!*

The mission was to get disaffected juniors and seniors to digest dry, crunchy grammar with no milk or fruit. Much of the semester involved diagramming sentences provided in the standard curriculum bible, the always thrilling *Warriner's English Grammar and Composition*. Something had to give. I made up stupid sentences that were perfectly diagrammable:

Although he is totally blind, Mr. Hagan still drives the school bus.
He ordered extra melted balloons on his pizza.

A weird thing developed during English class: We were having *fun.* Uh-oh.

My supervisor looked like she would have been better cast as a spinster schoolmarm or one of the last survivors from First Class on the *Titanic*. It was a cruel cosmic joke that I would draw the supervisor with the biggest stick up their ass. She no doubt had heard that long-haired hippie freak Maguire's class was having a little "F"-word. That she did not like the way I looked was palpable when we met for supervision, her eyes everywhere but looking into mine, alighting here and there on what they deemed offensive to normalcy. Admittedly, the idea of becoming an English teacher was beginning to show holes. After being forced to attend a school board meeting, I received an accelerated education. Having just built my Fortress of Solitude (sorry, Superman reference) in the North, I tried to ignore its whispered sweetness in my ear while being stuck at an overly-politicked, back-biting, tail-chasing excuse for a meeting. I had too much a taste of living right to reconcile myself to this scene. Being only two months from graduation, I thought it best to slog it out.

My supervisor, the only Thelma I ever knew, sat in on a class, another of those diagramming classes using whacked-out absurd sentences. The first mistake was laughter because if you're having fun, you can't be working, followed by enthusiastic participation and an actual demonstration of a degree of acumen. I guess that was bad too. After the class, Thelma Stick Up Her Ass went on the attack.

"You must stick to the curriculum!"

Having been beat-up a Catholic and the target of maladjusted, sadistic nuns, you could say I had a sore spot in the getting-yelled-at-by-teachers department. I tried to explain that the sentences made sense, at least for diagramming, and the kids had fun *and* learned something. I shouldn't have used the "F"-word.

It was no use. She ranted on about having to use the sentences provided in Warriner's English Grammar book. In the middle of gutting me, I noticed she was staring at my mouth. Now what? *What's wrong with my fucking mouth?* She noticed me noticing her noticing my mouth and broke off the inquisition, triumphantly declaring, "So you *were* chewing gum!" She forgot to say, "Aha!"

Well, I was, but I was not making a big show of it with only an occasional surreptitious chew. It was a great moment for her, my having been caught with the secrets to the hydrogen bomb in my mouth and trying to sell them to the Russians. With the Fraser Road whispering seductive entreaties in my ear (okay, it had its *tongue* in my ear), I picked up the *Warriner's English Grammar* book from the desk.

"You know what?" I said, "This I what I think of your curriculum."

I threw the book to the back of the classroom, where it hit the wall and fell to the floor. Not expecting this, she gave up the gum tirade.

"I'm done," I said and turned toward the door.

"But you won't graduate!" she called after me when she found her voice.

"I just did," I said from the hallway.

It was useless. I was probably one of the fellows that Robert Service called "The Men Who Don't Fit In." I thought I could make a go of it in the real world. In January, I had interviewed at two high schools in Nova Scotia, and they were both interested. It would have given me the necessary qualifications to become a "landed immigrant," granting me all the rights of a Canadian citizen, except voting. I didn't know who I was fooling, somehow *thinking* I could fit in. What happened instead was a collect call from a payphone to my mom, informing her that I had walked out of college two months before graduation and that I was hitch-hiking to Nova Scotia, which went over like a fart in a diving bell. What a waste, though. I might have made a decent English teacher.

I did hitch and spent two weeks in Scotia during spring break, but then decided to go back and talk to my advisor, the incomparable English professor Dr. Nathan Karb. I had sailed through his graduate-level course on the English Romantics with an A-plus. He said in that class once, "With Shelley, the 'soul mate' (a big theme in Romanticism) is never abstract. From poetry to bed in one easy leap." Yeah. What's not to like there? He recommended that I take a short class since I had taken five years to graduate and only needed one or two credits. He convinced me to at least get my BA in English. I took "Art Appreciation" and got an "A," and Mom was happy to attend my graduation. At the English House after the ceremony, Dr. Karb introduced Mom and me to the artist in residence, writer James T. Farrell, he of "Studs Lonigan" fame. He said to Farrell, "Mickey is going to be very successful. At what, we don't know, but very successful."

(Update on that: Social work saved my sorry ass. Next memoir, maybe. A life of service with the disenfranchised uncovered what I came to believe was what God wanted of me. This Tagore quote comes closest to explaining what happened: "I slept and dreamt that life was joy. I awoke and saw that life was service. I acted and behold, service was joy."—Rabindranath Tagore)

## A Wheelchair in Maine

**During the summer** of 1976, I played in a rock band at a bar just off the boardwalk in Atlantic City. Bill was already in Nova Scotia, cutting logs for his project. Once the summer and bar gig was over, I hitched to Nova Scotia to join him. Mostly, I got my rides from fellow freaks. A VW bus always meant a ride and sometimes a shared joint. Mary Lou dropped me off on I-684 just north of New York City. Soon after she pulled away, a New York State Trooper picked me up and deposited me on a dinky minor county road on the wrong side of a tall cyclone fence. He pointed at I-684 through the fence.

"I'm going to swing back later," he said, "If I see you on that highway, you're going to jail."

Hitching to the cabin from New York State, 1977.

As he pulled away, I assessed the situation. I needed to make Bangor, Maine, well before nightfall to catch the midnight ferry to Digby, Nova Scotia. I was on this little road where, even if I got a ride, it would lead to nowhere. Being a risk I had to take if I wanted out of New York, I scaled the fence with my backpack and stuck out my thumb on I-684. I was picked up immediately by a medical student headed to Boston. He said he would take me there if I read from a medical technical manual as he was cramming for an exam.

On a few occasions, I got rides with truckers. It is another world riding in the cab of a semi, so high up, almost like a low-flying aircraft. Yeah, they can see what you are doing in your low little cars as they pass you. Always friendly and helpful, I think the truckers felt a certain sympathy for intrepid hitchhikers. Perhaps starved for human conversation, they always seemed chatty. CB radio was their connection to the world of trucking, and each had their own CB "handle." On one of these trips, I got picked up by "Blue Max," who was only going halfway to Bangor. "Blue Max" got on the CB and canvassed other truckers, and arranged a meet at a trucker's stop where I was handed off to a Bangor-bound semi.

But this time, as I stood on I-95 just past the first toll in Maine, a big sedan pulled over, and I was surprised a middle-aged couple had stopped for me. I thanked them and tossed my gear into the back seat. They asked me where I was headed, and I told them of my log cabin in Nova Scotia.

"You remind us so much of our son," the wife said. "He has a jacket just like yours."

She was referring to my buckskin fringe jacket. On their way to visit this son, there was something about how she talked about him that made me think he might be dead. But they were going to see him now. Could their destination be the cemetery? But no, they were still talking present tense about him. I could not figure it out. There was pain, grief in her voice. I looked at dad and could tell he would find speaking at this moment a challenge. But then the answer came.

"Our son Dennis was in an accident. He was thrown from a Jeep and broke his neck," she took a deep breath, "He is paralyzed. We are going to visit him in a rehab facility."

"Oh, I am so sorry," I said.

They went on to tell me about his hitchhiking trips and that he was a writer of poetry. We were the same age and had been on similar tracks, but his life changed after ejection from a Jeep. I felt guilty being whole and walking around, riding the crest, living my dream.

"Would you like to visit him with us? I am sure he would love to meet you. Of course, if you are in a hurry, we understand."

I was trying to make the ferry, but, "Sure, I would love to meet him," came out.

We arrived at the rehab, where they ushered me to their son's room. Dennis Daigle was sitting up in a raised hospital bed, his hair curly and longish. Greeting me with a big open smile, he was pale, and his hands were withered, contracted. His accident had happened not that long ago, but somehow he emanated an air of acceptance. I was having a more difficult time with this meeting than he. We talked about our remarkably similar passions. When we got around to poetry, he showed me how he wrote his poems. He had an electric typewriter set up in front of him and a pencil-like stick he gripped in his mouth with a flexible flap attached to one end. He depressed the typewriter keys with this stick in his mouth. I told him how cool that was. I am not sure if he saw the tears welling up in my face like they are right now as I write this all these years later. His bravery was almost more than I could bear. Why him and not me? It felt as if my journey, my cabin, my freedom was like taunting. I had no right to these things.

Author and Dennis Daigle. Note the device he held in his teeth to type his poetry.

Dennis and I corresponded for a few years after that meeting, sending each other our latest poetic efforts. His letters and poems were always neatly typed, but I could not shake the image of the agonizing process with that stick clenched in his teeth, every word a product of passion and determination. It felt like I was insensitive, sending my handwritten verse. I felt guilty even existing.

We eventually lost touch. A few years ago, I searched for him on the internet, hoping to get in touch again, and got a hit on an article written about him. A posthumous article. He had gone to school in the south somewhere; I want to say Virginia. He became a fixture there and was much loved. There were written testimonials from the many people he had touched, inspired. The article spoke of his humor, grace, and strength. Dennis Daigle had found a way to be fruitful, to make his mark, even after so much loss. It said that his mom had taken care of him every day of his life since the accident, but when she died, he followed her five months later. Rest, my poet friend. I will never forget you.

## Banjo Pickin' and Dust Bowl Days

**I arrived at** 3:00 A.M. in Digby via the ferry and managed to get a ride as far as Clementsport, five miles from my hill. Leaving the blacktop and onto the dirt roads, it is a long hike in the dark with full gear and a guitar. The Guinea Hill is a steep incline that I doubt I could do today *without* a backpack. After a two-mile uphill trudge, the back end of the Fraser Road began the last two relatively level miles. In those days, I recall, getting up a good deal of momentum to attack the sharply pitched trail that led to the cabin, then practically gliding up the crazy rainbow steps to the porch, and BAM! I'd kick open the front door. This time, like a security alarm, screams came from my bed, and two shadowy forms sat bolt upright. I screamed right back at them, a purely reflexive response. Once the primal yelling was over, a staccato of questions and answers followed. It was Goldilocks and the Three Bears redux.

"Who are you?" from the bed.

"I'm Mickey Maguire. This is my cabin. (I thought it important to establish this right off.) Who are you?"

"We're friends of George and Rhonda. They said you wouldn't mind if we stayed here."

OK. Acceptable response. They must have been relieved I did not announce myself as Crazy Pete, The Backwoods Ax Murderer. They introduced themselves in their nightclothes as Greg and Beth and explained they were building a place of their own a few miles away. They needed a place to stay during the project. Once we all felt confident no one was going to die that night, we lit a few lamps and wasted no time finding out we were all cool. Overall, warmth and civility came easy in those days; we all, the freaks, that is, shared a commonality of purpose and cherished similar values. And reefer. They said they would move out, but I thought *Nonsense. We can make this work.*

For the next couple of weeks, Greg, Beth, and I were cabin mates during one of the most magnificent times of year to be in Nova Scotia: Fall. Warm enough in the daytime to hang out on the porch but with the crispness in the air that whispers of coming winter, yet cold enough at night and in the early

Digby Gut with Bay of Fundy beyond.

morning to need a fire in the cookstove, fall is prime time to be in the Maritime Provinces.

Hailing from East Texas, Greg Hunter was short of stature with long wavy blonde hair, blue eyes, and only a few front teeth. An agreeable, jovial sort, nothing seemed to rile him much. Beth, a lawyer by profession, seemed to take to this woodsy counterculture scene naturally. It seemed to me the lawyer thing was a stretch for her.

None of us had much money. Greg and Beth were building, so that's where theirs was going. Food was an afterthought. I had a can of Campbell's chicken noodle soup and an ear of corn so dried out it really should have been hung on a door as a Fall or Thanksgiving decoration. (As an older feller, I wonder how I could arrive at the cabin with only a can of soup and an ear of corn. Kids.) Since there were three of us, I added an extra can of water to the soup. We sat down and had our watery broth and took turns taking a bite from the ear of that nearly inedible corn. It was pitiful. We broke out in a fit of laughter and, sitting in this log cabin with the kerosene lamps and wood stove heat. It suggested what it might have looked like in the Dust Bowl days, albeit for just a second, though our poverty was willful and self-inflicted.

After our Dust Bowl feast, Greg opened a beat-up banjo case and took out a 5-string Baldwin "Ode" banjo. Armed with metal fingerpicks, he launched into a daring musical tirade. A skillfully executed up-tempo banjo instrumental with its ever-cascading impossibility of notes, referred to in the genre as a "break-down," hits you like a symphony and a drive-by shooting simultaneously. His playing was fluid and powerful, loud and melodic, dominant and commanding. The assault of notes passed through me somehow, like cosmic rays. I always loved the term "gobsmacked," and there is no better way to describe my reaction. And he looked so perfect there in the lamplight with his long blonde hair and unshaven face, digging into that Ode, his dutiful slave. When Greg played, he put himself in an otherworldly zone signified by the tongue he would stick out the side of his mouth through the spaces left by the absence of certain teeth. I had trouble breathing during that, or rather, I forgot to breathe. He invited me to accompany him on guitar, and this was the first time playing what was new music to me, this sort of earthy jazz. This was the bluegrass banjo seed, planted on a cool fall night in the North. I could not know then, but this would sprout years later when I would study the instrument with banjo master Tony Trischka, tour, and record with bluegrass bands James Reams & The Barnstormers and String Fever.

Looking out for varmints, 1977.

## *Springing Roof*

**Bill Watson was** in Newfoundland upon my return and returned to NS a few weeks later after Greg and Beth moved into their camp. Reunited, we stayed at my place while we worked on his cabin. Living on the Fraser Road that fall and early winter produced what I think of as the centerpiece of our deep friendship, a time we thereafter dubbed "The Log Cabin Days."

Leaving ourselves open to being justifiably accused of having too much time on our hands, we were not at a loss when it came to amusing ourselves. Music was our main staple, probably more than food. (Our diet mainly consisted of rice, cheese, eggs, and wild rabbit.) One of our favorite wastes of time was speaking in Spoonerisms in our everyday conversation; you know, "pouring rain" becomes "roaring pain." To this day, we can weak this spay right off the hop of our teds without thuch mought. We did this a lot with other people around who could barely stunderand sut we were whaying.

Interior, 1977.

As Billy's cabin grew, it became the number one topic of conversation of all who visited. It was something special and reflected the care and precision with which he approaches everything. A trash picker at heart, Bill had brought back a thick spring from a wrecked car and installed it atop a corner of the walls, prompting inevitable questions. That, he would say, was for the springing roof. *The what?* Yes, we would tell bewildered guests, *the springing roof.* Heavy springs would be installed on the top of the four corners of the cabin and the roof built atop them. There would be clamp-like devices that would keep it all battened down. But when you wanted, you could loosen the battens, and the roof would spring, you know, like *boing, boing!* But why?

We would tell them that is for when you eat *waffles,* you can go up there and eat them on the springing roof. Get it? Waffles/springing roof? Gotta have a springing roof for when you eat your waffles, right? The only thing people "got" was that there were two weird guys from New Jersey back in the woods doing dumb stuff to a log cabin.

## *God Makes a House Call*

**Having been beat** up a Catholic and somehow surviving twelve years of schooling at Our Lady of the Bleeding Knuckles, I had a well-developed aversion to all things conventionally religious and, in some ways, still do. I did not, however, go atheistic. I had a real sense of something greater than ourselves. At first, after having been taught the Gospel of Love with a fist (see "Nuns and Demeaning Sadism," Chapter 12), I went all pantheistic. I found God in the natural world around me. But it was missing something. I saw His signature, but not Him. Being at the cabin was like being in a safe room where you had the time and perspective to ponder what was going on *back there*. With Tolkien's *Lord of the Rings* still fresh in our souls, we called the world to the south "Mordor" while holding "High Council" in the North (think *The Council of Elrond)*. The world outside of our retreat on the hill just did not seem to make much sense. Though naturally buoyant, I found myself feeling hopeless and depressed about the way the world was going. (Author's note to younger self: You ain't seen nuthin' yet, bud.) Bill and I read aloud many nights. We flipped out over my English

Playing Bill's classical guitar.

Romantics. Bill was particularly enthralled with Wordsworth's "Tintern Abbey" lines. When it was his turn, Bill read Scripture.

During a late-night reading from the New Testament, I came across a passage where Jesus addressed the disciples. He spoke of how difficult our trials would become and how tough times would be. In the end, he said to them, "But be of good cheer, for I have overcome the world." That was the moment when the water soaked into the fine powder and became clay. I did not have to overcome the world. He had already done that. This changed everything. Yeah, I step off the path. But now, there *is* a path.

## No Door Locks and the Three Bears

**Of all the** questions I have been asked through the years about this log cabin experience, the most frequent are the "bear" questions: Did I ever see any? Are there any around? Did I ever have a problem with them? In over forty years, I never laid eyes on a live bear. There is a den purportedly a mile behind the property near Skull Lake. The bears in Nova Scotia are wilder and less accustomed to human presence than, say, the black bears in New Jersey, where they go from trash can to trash can. In Nova Scotia, the axiom that the bears are more afraid of us than we are of them is probably true. They hear us before we get near and are usually gone undetected.

There are exceptions, however. My dear departed friend and the long-time guardian angel of the cabin, "Miffer" Milner, came over to my place some years ago with a roast of bear for me. About two miles from me, a neighbor of his was cooking bacon on his stove one morning. He left the room for a moment. When he returned, he found a black bear had forced his way into the house and was eating the bacon out of the pan. The neighbor retreated to the living room, got his rifle, and shot the bear right in front of the kitchen stove. The roast I was given from that bear, with onions and salt and pepper and baked in the woodstove, was some of the finest red meat ever. On another occasion, I helped someone skin a bear and got gorgeous steaks for my efforts.

A sub-category in the bear questions is: "What does it taste like?" The key to good-tasting bear meat is meticulously removing all the fat and membranous tissue from the meat. Bear fat is the origin of that "gamey" taste, and its successful removal results in a quintessential red meat flavor, beef on testosterone.

Although I had never seen a bear nearby, there were three occasions when I heard them. The first was when I was accused of seeing a Sasquatch, chronicled earlier. The other two incidents occurred after I moved into the cabin.

During the fall when Bill was building, we were holding High Council one night when we heard it: something big right by the back door. We could sense its sheer mass by the deep "huff" of its lungs. The volume of expelled air could not be coming from anything but a beast.

Author (L) and Bill Watson, August 1977.

The door was lockless in those days. All a creature had to do was gently push with the smallest of its claws to gain entrance. Bill and I dove for the firearms. One of us had a single-shot 12-gauge shotgun, and the other had a .303 Lee-Enfield rifle, standing side-by-side, weapons cocked. He clawed the log wall on the outside, huffed some more, and . . . nothing. The bear lost interest and left, his tracks leading up behind the cabin toward Skull Lake. As scared as we were, we stood up admirably well. But the second incident explains the courage of the first.

On the second occasion, jumping ahead a couple of years, the scenario was similar. There was that same huffing from massive lungs just the other side of the door. The difference was that I was alone. Bravado on display when Bill and I faced this together, I believe, was for show. When you are with another, you have someone for which to be brave. But alone, there is no such artifice. It's just you, the bear and fear creeping into your every bone. I stood there facing the back door with the shotgun cocked in my hands, the rifle with its clip of nine shells slung on my shoulder by the strap. The plan: The bear comes crashing through the door, and I let him have a rifled slug from the single-action shotgun to make him feel ill, drop the gun, unsling the bolt action rifle and begin squeezing off as many shells as I could before he devours me. He never came in, but this was as scary as any crisis experienced at sea. I felt a lot less brave when I had no one to play to but myself. Now there is a kick-ass bolt installed on that door.

## *Cabin Fever and the Five-Step Kahlua Aging Process*

**As winter approached,** nights got longer and colder. We had no dry wood in, so we cut down a green maple or birch in the dusk after Bill finished work at the building site every night. Then we climbed up on a collar beam and called it "the loft," it being far warmer up there. Over in the kitchen area, the dishwater froze.

We got more inventive, finding ways to amuse ourselves. Knife throwing was always on our dance card. I have gone through three back doors over the years due to continual knife throwing. We often did this at night with the kerosene lamps lit. Sometimes an errant throw would hit the door at a wrong angle, and you would hear the steel of the knife ring instead of a solid thud. That ring meant the knife did not stick, bouncing back at us, a spinning

The old bullet-ridden outhouse.

airborne projectile, and in the dim light of the kerosene lamps, it was fast and invisible. The only thing to do was duck and hope it didn't stick us in the back or break one of the lit kerosene lamps. You can't say we didn't know how to have a good time.

We got what is commonly referred to as cabin fever, resulting in such symptoms as an indoor snowball fight and shooting the outhouse with a rifle and a shotgun. The old outhouse had many gunshot holes in its walls.

Bill came across a recipe for making homemade Kahlua consisting of vodka, Yuban coffee, and a few other ingredients that required cooking on the woodstove. Once properly mixed and heated, the dark sludge was to be aged five days before consumption. We had a good laugh that we indeed aged it five . . . five footsteps that is, from the woodstove to the dining table. Cool enough to drink yet? Yep. Down the hatch, baby.

Our enduring friendship was tempered by these long, cold nights in the North Woods. We left for New Jersey with winter biting at our heels in mid-December 1976. Bill had completed his walls and would return the following spring to put the roof on. The next time we were there together was in August of 1977, one month before I fell into commercial fishing.

That's the log cabin back story. We're up to speed now. Two boats and several near-death experiences later, Susan Renehan and I left Provincetown, headed for Nova Scotia.

## Fall of 1978: Carol Out/Susan In

**After a successful** summer fishing on the *Bay of Isles*, Susan and I arrived in Princedale with the Milbys on September 20, 1978. Nova Scotia was strutting its fall coat. The cabin has two stoves, both a century old. One is for heat only, and the other is an old-fashioned cookstove with an oven, warming oven up top, and a copper side tank for keeping a supply of hot water for washing. In the fall, the cookstove is sufficient to heat the living space.

Frank Milby is a gifted Provincetown watercolor artist. I submit that he is equally talented in the kitchen. Cooking most of the meals during their visit, Frank produced several masterpieces on that woodstove. He painted a watercolor of the cabin, too.

One afternoon we returned from a day trip, and on the table was a note. From *Carol.*

"So you *are* here and not at the bottom of the ocean somewhere," it read in total. It was unsigned, but it was in her recognizable hand.

Oh, man. For a guy so deep, I could prove to be shockingly shallow. I called her from a payphone in town and did my best to ameliorate the "Susan in/Carol out" situation, but there was no way to sugar-coat complete douchebaggery. Carol surprised me, though. She wanted to come down to meet Susan. They met and became good friends. Major bullet: Dodged. Not that I was deserving. My comeuppance was coming up, though.

## Killing Time

**The worst part** about going to Nova Scotia is that there will be a day you will have to leave. A dark dread settles in as you count down to Departure Date. In those days, there was the 5:00 A.M. ferry out of Digby to St. John, New Brunswick.

You had to be at the ferry one hour before departure, meaning you had to leave by 3:30 A.M. Since you'd be driving all day, it was essential to get some sleep. There was a Westclox wind-up alarm clock that I used only for departures. It jarred you into existence at 3:00 A.M. to begin the mad rush to catch the Digby ferry in the blackness. It was a dreadful, hated thing, always hidden, so I would not have to look at its face until DD.

This trip was different. I was sitting on $5000 and staying a year. Departure Day seemed like old age to a fifteen-year-old. I committed a symbolic act, loading my 12-gauge shotgun with a rifled slug, a single plug of lead (not BBs, but a single thick projectile), and took that clock, so long a harbinger of bad news for me, setting the alarm for five minutes. After placing it on Fr. Joe's table twenty yards from the cabin, I sat and waited from the front porch. When the alarm rang, I pulled and put the slug right dead center of that clock and blew it all to hell. Ahhhh. So satisfying. At the same time, my friends Greg McEwan and Brian Harris were coming up the trail for an impromptu visit and started hooting and hollering so I wouldn't blow their heads off. Good idea. There have been many alarm clocks since that I would gladly accommodate thus.

Greg (L) and me sitting on the front porch, October, 1978 (courtesy Susan Renehan).

# *Simple Math*

**Susan stayed till** January and left for Colorado to work with her sister in Steamboat Springs, leaving quiet winter to settle in. Though I talked with myself at times, listening skills improved, supporting the theory that one should shut up in case they might learn something. Hearing the daily litany of all creatures and the entire ecosystem around me, in time, it felt like I was more a participant than an auditor, the sound of splitting wood no different than the woodpecker's earth-tone jackhammer. This was the first sustained separation from the distracting buzz of mainstream life I had ever experienced. I had much unlearning ahead.

Wednesdays became the designated bread day, baking four loaves of whole wheat and usually a cast iron pan fruit pie or crisp. I ate almost half a loaf hot from the woodstove oven with fresh butter from Art and Alice's farm.

It was unusual to go three days without at least a couple inches of snow that winter, and the Fraser Road was a low priority for plowing. After some of the heavy storms, it could be five days before they plowed the road, making for lengthy periods of solitude. I didn't have a car anyway, but nobody was driving out to the cabin to visit if the road was unplowed.

The leaves have all fallen by then, so when the wind sweeps across the valley toward the hill, it is cut by pine, spruce, and fir needles, creating a dire North Woods whooshing sound, an ethereal hiss, not the softer rustle of the broadleaf trees during other seasons. Sometimes you can hear it from a couple of miles away, sounding like what you'd expect to hear in the Arctic Circle, a sweeping scythe of winter cutting cold across the valley, whispering, hissing: "I am Winter. Are you prepared for me?" and then suddenly it is all around you. The cabin might creak a bit when buffeted by the icy blast. Snow jumps out of the trees in clumps. Nova Scotia, a coy mistress, says, "You love me, you say, in summer and fall. Do you love me now?" You put another stick of wood in both stoves and sip on a hot tea. Or maybe something more potent. *Yes. I love thee.*

To this day, when I am there during winter, no night is complete without bundling up and taking in the falling snow outside, coming down so hard you

The wood-burning cookstove.

can hear it, watching smoke come out the chimneys, the cabin resembling a wooden stove. You must wait till the freeze drives you back to the warmth and aroma of wood heat. Then you can genuinely appreciate the cabin on the most elemental level. I'm good for that two, three times a night. Never good at math, I cling to the easy equations, like: "If I don't split some firewood today, I will die tonight." This is the only math that makes a lick of sense to me. I slipped comfortably into the simple math class of a northern winter.

Contemporary winter view.

## Boston Blackie: Magician, Thief, Life Saver

**Susan departed for** Colorado, leaving me to my winter "Fortress of Solitude." She left me her best bud in the world, Boston, a black lab named for a fictitious reformed jewel thief turned detective, Boston Blackie. The character first appeared in novels at the beginning of the 20th century, then in silent films, talkies, and cartoons right up into the 1940s. It turned out that at least in one instance, Susan's lab was aptly named. Boston and I shared the planet well together, and we had many a deep conversation on cold nights.

I spotted what looked like a worm coming out of his butt when he walked by me one afternoon. He had them before, and we had to take him to the vet to get dewormed. On closer inspection, I saw that it was not a worm but a white piece of fabric. I put on a scalloper's glove, pinched the small amount of cloth, and thought to pull it out. Figuring it to be about an inch or so long, I pulled. There was more resistance than expected, and soon I had about three or four inches of the white fabric, and it was getting thicker. *What the hell?* I kept pulling, and it kept coming. When I had about two feet of fabric exposed, it dawned on me that Boston had ingested a (formerly) white dishtowel. I had been looking for that thing but was now not glad to have found it. Pulled out by the corner on the diagonal, it was almost three feet long.

Boston was now the clown magician. *Hey, watch me pull a never-ending hankie out of my butt!* But this was the first time through for this trick. He turned his head back towards me, eyes imploring, *What the fuck? What the FUCK!* The dishtowel must have had food smells that made it a delectable appetizer for Boston. He was greatly relieved when this red-neck canine colon cleanse was finally over.

I hitched into Bear River for supplies and stopped at Aly's, a local grocery and butcher shop built atop hackmatack stilts in the tidal river. My gaze was captivated by an expensive roast of beef, so perfect it looked more like a cartoon than a real piece of meat. Cut like a steak about four inches thick, this artist's rendering of a roast had a small round bone in the middle, unmarbled, pure red meat, and about an inch of white fat ringing the outside. It looked like a

Contemporary cabin shot.

steak that Popeye's rival, Brutus, would eat in a gobble. It was more than I could afford, but it might feed me for a week and provide a break from brown rice and wild rabbit.

On arrival back at the Fraser Road, I fired up the cookstove and proceeded to roast it in the oven. The essence of browning beef in conspiracy with sliced onion and ambient woodstove smoke promised a greatly improved immediate future. Boston knew something special was happening here, too. I told him that I intended to share it with him. He knew he was in and wagged his tail.

Having cut all my winter's wood that fall, I piled it beside the cabin in four-foot lengths. You could climb the woodpile and walk right onto the roof. Every so often, I would have to go out and "junk it up," as they say in the Maritimes: that is, cut it with the chain saw, split it with an ax, and carry it to the indoor woodpile. That day I was running low on woodstove-ready wood, and a trip to the woodpile was in order. The roast was done and had to be pulled out of the oven before wood splitting duties could commence. Sizzling from the oven, it was fall-apart tender, and the flavor absolutely smoked wild rabbit. I sat down and sampled it and gave Boston what was probably more than I should have given a dog, but I am a generous soul, and we were in this together, right?

I put the roast on the counter and went outside to woodcutting duties. After an hour, I had enough wood for about a week, cut and split. I came inside for what was going to be the best lunch in months. I went to the counter and found (queue up the Hitchcockian "shocking discovery" music) an empty plate

Bear River, Nova Scotia.

that was miraculously uncontaminated by roast. There wasn't even a hint of the au jus. Was this roast just a Fig Newton of my imagination? It was like Penn and Teller made the Statue of freaking Liberty disappear. *It couldn't possibly have vanished.* But it had, and one black cohabitant of the premises looked guilty and started to whimper without my having said a word.

"You got up on the counter? And ate the roast we were going to eat for a week? The entire thing? After I had already given you more than I could afford?"

He did not deny these allegations and did his best to trade the guilty act for leniency.

"Very well," I said, "You want up on the counter, then that's what you'll get."

I lifted him to the counter and sat him down on the scene of the crime, put my finger in his face, and said in my best Clint Eastwood, "Don't—you— move." He did not. After about an hour, I put his water bowl up there for him. I let him down to go out and do his business, but it was right back up on the counter for Boston after that. I had seething brown rice with a contemptuous bay leaf in it for dinner (page 67 from "Dust Bowl Recipes"), and that night when I was blowing the lamps out for bedtime, I released Boston from prison. He never went near the counter again. But then, I never put a roast there again either. We both learned something, I guess.

During those days in the '70s, a popular form of mind expansion in Nova Scotia was hallucinogenic mushrooms. Harvested in cow dung in the fields,

From the front porch, 2019.

they were small but effective in good doses. A typical mushroom trip took about 25 small mushrooms. One cold winter's day, I did 28 of them. Things were going along swimmingly until that familiar thought came over me, *What if someone visits me?* Tripping was cool with other people around, but only if they were tripping, too. If you were tripped out around someone not turned on, you felt exposed and vulnerable. OK, I'll say it: *paranoid.* So I figured Boston and I would take a paranoia-driven walk in the woods. We went out the back door and headed towards Skull Lake.

Drifted snow made the journey quite a trudge, and it was Nova Scotia-frigid. After we got about a mile back, I stopped and began ruminating on pine needles with snow on them, and, *What's that?* Whining. A dog whining. I looked down, and there was the source, Boston downright shivering and whining and *pleading* with me, *"We've meditated on pine needles with snow on them for an hour in the frozen North Country. If we don't move, we are going to die, numbnuts."* Yep. At least, that's what I heard.

"You're right, old boy," I said. I had no idea I had spent so much time looking at pine needles. Mushroom time and dog time are different.

"We'd better get back to the cabin."

The only one in the party with any sense, Boston might have saved our lives that day.

# The Anvil Chorus

**Being without a** vehicle, I walked everywhere. Luuk and Karen Geerligs lived about a mile hike on the dirt road. Luuk was a blacksmith of Dutch extraction, and he and Karen were already my friends when he invited me to work for him on a government project. He had made primitive hand-forged hinges for my cabin doors four years earlier when I was building. Luuk had a contract with the Province of Nova Scotia for authentic restoration work on the fortress at Louisbourg in Cape Breton and the Citadel in Halifax. These fortresses had outsized doors with long "strap" hinges. They all had to be replaced and produced with the same methods blacksmiths used 200 years ago. No twentieth-century shortcuts were allowed, except for the use of steel, since pure iron is no longer available. The hinge had to be bent back upon itself at one end, forming a loop that would fit down over a vertical pin driven into a beam of the door frame.

My flat screen (only one channel but it's HD).

The trick here was they had to be "welded" the way they did long ago. The weld took place where the steel looped back onto itself. Luuk made a weld by heating the steel to the right temperature and adding a powdery mixture called "flux" between the two joining parts.

Then the pounding began in earnest, the super-heated flux creating showers of flying sparks with each hammer strike. Sometimes the weld failed, and the whole hinge had to be scrapped. If successful, the metal where it looped back on itself became seamlessly one. My role was that of a "striker." I stood opposite Luuk, the anvil between us, equipped with a sledgehammer. Luuk had a maul, a smaller but heavy hammer. The idea was that Luuk would direct my sledgehammer by hitting a specific area of the hinge. Wherever he struck, that is where I struck. Bang! Clang! Bang! Clang! We would get a self-perpetuating rhythm going, a groove that carried us along.

Art White stopped over in the middle of this and vocalized the melody of Verdi's "Anvil Chorus" in time with our percussion. I worked with Luuk for several months and became his de facto apprentice during that time. He showed me how to tell the temperature of the steel by the color of the glow. Temperature was everything; the steel would not behave the way you wished unless right. I learned steel burns if it gets too hot. I burned my first couple of

Contemporary view.

attempts to make something solo. If it gets too hot, when you remove the steel from the coals, it will burn like a sparkler, consuming itself. If you ever get to the fortress at Louisbourg in Cape Breton or the Citadel at Halifax, look for those long strap hinges on all the big doors. Those are ours.

## What Month of the Year Is It, Anyway?

**One of the** goals for this year-long stay at the cabin was to lose track of what day of the week it was and the month of the year. No calendars, watches, or clocks of the un-shot variety were in evidence up on the hill. With these things constantly prodding us toward thinking about tomorrow, next week, or next month, it is little wonder we have such trouble being in the now. With such reminders purged from my environment, I rose with the sun and whispered to the moon. As it should be.

It was surprising how long it took me to become unsure of the day of the week. Programmed by linear thinking, the brain keeps an accounting of the days of the week despite its aim to lose track. It could go a good string of days, but as the holidays approached, I found it impossible to ignore Christmas Day and New Year's Day and had to start from scratch. Making another attempt in January, after several weeks, time got very vague indeed.

On a snowy afternoon, Richard Milner hiked back through the woods to see me as the road had not been plowed for several days. The knock on the cabin door startled me, for I knew the road to be impassable. We had a beer together, and he mentioned it was hard to believe it was already March.

"It's March?" I asked. I couldn't believe it either.

"It's March 5th," Richard said.

Wow. It was March for a whole five days, and I still thought it was February. I had succeeded. Never again in my life did a month set up shop for five days without my realizing it. It would be nice to try again someday, though.

# Indian Hill

**I have been** in Nova Scotia through all the winter months, February being the most brutal. By February, you start getting a little antsy for winter to be over. But winter digs in hard with no intentions of letting go, and it has saved its coldest temperatures and worst storms for the winter-weary. It is telling you this ain't the Mid-Atlantic States, punk.

In February, Greg McEwan and Alan Harlow and his wife, Viola, came out to Princedale and took me back to the Bear River Reservation. Back then, people mostly called it Indian Hill. It is now properly called "First Nations," home of Nova Scotia's first inhabitants, the Mi'kmaq peoples. It was an excursion to Greg's cabin, sitting high on a hill commanding a crazy view of the Bear River valley. When we had driven as far as we could, we began the one-mile walk through the deep freeze, the snow sounding more like crunching Styrofoam. It was single digits Fahrenheit with a persistent wind. Greg had not been there since the day before, so his fire was long since out. He was low on firewood, too, so he ripped up a floorboard, broke it up, and put it in the stove. This place was more extensive than mine: 25X30 with an upstairs bedroom. We retreated upstairs where it would be warmer but not by a lot. We tried playing guitars but soon gave up because our fingers were so cold. Annoyed, Greg went outside and knocked an entire wall of boards off the outhouse, bringing them in to burn.

"The snow will blow all around in the outhouse now," I said.

"The snow already blows all around in there," he said.

He talked of what a great time he would have next summer, punctuated with his McEwan chuckle. Within the next few years, Greg would become Chief and implement many changes up on the reservation. Until his sad and sudden passing in 2014, he was a master basket maker and, with his woman Margaret, operated Beartown Baskets. Till we meet again, brother.

# The Naked Lathered Wild Man

**One of the** luxuries we all enjoyed was the sauna that Mike Phillips had built by a stream on his property. It was just big enough for a woodstove and benches to sit down. The stove sheathed with rocks, we would pour water on them and produce billows steam. A thermometer mounted on the wall allowed us to monitor the temperature. The idea was to get the sauna up to about 170 degrees, which is just about how hot we could stand it before passing out, lather up with Dr. Bronner's Peppermint Hippie-Freak Soap, bolt out the door, and jump through a hole in the ice. It was a shallow brook but deep enough to slip through the ice and lay down entirely underwater. Most folks deem it crazy when I relate this, but it is just as crazy to get that hot as it is to get that cold. After submerging yourself in the freezing water, you could stand outside in merciless winter air, naked in the snow, with the steam rolling off your body. The two extremes cancel each other out. I would never jump through a hole in the ice without first absorbing all that heat. I have never experienced that kind of clean since those sauna days. It was more than a physical condition. It was a state of mind that stayed with you all day.

In early spring, I decided to take a sauna. One of the locals, Cat Winchester, called it a sonar. We were all amused by that, so the name stuck. A freak storm struck Nova Scotia in February of 1976, known as the Groundhog's Day Storm. It caused hurricane-like damage throughout the province, with many a roof blown off that day.

A minor casualty on the Fraser Road was the door to Mike and Sharon's "sonar." The hinges ripped from the door frame, leaving a splintered mess. I found the door intact, lying on the ground. It looked pretty good except for the pieces of door frame the hinges had brought with it. I built my fire and had to wedge the door in there tightly to minimize heat leakage. As it approached 170 degrees, feeling like I was going to pass out, I lathered up with the peppermint hippie soap from hair to toes and started for the door.

Mike and Sharon had recently had a baby. On the day of my sauna, a public health nurse was doing a check-up on the infant, probably because the baby was being raised off the grid: no power, woodstove heat, no running water. The nurse had left her car on Fraser Road, correctly surmising that her vehicle would not make it back to the cabin site. She then commenced with the quarter-mile walk back.

Having never been there, she took a right on the first footpath she saw, figuring this tiny shack of a sauna with the smoke rising from the stovepipe was probably the "house." I can only guess what report was beginning to generate in her head: "Recommend immediate removal of the child. It's an outhouse with a stove."

Just as our circumspect nurse was approaching what she thought was a sorry excuse for a home, I was discovering that the door I had so carefully wedged into place would not budge. I pushed, pulled, and banged on it. No good. There was an urgency to deal with, too. I had maybe ten more seconds before I passed out, the stove glowing cherry red. *Oh my God, I can't believe he died taking a sauna. Yes, but he looks SO clean.*

There it was, my last shot at getting out. I kicked at the door with the sole of my foot, the door broke away and fell out flat to the ground with a bang, and my long-haired, lathered-up, naked, screaming wild-man body came running out over it, right toward the public health nurse who was startled out of her report-writing reverie. She screamed too. We both stood there for a moment screaming at each other. But I won this freaking battle. Being naked and in a lather gave me an unfair advantage. She turned and ran up the hill and went out of sight. I jumped into the frigid brook and rinsed off with a scream.

After dressing, I walked back to Mike and Sharon's place to say hello. There I found my nurse, who had discovered the correct address by default. Sharon introduced me.

"We've met," I said.

# Down on the Farm

**In the winter** of '78/'79, we had poetry readings with a different host each time. It was a nice break from the sameness of white-out. Two of our hosts were Debbie and Ross Waters at their farm in Bear River East. Ross invited me to work for him on the farm come spring. It sounded like just the thing, but I didn't have a vehicle to get back and forth.

"That's easy. You'll stay here. We have a room for you," Ross said.

Indeed they did. They lived in a big old farmhouse, and come spring, I moved in and worked for Farmer Ross. He taught me how to operate the beast of a farm tractor, sending me out to disc the fields. Towing a rig behind me with a series of big metal rolling discs, I was to drive over every inch of the field. The discs turned the soil over before planting alfalfa.

High up on the tractor, turning up the fields in the spring air, I felt like I had achieved a significant milestone, working the earth and feeling like I could do nothing more relevant. Even today, sitting on a dinky lawn tractor, I think of that day astride that big old machine, atop the world on a Nova Scotian spring day.

We seeded the fields, built a bridge across a creek, tended to animals, dug a root cellar by hand, and did various fix-it operations around the farm. The alfalfa came in lush and green. Harvesting the crop was the tricky part. Once the hay was cut, it had to dry in the field under the sun for two to three days. If it rained during that time, the crop was lost. Midway through the drying process, the hay had to be turned over to dry on the other side. An attachment called a "teader" was hooked up to the tractor. It had a series of sharp revolving pitchforks on cams that turned over the hay as it passed.

If the hay dried completely with no rain, then it was time for the baler. This was a big machine that passed over the crop and compressed the hay into seventy-pound bales. Now came the fun part. If anyone ever tells you they have been haying, you know that they have worked as hard as anyone can claim on the planet. When you are haying, properly pronounced "hayin," you walk across the field with a truck following alongside. The seventy-pound bales had to be picked up by hand and thrown on the truck. Seventy pounds is not an excessive weight but, in the form of a bulky bale held together with two twine loops, it is an awkward load, and the hundredth bale feels plenty heavier than the first ten.

There is a method to picking them up and throwing that I had to learn for myself on the spot. Bale tossing muscles must be different than scallop boat muscles, so things were stretching, popping, and snapping in my shoulders and back. One guy on the truck stacks the bales as they are tossed up, but this job doesn't get easier as you go, no. The more bales on the truck, the higher you must throw them. When we finished, I was numb. Greenhorn again.

A friend and I tore down an old barn, he for the beams, me for the barn boards. I wanted to do my inside gable ends with them. There was one obstacle before we could begin the demolition: it was filled with hay almost to the roof. The farmer who wanted the barn down called in a baling machine.

Joining a couple of greyed farmers who looked like their best field days were behind them, we pitchforked the mountain of hay into the hungry baler. This went on for some time. It takes a good while to empty a barnful of hay with four men. The chafe stuck to my torso like a layer of clothing, hands ached, and my arms did not feel like they were mine. The mound down to about half, I

Barn board showing in the gable end.

leaned on the pitchfork and said something about taking a break to one of the elderly farmers.

"Son," he said, "Once we turn on that baling machine, we don't turn it off till the barn is empty."

Then those elderly farmers worked circles around my young, in-need-of-a-break body. Yeah. That put my urban ass in place. The barn board gable ends are still there, as well as a picture in my mind of that Everest of hay and the old guys who redefined hard work for me. Son.

## Elopement in the Rain

**Susan returned from** Colorado that summer and, despite some indications that we were not built for the long haul, we entertained the idea of marriage. Love is that way. It makes you do stuff, often stupid. The summer passed, working at the farm and with Luuk in the forge. There were a few stints shucking scallops on Reggie Hazelton's boat out of Digby. That we were to get married was definite. The "how" of it vexed us, and we vacillated from a big wedding in Provincetown to elopement in Nova Scotia. In any case, we went to get a marriage license locally. We had to go to the residence of a Mrs. Hatfield Who Didn't Like Young People. Well, her real name was shorter than that, but her disapproval of us was barely disguised. She asked me my occupation but the way she asked, I knew she thought *Does he even have a job?*

I looked at Susan.

"What's my occupation?" I asked, more to feed her disdain than anything.

"Poet," she said as if I should have known. *Perfect. That should bring her to the next level.*

Mrs. Hatfield, predictably, did not care for that at all but was forced to put it on the marriage license. She wanted to know if either of us had been married before. We had not. The license read like this: "Mickey Maguire, Poet of Princedale" and "Susan Renehan, Photographer of Provincetown."

It also stated that I was a bachelor and Susan a "spinster."

We bought a junker car from George Goodin. It was an English car, an Epic made by Viva Vauxhall, and an unpredictable machine. We stopped calling it the Epic and started calling it the Epidemic. Sometimes it wouldn't start, so we always parked it facing down the hill on the Fraser Road so we could push-start it with ease.

We had gone back and forth about when and how we were going to get married. The big church wedding thing wasn't ringing our bells. Elopement was on the menu, and on the morning of October 9, it became the entrée.

"Let's go," I said.

"Where?"

Provincetown from the wharf.

"Bear River. To get married."

Susan smiled. It was raining. We push-started the car down the hill and drove to the home of Rev. Earl Waterman to ask if he would marry us. He agreed but wanted to shave first. His wife Pat put on a dress and played "Here Comes the Bride" on the piano and told Susan to take a few turns around the room. After the ceremony, having brought our shucking gear, we drove to Digby to see if any scallopers were in, but the whole fleet was out. We went grocery shopping and came back to Princedale and drank a bottle of champagne with Luuk and Karen. Then back to the cabin where we cut down some trees for firewood in the rain, for we had run out. Our wedding feast was celery and peanut butter. You can't say we didn't have style. We were married. It was the beginning of the end. The marriage would not last six months.

With money running out, no firewood, and winter setting in, we had to get back to Provincetown, where work could be found. By the end of the month, we headed back to the Cape in the Epidemic. I had my year at the cabin. What I did not know was that I would never spend an entire year there again. So far.

~ ~ ~

# PART IV

Ship's Cook

# *F/V* Little Infant

**They tore us** apart at the border. Yeah, not hard to figure. Two hippies in a junker car with a dog and a guitar. Susan had packed a lot of staples from the kitchen. The customs officers thought they had a bust when they found her baggie of powdered milk and justified their zealous search by telling us they found a single marijuana seed on the floor of the car.

We hit Provincetown on October 26th and stayed with friends of Susan's alternately until we could get some cash flowing and get a place of our own. One of her friends had a farmhouse at Corn Hill, and we stayed there most often. Susan got work immediately at the Edwige, where she had worked before. Jingles hired her to manage the café. I hit pay dirt down at the harbor.

Former shipmate Lawrence Schuster's dune shack.

At the end of the wharf, after dark, I saw Captain Gerald Costa's maroon diesel pickup truck idling. Capt. Costa was one of the better-known captains in the fleet. He had lived his whole life fishing out of P'town, as did his father before him. The story was that his father tied him to the mainmast during a gale when he was five years old. Whether that was true or not was irrelevant. It *could* have been true. He owned and operated the F/V *Little Infant*, arguably the best boat in the fleet.

The *Infant*, as she was known in the familiar and named for the Baby Jesus, was a Harvey Gamage, Maine-built eastern rigged wooden boat. Gamage was like Lloyd Loar to mandolins, Delorean to cars, Stradivarius to violins. He lovingly built some of the most beautiful and seaworthy vessels that ever graced the North Atlantic. He must have had a soft spot for the *Little Infant*. Hardly little, she was about ninety feet in length and looked huge to me after the fifty-six-foot *Bay of Isles*. She was deep and had an elliptical stern; following seas would break around her. The *Little Infant* was eminently seaworthy and well-maintained. Getting a site on her would be a dream come true; she could be my first safe boat.

I approached the truck, and Gerald rolled down the window. I introduced myself and went over my qualifications, seeing that my first aborted season on the *Janet and Jean* did not impress him. But that I had fished a whole summer with George Hann, hooked up for Richard Dickey, and learned to run the winch from Dickey and Joe Lisbon made a better impression. He hired me on the spot as a deckhand. After my difficulty getting on the *Bay of Isles*, I did not expect such immediate good fortune. I had just gotten on the best boat with the best skipper in the fleet.

Getting a site on the *Infant* reunited me with old *Janet and Jean* shipmate Skip Albanese, now the cook. The *Infant*'s first mate was Wayne Costa, one of the most likable and respected fishermen in Provincetown. Wayne knew fishing, had a great sense of humor, and always saw the upside of everything. He was even-keeled, easy-going, and I believe I never saw him get upset about anything. He wouldn't say a bad word about anyone. The only negative thing that I ever heard Wayne say was at the beginning of every watch, though I believe it was said more as a joke. He would find his way into the fo'c'sle half asleep, pour a cup of sludgy coffee and say with sleep in his eyes, "Fuck this business." Every watch.

I was assigned to Wayne's (the mate's) watch. Showing up for gear work the next day was way different than showing up on the *Janet and Jean* or even the *Bay of Isles*. I knew enough about what was going on that I didn't have a "greenhorn" bullseye painted on my back and "horse's ass" stapled to my forehead.

Gamage-built eastern rigged scalloper F/V *Little Infant* in Provincetown Harbor, circa 1978 (courtesy David Meads).

We finished gear work and put to sea. Boy, the *Little Infant* sure felt so natural in the water. Though she was capable of a fight, her usual demeanor was one of cooperation with the sea. On the way out, Stevie Perry, a fellow Scorpio and fun-loving character, said it was his birthday the next day. I told him mine was two days after that. We headed for the "peanut pile." A peanut, as mentioned before, is a small scallop. When you fish the peanut pile, there are usually tons of them, but the shucking is hard going because it takes about 1600 of them to fill a bucket. I counted. Nobody liked fishing the peanut pile. This particular pile was located at Fippennies Ledge in the waters between Maine and Nova Scotia. From the Cape, we steamed 60 degrees for seven hours.

Skippers liked to withhold info about where we were going. This held true on the *Infant*. (What is that all about?) But that season, all we had to do was look at the compass. *60 fucking degrees. Fippennies Ledge.*

One trip, we steamed the whole seven hours out there, and it really started to blow. Gerald decided not to set the gear out and just go home. We had breakfast and then headed for the barn. I called that trip "Breakfast at Fippennies."

On this first trip, we arrived at Fippennies and started in on the peanut pile. I knew the drill. Scallops in the basket, everything not a scallop: over the side every twenty minutes. Ah yes, I remember the drudgery of this. Wayne's comment at the beginning of every watch made lots of sense at times like this. While he was working, Stevie Perry always had some kind of rap going. This time he was saying, "So, you wanna be a scalloper, eh? Well, suffer, you bastard!"

Everyone laughed. We all started saying it, becoming a season-long mantra. Amidst our hard work, as we were all bent over picking scallops, assholes, and elbows in the dark, a dreary cold mist making everything wet, I yelled out to Stevie.

"Hey, Stevie." I think I startled him. He popped his head up.

"What?"

"Happy birthday." A big smile washed across his face like a wave on a beach.

"Thanks, man," he said. We all sang to him. It was a nice moment.

The trip dragged on, and it was cold by early November in the Gulf of Maine. On the night of November 2nd, we were all hunched over our work on deck. I heard a voice yell out.

"Hey, Mickey."

I looked up. It was Stevie. "What?"

"Happy birthday."

More singing. Stevie came over and reached into his pocket and pulled out a lime sour ball hard candy, and handed it to me.

"It's not much. But I really appreciated your remembering my birthday the other day. Happy birthday, man."

I thanked him. Out there in the dark, miles from shore, in the cold, and the early part of a trip that would surely never end, that sour ball was one of the finest birthday presents I ever received. I was 26 years old. About a month later, Stevie, who had his demons, would die of an overdose. I never forgot him. I never forget a good heart.

# Career Move: Ship's Cook

**Skip did a** good job, having *Joy of Cooking* as a blueprint and an unlimited budget. He once made a double meatloaf in the shape of two voluptuous breasts with nipples—fishing *and* Anatomy Class all on one trip. As far as dishes go, the guys had pedestrian tastes, and if you were able to produce middle-of-the-road meat and potatoes comfort-food style meals, you would be considered acceptable. The trouble was Skip disliked the job. It was more than the cooking, I think, that wore on him. There was menu planning for both watches, shopping, icing perishables, cleaning the galley after trips, doing dishes after every meal, and on and on. When Cookie finished a meal and clean-up, it was up on deck to work with the crew. Some cooks "hid behind the apron" and found busy work to keep them off deck as much as possible. Others were right up on deck like a deckhand. Skip was on deck a lot. He just wanted to be up there working where there was no organizing, planning, or coordinating. If only someone else would take over as cook.

Beneath that happy-go-lucky exterior was a schemer, and Skip was looking for his mark. I was friendly with him, and he had been a tremendous help to me when I was trying to break in as a greenhorn back on the *Janet and Jean*, so I felt indebted to him in that sense. He was not above using that to advantage. After going deckhand my first two trips on the *Infant*, Skip approached me at the starboard shucking box between tows and told me he quit as cook. We were only three days out, and I thought, *How can somebody quit a job way out here?* Answer: *If you have a complete idiot willing to take over for you.*

I liked Skip, and he could be persuasive. The idea was not a stretch. My two older sisters, Ree and Kathy, started me out making eggs and such for breakfast as soon as my eyes could clear the stove. I had produced complicated meals on open fires with the scout troop and was at home on the cast iron stove in Nova Scotia, very much like the *Infant*'s stove. Skip made sure I knew the cook made an extra $100 as well as the engineer. I agreed.

So began a hit-the-ground-running crash course in maritime cookery. His daily written menu instantly became the new blueprint for my life for the next

week or so. I learned how to use the kerosene-fed cast iron stove, crucial icing techniques and protocol for the food in the fish hold, nuance things like
making sure there was a backup deck of cards, and how the captain and mate
preferred their coffee. Being in his best interest that I succeed, Skip's instruction
was thorough.

Not being a great believer in luck, I see God's hand on my shoulder here,
for not only was this position ideally suited to my sensibilities, it prepared me
for my lifelong career. There was more to this gig than just putting food in front
of fishermen. Skip showed me all the ropes, including cleaning the galley and
fo'c'sle at the end of a trip. Cookie brings the deck hose down into the foc's'le
and signals to the engineer to turn on the pump. A gushing column of seawater
washes the entire galley/fo'c'sle, draining down into the bilges through drilled
holes in the deck. The engineer would pump it out later. That would be a great
feature for a house: Hosing down a room into holes drilled in the floor where
dust bunnies go to die. *Die, bitches! Ha! Ha!*

Between trips, the cook made the menu covering every day of the next trip,
three meals a day for both watches. If you were making roast beef, you had to do
two roasts because the upcoming watch would surely polish off theirs.

Skip went with me the first time to the Provincetown A&P and showed
me how he did it. On average, he'd get nine or ten shopping carts rounded
right over with goods, three of them just for meats. Twenty-six gallons of milk
stacked in crates alongside the carts; you would not want to get behind a ship's
cook in line at the check-out. We rang up a bill of more than $1000, which
probably translates to a lot more money in today's prices. Most of the fleet ran
tabs, so money never changed hands on shopping day. If you were practiced and
a madman, you could do the shopping in about two hours.

The pickup truck would arrive with some of the crew for loading. The
whole crew would act as a conveyer belt at the wharf to offload the grub and
pass it down to the fish hold, where the cook would ice it up properly for the
trip. Then the icebox in the galley would be stocked with a few gallons of milk,
cold cuts, and other perishables needed more immediately.

I settled into a groove and completely inhabited the gig in just a few days.
The first advantage I discovered was the schedule: Sixteen hours on and eight
off. A sixteen-hour day sounds grueling, but eight uninterrupted hours off was
so much better than the six and six. On the latter watch, you were lucky to get
four and a half hours of sleep twice a day. Interrupted like that, it gets old by
day six. Eight hours off had the feel of normalcy. I was now working with both

watches and had discourse with everyone. As a deckhand, most of your interactions are with guys on your own watch.

The cook's day starts at 4:00 A.M., making a couple of fresh pots of coffee after tossing the old stuff from the dog watch. Consulting the day's menu, he lists all items needed from the fish hold: lamb legs, roasts of beef, cheese for lasagna, supply of milk, juice, breakfast meats, eggs, or bread. Then out onto the deck to say hello to the dog watch on deck since midnight, ask them how the fishing has been, and hear an account of whatever funny or hairy events might have taken place. He times his trip to the fish hold, going after the gear has been set out, and the tow has begun, not wanting to be in the hole with the hatch cover off when the gear is coming up over the rail. If I were still in the hole when the dredges were coming up, the hatch cover would be replaced for safety, and I would be stuck down there until the rakes were aboard, dumped, and set on the rails for the next tow.

I would pass up all food needed for the day to waiting deckhands, redistribute the ice over what remained and climb back up the ladder. The crew would then pass the goods down to the galley through the doghouse, where I would store all the food for lunch and dinner in the icebox. Then I began cooking breakfast meats in the dark. The boys always had to have lots of bacon, sausage, and linguica, a spicy Portuguese sausage. A lot of cooks would just scramble up a bunch of eggs. I always made them to order, the crew having their choice of sunny side up, over easy or scrambled. We had individual omelets on occasion, cast iron stove toast, toasted English muffins, home fries, pancakes, syrup, cereal, and fruit.

The olfactory aspect of being at sea is predominantly raw and unvaried day in and day out: saline spray, salty air mixed with a hint of diesel fumes, and the fishy presence of whatever we happened to dredge up from the bottom. Potent primeval odors of wet, squirming things hidden from daylight, now scraped violently from the deep by the rake, constantly reminded us that this, like outer space, was not our home. Step outside the spaceship, you die.

During the mate's watch at 4:00 A.M. in the dark, Cookie has gotten up, brewing fresh coffee and cooking breakfast meats. The Coffee and Bacon Genie wafts up out of the doghouse, tantalizing everyone on deck above with a breath of terra firma, bounteous home, and its ample larders, its impact all the greater out far from shore in this cold and blowy wasteland. It promises that in an hour or so, they would be warm and dry, sitting at the fo'c'sle table having a hard-earned, much-appreciated breakfast with their mates. It is a good time.

At 5:30 A.M. Cookie wakes the captain's watch, slapping guys on the feet to stay away from flailing arms with fists at the end. (Learned that during Skip's crash tutorial.) The crew would drift, half-awake, toward the fo'c'sle table where they would suck up coffee and shovel down breakfast. They had about twenty minutes before they had to be awake enough to avoid getting maimed or worse up on deck.

At 6:00 A.M., the captain's watch went up on deck. The mate's watch would proceed to wash, bag up and stow the scallops in the hold before they could go below for breakfast. This was Wayne's watch, and this crew carried themselves differently, having worked since midnight. The upcoming watch would eat their breakfast with a more restrained, almost human bearing. Coming off six hours of hard labor in sometimes brutal conditions, the off watch attacked their food as if it might otherwise escape. As they dove into breakfast, I would hear all the stories of what occurred during the dogwatch, good-natured ball-busting and filthy jokes all on the menu.

Once they had eaten, most guys hit their bunks as soon as they could, for I would be slapping their foot at 11:30 A.M. to get ready to do it all over again. Breakfast finished, the cook washed the dishes. We had a hand pump on the *Little Infant*, and I heated the water for dishes on the cast iron stove in a big pot like at the cabin. With the galley tidied up, I went up on deck and worked with the captain's watch picking the pile and shucking scallops. Gerald once told me that of all the cooks he had ever had on his boats, I spent more time on deck working than any of them.

Around 10:00 or 10:30 A.M., it was back down into the galley to prepare the next meal. At 11:30, the mate's watch was awakened and fed. They were up on deck at noon, and the captain's watch washed, bagged, stowed the scallops, and came down for lunch. Then it was clean up the galley, wash the dishes, and back up on deck for more picking and shucking. At around 3:00 or 3:30, I was back down into the galley to prepare dinner.

At 5:30 P.M., the captain's watch was awakened and fed. The mate's watch, coming off deck after their six hours, was fed at 6:00. After clean-up, it was back up on deck for picking the pile and shucking till 8:00 P.M., and then it was off-watch for Cookie.

There was time, a commodity I never felt I possessed as a deckhand. Sometimes I would do prep work like peel potatoes for the next day's hand-mashed potatoes, storing them in cold water on ice so they wouldn't go brown. My friend and shipmate Lawrence Schuster would often help me peel to pass the time.

I liked to go up on deck and find a spot to enjoy the open ocean, an ever-changing painting. In good weather, I would sometimes lay down in the dory on the roof of the wheelhouse, looking up to the three-dimensional field of night stars unobscured by light pollution. It was only here at sea or up in Nova Scotia that I ever saw stars like this. Sometimes I would go into the shucking house with the captain's watch and cut off a bucket of scallops for the hell of it. Eight hours off made a big difference to me. Long days but there was the feel of a normal day in getting a decent night's sleep.

Written down like this, it all seems simple, but variable weather creates its own reality. Lasagna is not intended to be constructed in a full gale, which became a maxim after chasing and losing ingredients to the galley deck. "Cold cuts for lunch, boys!" Cooking and serving in heavy weather can become quite acrobatic. There's a loose choreography with room for improv:

> Three steps forward
> Two back
> Four steps forward
> Grab hot coffee pot
> Six steps to starboard
> Jump over sliding milk crate
> Execute half-turn
> Smash back against icebox
> Lunge for fo'c'sle table
> Pour coffee with roll to starboard
> Three steps to galley
> Bad roll to port
> Grab ladder and spin to stove
> Release coffee

Confident that I was doing a decent job cooking for these guys, it wouldn't do to get too fancy. I went to the trouble of making fettuccini alfredo from scratch. They came down, opened the lid, and asked what it was. I identified it as fettuccini alfredo. The cover was promptly replaced, and no one tasted it. It might have been wiser to have said it was spaghetti with cheese sauce. The cook, however, had an excellent pasta dish that evening. We had some of the finest seafood coming up in the dredges, but the guys would not touch any of it except lobster. The only fish I could ever get them to eat was Mrs. Paul's fish sticks. If we weren't shacking the lobster, we cooked it and ate the tails like hot dogs.

I brought a used tuxedo that I picked up on the cheap and late into a trip, I put it on when dinner was ready, wearing it up on deck with a white towel draped over my arm, solemnly announcing that "dinner is served," in my best snooty British butler accent. Something like this was way funny about eight days out.

David Meads used to kid me and call my pancakes bunker plates. One morning he was served an actual bunker plate with syrup and a pat of butter.

A tradition in the fleet, or at least on the *Little Infant*, was a full turkey dinner for the last meal before heading for the barn. Roast turkey right out of the cast-iron oven, hand-mashed potatoes, gravy, cranberry sauce, stuffing, brown and serve rolls, pumpkin pie, and whipped cream: the works. This meal was always somewhat celebratory, knowing the ordeal was finally at an end, and we were steaming back to port with a big fat wallet and all the pleasures of our beautiful Provincetown waiting for us.

During winter, when it was difficult to get five days in a row fishing without getting blown in by a storm, boats would shell stock: loading up with unshucked scallops and cutting them off in the harbor. Many boats would come in around the same time because we were all slaves to the same weather. The boats would load up with cutters who worked for $20 a bucket. Part of the package was that the cook made a big lunch for all, crew and cutters. Word had gotten out that I was a competent cook. The crowd to get on the *Little Infant* was always thicker, not only because of Gerald's reputation and the *Infant*'s status in the fleet but also because they knew they would get a decent meal come lunchtime.

Though not immediately apparent, there was an esoteric quality to this role that revealed itself as the weeks turned into months on the job. I sensed that there was a hint of a difference in how the crew interacts with the cook. He is, after all, the one who *feeds* them. After an entire winter season fishing, one crew member, Moko, said to me, "Wow. You kept me alive all winter."

Cookie is often an advocate for the crew to the wheelhouse, a well-meaning advisor to greenhorns, keeper of the books in poker games, officer in charge of morale, ship's doctor, and referee in brawls. Cookie often knows where we are headed. How? By carefully timing his first gift of hot coffee to the wheelhouse while the captain is plotting a course on the chart—a time-honored tradition. He knows the latest rumor, the weather forecast, and the punchline to that raunchy joke told at the foc's'le table last watch. He is aware that the head is down to one roll of toilet paper, the captain loves custard pie, and Wayne likes flavored Tums, not Rolaids. His mind is always somewhere between scallops and scalloped potatoes. He is the boss of the galley.

I could not know this, but being cook on a fishing vessel would be a badass boot camp for a social work career. Looking back after 39 years in the field, the cook *is* the ship's social worker. Going from deckhand to cook was a shift from surviving amongst the ruffians to taking care of them. I went from treading water to actually swimming somewhere. Now there was purpose beyond mere adventure and the model for my professional life.

## Projectile Dinty Moore

**Gerald hired two** shuckers for a trip. Greenhorns both, they didn't work the gear but stayed in the shucking house and cut for $20 a bucket. They were average shuckers but had not spent any kind of time at sea. And they were arrogant, which never shows well on a greenhorn. Besides the cockiness, there was something about these two that nobody liked. It was winter in the Gulf of Maine, and even without a storm, seas could be turbulent at baseline. One night it was blowing half a gale, as they say, and our cutters were borderline seasick. They were a bit green in the cheeks but hanging on. There was a regular status report among the crew regarding the progress of their nausea. Nobody was puking, however, a pleasure we all wished on them.

One of the "talents" I utilized to great advantage in Catholic grammar school was making vomiting sounds that evinced images of someone throwing up their lungs. Run up to the front of the class, bend over the trash can next to the nun's desk and start retching. It was enough to gag a jackal, and it was good for a ten-minute disruption as the nun tried to regain control of the class. This effect is achieved by belching while making retching sounds. (Still in the repertoire.)

That night on a chopped-up sea, Cookie had a special surprise for our two green at the gills shuckers. I opened a can of Dinty Moore beef stew and shoved as much of it in my mouth as possible without bursting. Up on deck and into the shucking house where our cutters were hanging on, I leaned over into the shucking box between them and started my visceral retching sounds while expelling clods of beef stew all over the scallop shells. Tipping the scales in their battle with nausea, they bolted back aft and lost their dinners over the rail into the blackness. At last, everyone in the fo'c'sle was satisfied. So, you wanna be a scalloper, eh?

## Dart Boards, Thieves, and Beer

**On the same** trip, we got blown into Gloucester for a few days. We sold off a few bags of scallops, so we had some beer money and hit the bars. We were in the one featured in the film *The Perfect Storm*, and another one a couple of blocks away that reminded me of a bowling alley, only instead of pins at the end of the lanes, there were dartboards.

I was a fair dart thrower. We had a board in the house growing up because Dad shot darts. We wound up playing for pitchers of beer with some regulars who knew their way around a dartboard. Eventually, I was the only one left of the crew throwing in the beer tournament. I picked that day to have the best day I ever had at a dartboard. Even the bad shots were pretty good, and a scalloping crew was kept in free beer all afternoon. My stock on *Little Infant* was never higher.

While most of the crew were out partying, Lawrence Schuster and Ricky Merrill were hanging out back on the boat. That night they heard someone down in the fish hold when no one had any business being there. They looked around for weapons and found only a hatchet and a cast iron pan to protect our catch.

"Which one do you want?" Ricky asked Lawrence.

"The hatchet."

"OK. You go first." Hatchet trumps frying pan every time.

They found our Dinty Moore greenhorns on deck, fresh out of the fish hold and trying to pinch a few bags of our hard-earned catch. We found out later that was their aim all along. They were junkies looking for fix money. We all felt vindicated in our dislike of these two dirtbags.

Lawrence held the hatchet over one of their heads and threatened to use it if they did not disappear and never come back. They did, and when we finally put to sea, we threw their gear unceremoniously over the side. And hopefully, beef stew had lost some of its appeal for them for years to come.

# January Blow

**In January of** 1980, we traveled up to the Gulf of Maine and got pounded by a most peculiar storm. When it hit, it was blowing around 50 mph and picked up through the day, peaking with sustained winds of 70 mph. The strange part was that the sun was bright and the sky a brilliant blue with white billowy clouds. It was a beautiful day, just blowing 70. Naturally, we couldn't fish in that kind of weather. Gerald always ordered the rakes aboard when it started blowing higher than 55. The forecast called for sustained winds for a couple of days, so he decided to head for the barn. I loved times like these when there was little work, and you could take in the wonder of these storms so far out at sea.

It was a stunning day, the kind that makes even a bunch of jaded fishermen stop and stare, drinking it all in, in respectful silence, no matter how many times they had seen it. At first, we were heading into it, so the bow of the *Little Infant* would hit 30 to 40-foot seas head-on in violent collisions, breaking over the bow and all the way aft where they would smash at the wheelhouse windows. We all hoped the windows would hold. You had to time your dash from the shucking house forward to the dog house to get down to the warmth of the fo'c'sle, or else you would get drenched and possibly knocked over by the frigid seas coming over the bow. Having made that dash and climbing down the doghouse ladder, someone asked me to close the whaleback door. The Infant had an enclosed bow called a whaleback for stowing gear. There was a vent to the fo'c'sle located here. It was getting cold down there, so the guys wanted the whaleback door closed. Having done that, I was standing next to the port side rail when we took a "queer sea," one that had come out of a different direction than usual, which hit the Infant broadside. The boat jerked violently, starboard side down, port side up, catapulting me straight up off the deck several feet. As I was going up, the boat rolled to starboard and away from me. I looked down and saw no boat under me, just white, turbulent, frigid Gulf of Maine ocean propelled by 70 mph winds. On my way down, I thought, "So this is how I die." I was in free fall with no coping strategy.

As I descended, thinking of the inevitable shock of the frigid waters that awaited, the Infant rolled back to port under me, and I landed on the rail, my left arm and leg outboard, my right inboard like I was sliding down a banister. I rolled over to starboard, landing back-first on the deck. I just lay there for a minute, knowing how close to an exit this was. The skipper, who saw the whole thing from the wheelhouse, lowered the window for a second between seas to laugh at me. You know, of the "Ha! Ha! You stupid fuck! You almost got killed!" variety.

Sitting at the fo'c'sle table, the enormity of what just happened washed over me. I'd have been fortunate to withstand two minutes of the January ocean temperatures. Even having accomplished that, there would have been no fishing me out of such turbulent waters. I would have been gone by the time Gerald could have gotten the vessel turned around, faced with the task of finding me in such fast-moving, chopped-up water. I said nothing to my mates. Gerald was the only one who had seen this. Later, I went halfway up the dog house ladder, held on, and watched the *Little Infant* bury her galluses and shucking houses in the angry North Atlantic and, as I always did, I thought of Mom and home and my friends and how they wouldn't believe it if they saw it. They would never really know. This is about as edgy as a fellow can get, I thought.

The wind picked up, and we did not go up on deck after 3:00 P.M. In the fo'c'sle, everyone had a cigarette or joint and hit the rack. The boat was taking a pounding. The fo'c'sle was noisy with creaking, groaning, and banging as the bow was taking it head-on. Dickey used to say the creaking was music to his ears. It meant that you were on a wooden boat, and she was stretching out, bending, and adapting to the environment. A steel boat does not do that. There's no give. It holds until it doesn't and pops a weld. Then, abruptly, it's game over.

Occasionally, we would take a bad one, and the boat would sound like it could be battered to pieces like someone drove a dump truck smack into the bow. That would stop the boat dead for just a second in its trough, and she would shiver her timbers successively from fore to aft. Then the Infant would shake it off like a veteran prizefighter who knew how to take a wicked chin punch and somehow groggily start forward again. On one of these seas, I was almost thrown from my berth. I stuck my head out of the bunk to find five other heads sticking out of their bunks, having all been lifted about a foot in the air. I had never heard a pounding like this. We all looked at each other, thinking the same thing.

"Baby! I thought that one was coming through," said Skip.

At about 6:00 P.M., we all arose, grubbed up, primarily sandwiches, because cooking was impossible and shot the shit around the fo'c'sle table. It turned dark, and the storm had not let up at all. As always, Capt. Gerald Costa was bringing us in. So many of these smashing seas felt like they would be the one to breach the hull and do us in. We had two things comforting us: Harvey Gamage knew how to build a boat, and Gerald knew how to handle her. No way the *Janet and Jean* or *Bay of Isles* could make it through this.

We were all hanging out in the fo'c'sle, and I decided skipper could probably use a cup of coffee. (See? Ship's cook/social worker.) So, I poured half a cup and made my way up the swaying doghouse ladder. Once on deck, I had to use the tow cable as a lifeline. It wouldn't do to get washed overboard in the dark. The deck lights were off as Gerald needed to see beyond the bow as best he could. I made my way up the wheelhouse steps, reached for the brass latch, and opened the door. The wind lashed, trying to relieve me of the cup of coffee and tear the door from my hand. Being lower on the steps, my eyes were almost level with the wheelhouse deck. Customarily dark inside, I looked up and saw the wheel steering through those terrible seas, the only light the faint glow of the radar screen. But there was no one behind the wheel as if a ghost were piloting the boat. *What the fuck.* Then I heard a moan. Where was it coming from? There it was again, coming from the deck just under the wheel. I looked closer and saw a body lying there in the darkness in a puddle of puke with one hand on the wheel, steering by feel.

"Gerald? Are you OK?"

"Yeah, I'll be alright," came a voice from the shadows. He somehow kept the *Infant* on course for Provincetown, lying down on the deck and steering with experience only. I let the wind rip the cup of coffee away.

"You sure you'll be OK?"

"Yeah, yeah, I'll be fine," he said.

I closed the door and made my way carefully back to the fo'c'sle and told this astonishing story to the crew, figuring they would be concerned as I was. What I got were peals of laughter of the *Ha! Ha! Ha! The skipper got seasick!* variety. (No mercy at sea.) Then they all hit the sack and were soon fast asleep. They all believed that Gerald Costa would bring us in even though he could not even stand up and look out the wheelhouse window. My faith in God was not even that strong, but I was outnumbered. With my hope for a safe return lying in a puddle of puke on the wheelhouse deck, I turned in and fell asleep amid the relentless pounding. How did I do that? I think a storm of this magnitude is as exhausting as the hard labor of deck work.

I was roused several hours later by some commotion on deck. Most of the guys were topside, and I recognized the sounds as those made by making ready to tie up at the wharf. The cook was not required to tie up, having other duties. Even the harbor behind the breakwater was sloppy that night, but we were indeed tying up. I had somehow slept through the Race Point rips in 70 mph winds. Captain Gerald Costa, Wayne Costa, Harvey Gamage, and the F/V *Little Infant* had gotten us home.

# The Great English Muffin War

**Around the core** of regulars, we had additional crew rotate in and out. Ronald Baker had been on the *Infant* the previous year and was now back for a few more trips. We seemed to get along well until the first breakfast of the trip. After cooking the bacon, sausage, and linguica, I made eggs to order for the guys, toasting English muffins right on the cast iron stovetop. Baker approached me in the galley.

"You don't toast these with butter?"

I wasn't sure what he was talking about.

"Here, I'll show you." (*a bit condescending*)

He placed a sheet of tinfoil on the stovetop, buttered up two English muffin halves, and put them butter side down on the tin foil. It was not long before the butter began to smoke and fill the galley with Eau-de-burnt butter. I let him continue his demonstration, but when finished, it was one smokey fo'c'sle. It seemed obvious, at least to me, that this was not a good idea.

"Sorry, Ronald, I don't think so," I said.

"Why not?"

I stood there in a smoke-filled enclosure, explaining that we were standing in a smoke-filled enclosure. It did not go over well. While cooking for two watches with men sleeping just a few feet away, the air quality was entrusted to the cook, who monitored it faithfully. But this was *I'm the townie fisherman and, you, you prick, are a wash-ashore.* I decided that just because I was newer to all this, I wouldn't let anyone get away with breaking a set tradition like the cook being boss of the galley. He would never have done this with a townie fisherman. He began the war by doing little malicious things.

During a meal, I stood by in the galley after serving. A stream of milk flowing down the pitch of the fo'c'sle deck from fore to aft caught my eye. Baker had an empty milk cup and the look of a third-grader who had just let a frog loose during class. He knew I was the guy who would clean that "accident."

Things escalated because this was, after all, serious business, me not butter-grilling his English muffins. He also knew the most sacred of galley/fo'c'sle laws:

Never leave dishes in the sink after mug-ups. The cook washes only breakfast, lunch, and dinner dishes.

So later at night, I discover a sink full of dishes when, after months with the old crew, never so much as a teaspoon. We all knew who I was talking about when I gave a generic warning to the crew. Next time around on Baker's watch, another sink full of dirty dishes but now with ketchup applied liberally. The plates had not been used otherwise. They were merely a vehicle to display the *fuck you* message of ketchup. OK. That was enough.

Baker was in the portside shucking house with Lawrence, Ricky, and others. I shattered dishes one at a time on the closed shucking house door, making a hell of a racket (like me and Chuckie's sheet metal cabinet). Then I started my diatribe, delivered between broken dishes, on how if it happened again, there'd be no fucking dishes left, and they'd have to eat off the fucking deck. Gerald, seeing (and hearing) this and came out of the wheelhouse and down to the deck.

"What the hell is going on?"

I brought him up to speed while smashing the dishes. That he wished me to stop breaking them was apparent, but I am pretty sure he did not like the disregard of galley rules and the particular nastiness of the ketchup signature. The dirty dishes stopped but not the animosity.

We were in port doing gear work when Baker tried to fight with me, and we got into it. Gerald broke it up and told Baker I was the best cook he'd ever had on his boat and that if he couldn't get along, he'd have to find another boat. I never saw Gerald that mad before or since. That pretty much put an end to the stunts. Thanks, Cap. There was no love lost between us, but at least the circus was over. He only made two trips with us that time around anyway. The war started over English muffins had ended. The cook was still boss of the galley.

## The Uneasy Rhythm

**I settled into** fishing life in winter. One significant difference was Provincetown was more habitable and enjoyable in the off-season. When I got back from a trip, we'd mix time at the Fo'c'sle or Old Colony, eating out a few times, finding a party (not difficult in P'town), or a poetry reading at the Fine Arts Work Center. We often visited Richard and Betty Dickey, hiked into the dunes, and once stayed in the dune shack "Euphoria."

The dune shacks of the Province Lands are rare jewels. Euphoria had a woodstove and kerosene lamps. They are cradled in the dunes and set you up to experience the seashore as it was meant to be. Lawrence Schuster, a friend, and former shipmate from the *Little Infant*, lived in one for probably 30 years.

I refer to this as an "uneasy" rhythm due to that nagging feeling that a phone call or quick visit from the captain would come at the least opportune time, and we would have to go out onto the half-frozen Atlantic. The various

Dunes with a shack left of center.

moods of the winter ocean made scheduling trips improvisational. We had not been fishing in nearly two weeks due to storms, and I had way too much time on my hands. Being the curious type, I sought some "killed the cat" kind of activities.

I bought a gram of opium from a gal we knew. Some of my favorite writers had their affairs with opium. Did not Coleridge write "Kublai Khan" after an opium dream? Shelley took laudanum, a derivative, often. Thomas DeQuincy wrote "Confessions of an Opium Eater" from experience. So I was ready to have my ticket to the sublime punched, baby. The opium itself was black and gummy, about the size of a marble.

"What's the best way to do this? Smoke it? Eat it? Tea?" I asked my friend.

"Stick it up your ass."

"Excuse me?"

"You stick it up your ass. That way, it all gets absorbed," she said.

OK, makes sense. I excused myself and deposited the ball of opium where it would do the most good. Susan and I were hosting a party in our apartment. When the wrecking ball hit the back of my skull, I settled into an overstuffed chair and began to recede. The party in front of me was getting smaller and smaller as I got farther away. The chair got softer, mingled with my skin. I *became* the chair. I didn't give a shit about anything. Chairs. That's just like them, right? They don't care. I was preoccupied with being purely a piece of

At sea on the F/V *Little Infant* (courtesy David Meads).

furniture, unsure where I ended, and it began. At some point, it dawned on me that this was no way to have fun. I envied the little partygoers *way* over there who did not have to be chairs. They were having a far better time. Any curiosity I may have had about "chairiness" satisfied, I never tried opium again. Staring my lack of genius square in the face, there was no "Kublai Khan" to be written here. Maybe a little drool.

## Winter Fishing

**Eventually, the boat** beckoned us back for the inevitable gear work in the biting cold at the wharf. I am often asked what it's like working in the January winds of the North Atlantic. Properly clothed, staying warm was rarely a problem. We worked enough to break a sweat, so it wouldn't do to wear too much. I always thought the gear work was colder, just because you're not moving as much.

During winter, we fit our schedule around storms and gales. As soon as there was a break, we'd try to get a trip in. Winter trips were generally shorter due to storm frequency. If you got five or six days out, that was a lot. If there were a three-day break in a bad weather pattern, we'd try to steam out there and shell stock like mad, running a 6 and 3 or a 9 and 3 watch for two days, run back to port, hire shuckers and cut it all off in the harbor. A trip like that was called a "pirate run." There were occasions when we broke watch, and all hands were on deck to break ice out of the rigging with mauls to prevent top-heaviness.

Author (L) and Lawrence Schuster on the *Little Infant*, waving at *Bay of Isles* at sea (courtesy Jennifra Hann-Norton).

During these times, I would come off the turbulent sea and find it difficult to walk on solid ground. It felt like it was shifting and undulating as I was so accustomed to pumping my legs to maintain equilibrium. We laughed at a phenomenon that usually happened when I took my first shower in our apartment after a winter trip. Our shower stall was phone booth small and made of thin sheet metal. When I went into this environment right from the boat, I found that I could not stand up steady or straight in the shower without constantly banging into the noisy metal. Boom! Boom! If we had a guest, Susan would have to explain all the noise. It was Mickey just in from sea, not being able to stand up steady in the shower.

Sometimes the call to be at the wharf would come around 11:00 at night. And although we timed our trips between blows as best we could, we still managed to get caught in our share. During the first week in February, we made another trip to Fippennies Ledge. I wrote in the journal it was a blizzard with 75 to 80 mph winds with gusts of 90. It was a nor'easter, so we luckily had fair wind all the way home. We were cutting in the shucking houses on the way, listening to Stevie Wonder, Van Morrison, and others on Ricky's tape player. A few of us were hanging out astern at the turtleback, watching the battle between blizzard and angry ocean.

## Bikers, Brass Knuckles, and Knives

**On Palm Sunday,** March 30th, I began recording a series of events in my journal that would recount what were probably the scariest experiences of my short fishing career, some of them occurring on dry land or tied up at the pier. We had gone out on March 20th and returned to port four days later, a busted trip owing to weather and poor fishing. We still had a ton of grub, fuel, and ice.

I was home asleep with Susan on the night of the 24th when, at 11:50 P.M., there came a knock at the door that I did not hear. Susan got up to answer. It Gerald to say we were going fishing at midnight. I had ten minutes to get ready and down to the wharf. I threw my seabag together (mostly dirty clothes) and headed for the waterfront at 11:55 P.M.

"And I wanted to be Popeye the Sailor," I muttered while packing, thinking of my childhood ambition. Susan chuckled at that. I met up with shipmate Kevin on the wharf. We walked slowly as neither of us was too enthused about going fishing on this bone-chilling night. Had we been two minutes later, we would have missed the boat as the Infant was pulling away from the wharf without us. Wishing we had been two minutes later, we made a run for it, threw our sea bags aboard, and jumped down onto the deck of the already moving vessel.

We were almost to the breakwater when we saw the flashing headlights of a vehicle, its horn blowing. It was our engineer, Paul Boyle. The captain turned around, picked him up, and then we were bound. Gerald gave us gear work to do, fun when you are only half-awake.

The handle from a pair of squeezers got away from Eric and opened a deep gash over his right eye. He did a massive job of bandaging it, which made it look worse than it was. We all joked about it, saying Skip had belted him. Word was we were going fishing for the big stuff off Gloucester. After the captain had turned in, word came from the wheel watch that we were indeed headed for Gloucester and not that discouraging 60 degrees for seven hours to Fippennies Ledge and the peanut pile.

I shot the shit with the gang till around 1:15 A.M. and got up at 4:00 A.M. to cook breakfast, which is one bad thing about being cook when you are bound at midnight: four hours till your day starts. We arrived off Gloucester around 6:00 A.M. On seeing no other scallopers around, the captain set a course for Fippennies Ledge, which did not cheer us.

I made lunch for the two watches, and since we had a few more hours of steaming before we got to the grounds, we hit the bunks. I fell into a deep sleep until awakened by a commotion in the fo'c'sle.

"What's up?" I asked from my berth.

"There's a fire in the engine room."

We were all up the doghouse ladder in a shot. Jimmy Perry, who had been back aft, had jumped down the ladder without hitting any rungs in-between and grabbed the galley's two fire extinguishers which meant the other three back aft had been exhausted.

The first sight to greet us on deck was the smoke. Everything from the winch aft was enveloped in black smoke pouring from every vent and porthole serving the engine room. I went back aft through the smoke-filled cutting house to the turtleback. Wayne was just staggering out of the engine room, eyes red and tearing. He leaned over the rail, gasping and choking. Wayne, Paul, Jimmy, and Skip alternately went down into the thick smoke with fire extinguishers for as long as they could stand it. Positioned in the turtleback, I could see flames shooting up from the engine, licking the wooden beams and deck planks above. The captain was in the wheelhouse on the radio.

"May Day! May Day! *Little Infant*! *Little Infant*! May Day!"

Gerald sent the May Day out over every channel. I had never been part of a May Day. Man, that's just for movies and television, right? But hearing the captain call it out repeatedly on the radio, it went through my skull like a spike. When he said, *Little Infant*, I felt like he was calling my name. The *Infant* was our world, and our world was in peril at about a ten-hour steam from the nearest land. There were already too many guys down in the black smoke of the engine room. Ricky and I stayed in the turtleback, ready to jump down should we be needed and standing by the deck hose should that be needed.

We were dead on the water, bobbing like a burning cork. With the engine out, Paul started the lister so we'd have electronics, pumps, and deck hose in working order. We watched the flames shooting upward.

"I'm handing you the deck hose," said the young Moko.

"No!" said Paul

"Oh yes, I am!" he said

"Not until the Captain gives the order!" said Paul.

Each time we thought the fire out, it would reignite like those trick birthday candles. I went forward to update Eric and Kevin, both in the fo'c'sle since there were enough crew members back aft. The reclined Kevin told the pacing Eric, "Look, if this boat blows up, it's not going to make much difference if you're back there or up here." Eric was no doubt thinking of the monstrous fuel tanks on either side of the burning engine.

Skip, Paul, Wayne, and Jimmy alternately went down into the engine room to fight the fire. A single man could only stay down there for just a few moments before being overcome. We were running low on our last extinguisher, and the fire still burned. Through it all, we could hear Gerald on the radio.

"May Day! May Day! *Little Infant!*"

At last, the radio crackled to life in response. It was a fish dragger named Theresa Marie from Wilmington, Delaware. Through the sizzle of radio static, they asked if we were alright.

"Yeah, we're alright, but we may have to use the life raft," said Gerald. Having to possibly use the life raft had me questioning his usage of the word "alright."

The only active part I had in the whole affair was when Paul went into the engine room after the fire was presumably out. I followed behind him and stayed at the threshold of the engineer's cabin and the engine room, should he need me. The flames erupted once again.

"It's still burning! Tell him it's still burning!" Paul hollered back to me.

I relayed the message to the captain. Paul finally put out the fire with the last few squirts of the last extinguisher.

The ship was out of immediate danger. We just bobbed in the water adrift for three hours or so. We all went down to the engine room to inspect the damage. Charred and blackened, it reeked of burnt fuel and white-hot metal. Everyone realized how fortunate we were, seeing those fuel tanks of the unexploded variety. Had that last extinguisher not done the job, we'd have had to abandon ship before she blew, adrift in a life raft ten hours from shore.

It was also our good fortune that it wasn't blowing a gale as we would not have been able to head into it or lay on a rake. The Infant would have laid broadside to seas like the *Janet and Jean* at Great Round Shoal off Nantucket in '77. But it was relatively calm, just a gentle swell, unusual for this time of year. We disconnected the rake and pulled out about 100 fathoms of wire from the winch, coiling it on the bow for towing. That done, we went below to the fo'c'sle and played poker.

After about four hours, someone up on deck spotted the Theresa Marie on the horizon and called down to us card players below. We went up on deck and cheered this most welcome sight. She looked glorious, cutting through the swells headed straight for us. The Theresa Marie cut her off her nets, leaving her gear in the water, marked with buoys, rather than take a half-hour to haul back. Yes, impressive. When she came within hailing distance, we hollered greetings and applauded her crew. We threw them a painter line tied to the cable, and soon we were under tow.

I cooked a steak dinner, then we all sat down to poker till about 10:30 P.M. when we saw the lights of coastal Maine. Gerald had gone up to the captain's bunk in the wheelhouse for some shut-eye, so I went up to wake him. The wheelhouse was dark, and where one usually feels the growl and vibration of the engine below, there was only an unnerving stillness. Yet the boat was doing nine or ten knots, gently rolling through the swells like a ghost ship under the power of some dark spell. It was eerie. The crackle of a voice on the radio broke the trance.

"*Little Infant. Little Infant.*"

The captain answered and learned that the *Theresa Marie* would cut us loose, and the Portland Coast Guard would tow us the rest of the way. It was all hands on deck to haul in 110 fathoms of cable after we disconnected. The wire was damned heavy and seemed to get caught up in the rocks with every haul. We could only pull a few fathoms at a time since we had no working winch and did it to the tune of "I've Been Working On The Railroad" and other inspirational songs, requiring a good half hour of toil.

The Coast Guard tied up on our starboard side and towed us from there, directly into a buoy. Then they boarded us to see if we had enough life preservers and performed other annoying inspections. This rankled Gerald.

And so, at midnight, twenty-four hours after we had left P'town, we were in Portland, Maine. We had survived a fire that came within a whisker of destroying our boat and were now safe. We thought. Our adventures had only begun.

The waterfront of any city is usually a rough section of town, and so it was with Portland in the 1970s and early '80s, before the gentrification that transformed the city. The town we saw was the one that inspired people to do something about it. It was a hard-looking place that had seen better days. The bars were all closed by the time we were tied up and the boat secured. No one had much money, so we were safe for the time being. It was the next morning that it all started. The captain gave everyone some cash, and by 10:30, we were in the bars. We broke up into a few groups. My group went to a bar where a massive Native American man, known colloquially as a BFI, sat down with us and said that Skip's forearm tattoos were worth money.

"Yeah? You can get money for these?" Skip said, playing along.

"We don't take scalps around here," the guy said. "We take tattoos. I'm gonna make a lampshade out of your arms."

Three of our crew who had been looking for us arrived, evening the odds somewhat. Skip kept his tattoos. By mid-afternoon, we all wound up in dives called "Shane's" or "The Factory," where we played pool and drank pitchers. Around 5:00 P.M., we went back to the boat to collect $30 more and eat something.

Some of the guys were already cooking bacon. We were all hungry, but none could match Moko's impatience. He grabbed several pieces of white, less than half-cooked bacon from the hot bubbling grease with bare fingers, gave them a shake or two to get the excess fat off, and quickly popped them into his mouth, the strips being way too hot for his fingers. Fishermen.

Thus refueled with food and funds, we continued our tear. As we were leaving the boat, a young guy about 18 years old approached us and introduced himself as Edgar Miller, known as Bub, he told us. He had hitchhiked down from Ellsworth, Maine "to look for a job on a scallop boat." I know he must have cursed the moment he hooked up with us, and I have often wondered if the rest of his front teeth finally fell out or not. Bub was an honest, forthright fellow, but, it turned out, he tended to say too much at the wrong time. There are few traits worse on a greenhorn.

Bub tagged along with us from bar to bar. He was looking for a site on a scalloper, and we were scallopers, so we were his best bet. Bub, Kevin, Jimmy Perry, and I made our way to the much-heralded Free St. Pub. Everywhere we went, barflies told us to hit this place. It was a cavernous club and a hot band, Renegade, belted out one rocker after another. Soon the rest of the crew arrived: Ricky Merrill, Paul, Skip, and the captain. Wayne had gone back to P'town because his mother was ill. A bouncer threw an unruly girl out of the bar rather roughly. Ricky, mortified by this treatment, intervened on her behalf. He got into the bouncer's face, and some of us had to pull him away. Ricky had a soft spot for the underdog and had a refined sense of fair play. Paul, who got nasty when he drank, tried to pick a fight with one of our crew members but to no avail. He left the bar after the captain spoke to him for a few minutes at the door. Later in the evening, we would hear from him after he had his fester on for a few hours.

As it neared closing time, the band was through playing, the house lights came up, and we were all sitting at a round table finishing our beverages. Gerald told Bub that he would give him a chance.

"I'll take you fishing at half share if you work hard," he said.

"I can work just as hard as anybody on the boat," was Bub's answer.

Whoa. Screeching halt like a needle scratching across a record. Everyone's head turned on that. "Fuck you, douche bag," would have been a better choice.

Skip's eyes lit up. I tried to give Bub the high sign to shut his trap, but it was no good. He went on about his working prowess.

"I want him." Skip said to Gerald. "Put him on my watch. I'm gonna break him."

Skip promised Bub that he would work him into the deck and Bub, digging the hole a little deeper, said he could handle anything Skip threw at him. He was alienating the guy who would be his best ally in a hostile environment besides me. Skip had been that for me when I broke in, but for Bub, well, he had just thrown that overboard wrapped in chains. This unfortunate exchange was interrupted by a savage fight between some tough-looking women. I have never seen scarier fights than those among the fairer sex. Some guys from a motorcycle club wearing cuts got involved, breaking up the melee, probably between their old ladies. Gerald got up and walked into the middle. Skip, who had done time and had experience with them on the inside, looked warily from his chair.

"I don't mess with bikers," he said, which proved to be a pretty good rule to have.

Jimmy tried to get Gerald away from them, having to pull him physically. Outside, the MC was involved in three different pockets of bloody fights, and Gerald walked between them like a religious zealot who believed a pit of rattlesnakes wouldn't bite him, preaching the gospel of You Don't Know What Life's All About. It was only a matter of time. Desperate, we hailed a cab and, with some difficulty, got Gerald into it along with me, Skip, Jimmy, Ricky, and our newly acquired shipmate. Welcome to commercial fishing, Bub.

Cabbie asked, "Where to?"

Somebody said, "Take us to where the hookers are."

He dropped us off on a major street a half block from Dunkin Donuts, where all the action was supposed to be. He had judged correctly. Being last to leave the cab, I found everyone congregating in the alcove of a closed store, sharing a joint with a painted girl who looked about 18 and dressed for trouble. She paired up with a strung-out-looking burnout with straggly hair and missing a couple of teeth. How the hell did they make this connection? I hadn't taken overly long getting out of the taxi. I got that same sense of foreboding as when your boat is headed straight into a squall. It never occurred to me to simply get off.

As if to confirm my anxieties, three bikers pulled up in a car next to us, and we were the focus of their attention. Oh, good. Windows down, tatted arms hanging out, one of them singled out Bub, who was standing next to me.

"You're an asshole," he said, pointing at our new greenhorn. Bub, having missed the enrollment period for Tact 101, said, "You're an asshole, too."

*Cool. He just called a biker an asshole.* According to script, the guy got out of the car, looking very much like a man with a plan. Backed up by a massive dude who had to be 350 pounds and dirty, like Pig Pen, they both approached us. The third remained behind the wheel, getaway.

He got in Bub's face, and Bub gave it right back. But this was an apparent mismatch. Not very bright, our greenhorn, though brave for a guy his age. The biker abandoned verbal intimidation in favor of something more visceral.

"I got something for you, mother fucker," he said.

He slipped his hand into a set of brass knuckles and pummeled Bub square in the teeth. The sound of brass on tooth still shoots through my mind. Bub lost a few front teeth that night; his lower lip split almost in two. He spat chips and blood, but the punch did not knock him down. He did not fight back but stood his ground and faced his attacker.

If this had happened to one of our actual crew members, we would have been all in and committed ourselves for good or ill, but Bub was just this guy hanging around with us for a few hours, so he was not covered by the full protection plan. But intervene, we did. One of our guys shoved a joint in the biker's mouth and tried the "Now why would you want to go and do a thing like that?" approach.

"I just wanted to fight, alright?" he said. A fellow has his rights, I guess.

Gerald then called the guy an asshole, but not to his face, an aside comment made in the crowd. But the junkie guy heard it and said that nobody calls that biker dude an asshole. I'm guessing he was a friend of the club. He threatened to make a phone call.

"*They'll* come . . . with guns," he said. Great. There are a lot more hornets back in the nest.

Man, I'm liking this night, ain't I? My crisis diplomacy skills on display, I told the junkie that he's just a drunk fisherman and didn't know what he was saying. I encouraged him to let it slide, and he did. See? Some things can go right on a night like this: no guns. Always a plus. A considerable crowd had now gathered, and everyone had something to say. Bub was finally not talking, probably absorbed with getting to know his new mouth.

The police arrived. The first person they singled out was me, perhaps because I fronted them directly with *Please stop this insanity* written on my face.

"Get moving."

"Right," I said, "That's fine with me."

I walked, but not far. After the police had dispersed the crowd, I went back. I found the entire crew had moved into a turbulent Dunkin Donuts, populated by painted hookers, junkies with glazed expressions, drunks pontificating, scallopers from Provincetown, but no bikers. I thought of Dickey's "trap in the drain of the world" expression. This place was indeed the trap in the drain of the evening, this Dunkin Donuts in Portland, the only place that would have this whacked-out crew at so late an hour.

Gerald was seated in the middle of it all, still telling everyone they didn't know what life was all about. Man, that was a real crowd-pleaser. He was having fun with them, baiting them, inciting pushback and screams of protest. One garishly made-up hooker left her seat, cocked her fist, and announced she was going to punch him in the mouth.

"Go ahead," he said without so much as a flinch.

Gerald continued throwing gas on the fire but, through it all, he bought coffee for everyone in the joint. I stayed for about twenty minutes and decided I'd had enough, thinking the ultimate climax for this scene would be bikers coming back with guns, the big windows disintegrating under a hail of gunfire.

Seeing our new shipmate with the mashed-up face, I thought I should get him to the boat to see what could be done for that lip and show him a bunk. I should have just left him there, and the night would have sorted itself out somehow. It was raining now, and it was nice walking in peace, though I did not relax until we got back to the boat.

The *Infant* was dark and quiet when we reached her. Once below in the fo'c'sle, I looked at that lip. It was split wide open vertically right down the middle, obviously requiring stitches. Bub refused to go to a hospital, so I cleaned and disinfected, but there wasn't much else I could do. (By tradition, an alternative name for Cookie was "Doc" since he also functioned as ship's doctor in the old sailing days.) The teeth were a mess; some knocked right out, others cracked to nubs at various heights. But this kid was determined to go fishing.

I thought he was headed for more trouble and offered him some advice, the kind that helps you not get a dredge dropped on you about two days out. Boasting: bad. Silence: good. Mouth shut, ears open, work your guts out. I went on and on, lecturing the poor lad, and he accepted the advice graciously enough, though it was shocking how quickly he would be tested.

I went up on deck as Bub got settled below. Paul Boyle, our engineer, was coming down the pier toward the *Infant* with the studied walk of someone who had overindulged. *First, this foot. Now the next.* Descended from a long line of Provincetown fishermen, Paul was a hell of an engineer and a good seaman. I trusted my life with him. Drinking, Paul turned nasty and had already tried to pick fights with two of our crew earlier. The boat was settled away from the pier, so he asked me to pull her in, which I did by pulling a spring line. He jumped down onto the deck. Ok, now what?

"I tried to fight with Eric, but he wouldn't fight," he said.

"What did you do that for?" I asked him, figuring I was next on his dance card.

"Nothing else to do."

Ah, boredom. He should have hooked up with the brass-knuckled biker for a date. They deserved each other. He looked down through the doghouse and spotted Bub below brushing his tooth.

"Isn't that right, Eric?" Paul shouted down.

No answer.

"Hey, Eric!"

Oh, no.

"I'm not Eric, I'm Bub," came this youthful voice up through the doghouse.

Paul looked at me in melodramatic surprise.

"Mickey, who the hell is that?"

What if I had not told the truth? Yeah, a question that repeats on me like an onion bagel. I suppose I could have come up with a better truth than the one I gave.

"He's Bub. The captain hired him half-share."

The truth served neat with a wicked finish. Paul erupted.

"What? Half-share my ass! You! Get the fuck off this boat! Now!"

A voice came from below: "But the captain hired me and . . ."

"I don't give a fuck who hired you. Get off this boat now!" He turned to me.

"I'm not gonna pay for no half-share greenhorn outta' my pocket. Mickey, is Gerald nuts? Half-share my ass."

I don't remember if I even said anything back. The journal says I just jumped down the ladder. Bub was not leaving for anything. He already ruined what could have been a decent prom picture, courtesy of a biker. A dickhead fisherman wasn't going to change his mind. We decided to turn out the lights, hit our bunks, and hope the storm blew over. We lay there for some time in the darkness, waiting. So far, so good, but then, footsteps, *determined* footsteps sending a message *(Fi, Fie, Fo, Fum!)*, crossing the deck and down the ladder, *click*, the fo'c'sle is flooded in light. Paul, eyes flaming, voice scorching: "You! Get the fuck off this boat!"

I was in an upper starboard bunk, Bub in the forwardmost lower. I heard his voice come back at Paul from below.

"The captain gave me a job, and I'm going to take it."

I felt like a guy whose chickens had just gotten out of the yard, running everywhere. I could not get them all back in the dooryard. This kid did not know how to cut his losses and shut up.

"Listen, I'm telling you to get the fuck outta here! You hear me? Get the fuck outta here!"

But Bub was still in his bunk answering Paul back. Paul came across the transom toward the bunk and positioned his foot close to Bub's face.

"I'm gonna push your face in!" I thought, well, not all of it. Someone already had a head start on you.

The heated exchange went back and forth, but Bub never caught on that the longer he stayed quiet, Paul would power down a little. He barraged him with zingers like, "I don't know what you've got against me," "You'll probably like me," (the speed date was over, lost cause, that) and Bub's Greatest Hit: "I Can Work Just As Hard As Anybody On This Boat" in the key of A-flat Greenhorn.

I begged and pleaded with Bub to be quiet to no avail. There were a couple of the guys sound asleep in their bunks, snoring away, sleeping off the drinking that had started in the morning, oblivious to all the yelling. I wanted so badly for them to wake up. These guys are used to sleeping through two locomotives dropping on deck every half hour. Or maybe they were awake and decided to skip this funfest we had going. No help there. It was just us three in this cozy scenario.

Paul had to have been wondering what it took to scare this kid off the boat. He turned and lunged over to the galley, grabbing the big chef's knife with the ten-inch blade. I had sharpened it two days before. The way he wielded it, it looked like a small cutlass. He screamed, more like a war cry, and drove the knife down into the table, nicking the chain that supports the fo'c'sle table on the way down. That took a nick out of the chef's knife, and every time I used it that winter, it brought me back to this moment, seeing that ding. He unstuck the blade from the table and came across the transom at Bub.

It's amazing all the full thoughts that can shoot across your brain in just a second. I planned different scenarios depending on how this unfolded. Paul would have to bend down to get at Bub in the lower bunk. I could roll out and be on Paul's back in a second. Some of my self-preservation advisors did not like this option. It went contrary to a bit of wisdom I think I came across in a Stephen King novel that goes thus: "Crowd a gun. Run from a knife."

Paul stopped well short of Bub. Then, in a menacing tone: "I'm gonna slice your balls off."

He moved the knife in such a way that Bub could fully appreciate his intentions. Whoa, the visual on that was effective, the foc's'le lights glinting on the blade. I pleaded with God to wake one of these sleeping shipmates, but only snoring came from those bunks.

"I'm gonna cut your heart out." (Before or after you cut off his balls? I think that would make a difference, to me at least.)

Would that some director would yell, "Cut!" and tell him this cutthroat pirate act was too over the top. I was hoping it was an act. Whatever diplomacy skills I had were now on full-tilt boogie. I told him that if Bub were as bad an idea as he seemed to think he was, Gerald would get rid of him when he came to his senses in the morning.

No good. Paul cursed more threats and flashed the blade. *That's OK, as long as he doesn't make a move for him.* It was then that Paul made a move. He surged towards Bub with the knife out front and, without thinking, my hand shot out of the bunk and clamped hard on his wrist. The forward motion of the knife stopped. Paul stood dead in his tracks and turned his head to face me.

"Paul," I said, "You put down that knife right now. That's serious business you've got in your hand."

I think he was stunned, more so than listening to what I had said. It was that someone was holding his knife arm that got his full attention. Though I had his wrist, he pivoted the knife away from Bub and toward my nose so that I could look down the length of it head-on from inches away. I glanced at it; *yeah, I know what it is* and sought out his eyes. Our eyes locked, and we stayed like that for a few moments in silence. Seemed like a long time. Then his glare seemed to flicker, to waiver. He took a slow step backward. I released his wrist.

"All right then," he yelled and threw the knife towards the galley, making a hell of a racket. "I'm gonna make your life miserable on this boat. I'll drop a rake on you. You're gonna disappear between here and Provincetown. It'll be an accident. You're gonna disappear, and nobody's ever going to hear from you again."

Nice. Bub had finally shut up. Paul turned and headed for the ladder. He turned the lights out and, climbing the ladder, he laughed, saying, "We'll see. We'll see." We heard him muttering as he crossed the deck to his engineer's cabin back aft. Yeah, he knew how to make an exit, too. We lay there in the darkness for some time before Bub broke the silence.

"I can't sleep," he said. That made me laugh. "Who the fuck *was* that?"

We talked for some time till the adrenalin subsided. I told him that Paul was a good guy and a great engineer and that none of us were ever happy to take on a project like a greenhorn who cuts into everyone's share. I was there myself just a few years before and told him about the engineer of the *Janet and Jean* punching the living shit out of me for "fun," and he was cold sober at the time. Bub was *still* intent on going fishing. We slept.

The remainder of the crew escaped the ordeal at Dunkin and found their way back to the boat. They all fell out of their bunks around 10:00 A.M. in pitiful shape, none of them aware of our little *Saturday Night at the Movies*. The captain came down to the fo'c'sle looking bad too, hair sticking out all over. He scanned the place till he found Bub with his puffy eyes. He never said a word. He just pointed with his index as if to say, "You." and motioned with his thumb, "Outta' here." Yeah. I figured that might happen. Paul, whose quarters were aft along with the captain's, had already said his piece with Gerald before he came down to the fo'c'sle.

Bub got up, his mashed face and dried blood looking worse in the stark daylight. He floated/stumbled his way to the ladder in a daze and went up, mumbling something like, "I'm sorry I didn't get a chance to . . ." and was gone. So you want to be a scalloper, eh?

After a couple of days in Portland, the experts said that this damage would take a while to repair, and we might as well go back to Provincetown. Bub wouldn't have seen a lick of fishing anyway. Edgar "Bub" Miller from Ellsworth, Maine, how did you make out? I hope you got your teeth fixed. No one would ever accuse you of not having the spirit. Looking back on it, Paul was probably just trying to scare him, and Bub's refusals and provocations called for ramping

Author (looking up) aboard F/V *Little Infant* with dredges on the rails ready to be set out (courtesy Jennifra Hann-Norton).

it up. If he had meant harm, it would have happened. Though, as a witness, I must say he was damned convincing. It remains one of the most frightening moments of my life. I don't think I would have stayed on that boat as long as he did. He does have a rearranged mouth as a memento of that whacked-out night in Portland.

Gerald rented a van, and we drove from Portland to Provincetown. We made it back later in the evening. A bunch of us hit the Fo'c'sle Bar first, all walking in together. That night there was a decent crowd, Mike Moon behind the bar presiding over many conversations—which immediately stopped. It got oddly quiet for the Fo'c'sle, and a lot of people just stared at us.

Moon broke the silence.

"We heard you were dead." He had a way with words, Moon.

*What?*

"There's a rumor going around. Someone heard on the VHF (marine radio) there was a May Day for the *Little Infant*. People are saying she burned to the waterline with all hands," he said. *Guess what? Not dead! Beer? Yeah, baby.* None of the *Infant* crew had to buy a drink that night. I was glad to be back in Provincetown, attending what seemed like our own funeral. Everyone was grateful not to have to add the *Little Infant* to the list of lost vessels.

## The Blessing of the Fleet, The Sequel (not as good as the original)

**Before my last** trip on the Infant, a trip skippered by Ricky Merrill, I bought all new oil gear. The stuff I had gotten with Chris Scanlan when I started on the *Janet and Jean* had taken a beating. I had repaired some rips and stuff (I still have the pants part. I gave the hooded jacket to a hitchhiker on a rainy day), but I was making good money and could afford a new set.

Susan and I separated. When you separate as a means to stay together, you're in serious trouble. Knowing what I know now, marriage was beyond me. Being married to a kid could not have been easy for her. I was in love with the idea of being in love and had no clue what it required. There we were, not even living together, coming up on the two-year anniversary of "us": The Blessing of the Fleet. I had a desperate bout of magical thinking. We would celebrate our anniversary at the Blessing and discover that under all the bullshit, there was a deep love that would breathe new life into this DOA marriage.

The plan was that as soon as she could break away from the Edwidge, she would get a motorboat ride out into the harbor and join me on the boat I was on. I did not record the name of this boat, and memory does not serve. Chris Scanlan was there. It was the last time I laid eyes on the man. P'town sweetheart Genie was there too. She knew how to shuck and was good on a boat. Her nickname was "Buckets," owing to her shucking ability. She was kind, sweet, personable, and everyone knew her.

It was overcast that day, but the fleet lined up, adorned with flags and revelers for the pass by the bishop, who blessed each vessel in turn. Then, as was the custom, all boats went out and anchored in the harbor for the parties. Everyone was having a great time, but all I could think about was Susan and the marriage that had never gotten off the ground. If we could have but one romantic day, our anniversary, we might be able to right this ship. The afternoon wore on, and no Susan. Genie saw my anxiety, so I let her know I was waiting for her. Everything was riding on this. She tried to comfort me.

"She'll be here, you'll see," she said.

Sunset at sea (courtesy David Meads).

I was not listening. All I could do was stand there at the rail and look back toward town, waiting for a sign of her, a fixated dog whose master has left him tied up outside a store. I caught sight of a sleek speedboat making its way out towards us and strained my eyes. When it got close enough, I spotted her. Susan was indeed in the boat with three guys. I didn't recognize any of them. Who were these guys? They were barreling towards us. Genie saw that it was her, too.

"See? I told you she would come," she said with her arm around my shoulder.

God, I must have looked pathetic. Susan stood, holding on for balance with one hand and a beer upraised in the other, wearing a smile I had not seen in some time. The boat sped towards us, and boy, they looked like they were having a great time. My eyes sought out hers as they came abreast of our boat, but she did not glance my way, even though she knew I was on this vessel.

The boat never slowed down, passing us by, and kept right on going to whatever good time lay ahead of them. It was in this way she let me know how important this anniversary was to her. To be fair, at that point, I was not responding to subtleties.

Genie, standing next to me, was almost as stunned as I was. Then the enormity of it all fell full on me like a sumo wrestler sitting on my chest, and I could barely breathe. That speeding boat sucked the life right out of me when it went by, carrying all my delusions of reparation with it. I knew I would lose it and made my way to the engine room, where there was a chance of being alone. Chris Scanlan was there, but I could not contain my grief and wept. Chris was a good guy and tried to be as supportive as possible, but no words of comfort would fix this mess. I stayed in that engine room for some time, trying to figure out what would come next.

Overcast and threatening all morning, it then rained hard as if to punctuate the tenor of the moment. This Blessing was the antithesis of 1978's sunny love fest. Most of the boats made their way back to tie up. The tide was out, the vessel way below the wharf with a long ladder climb ahead of me. As I put my hands on the rungs, I looked up, and there was Susan at the top waiting for me. A flicker of hope. When I gained the wharf, I hit her with: "Why didn't you stop? It's our anniversary." Nothing like the old guilt-bomb for openers. We can all see where this is going, right?

We walked down the wharf, the rain pounding like bullets on a pond. Our clothes saturated, the rain ran down into our eyes, my denim jacket heavy, having absorbed so much water. Under normal circumstances, a torrential downpour like that ushers you toward shelter unless you are working on deck in full oil gear, but with the world hanging by a thread, it didn't matter if it was raining nails. Standing there in a fierce summer squall, she then spoke the words that split my forehead like a hatchet.

"I don't think I love you anymore. I want a divorce."

# *Flight*


**Her mind made** up, there was no putting her off this. She had had enough. We parted on the wharf, and I walked in a daze through dark rain back to Lawrence's, where I was staying. I had no idea what to do. We had gotten married on a rainy day and ended it on one too. One thing became clear to me. I could not bear to be in the same small town, a town where it would be impossible not to know what the other was doing and everyone else would too. I had to get out of there.

Prospects were few. I was broke since I had bought Susan a nice 35mm SLR camera for $800 with my last fishing trip money. That eliminated the cabin from the equation. Though it was still late afternoon, the rainstorm made it almost dusk outside. I called home and talked to Mom, who, as a mother, was sensitive to the train wreck timbre of my voice. She said to come home if I wanted. Having no idea what I wanted to do, besides putting as much distance between Provincetown and myself, I decided to go home to Atlantic City. I needed money, and I appealed to Susan to help get me out of town. I figured me being gone would be an attractive option for her. She contributed a couple of hundred dollars to the "Make Mickey Disappear" fundraiser.

Heading for Provincetown airport, I saw it all—the hard-fought succession from greenhorn shacker to deckhand, winchman and ship's cook, even the brand-new oil gear hanging in the *Infant*'s shucking house, the friends and shipmates, the unsurpassed beauty of Cape Cod, I saw it fade all at once into a used-to-be life—the next chapter: figuring out how to exist with my new roommate, Failure.

Heartbreak. This was a new thing. Up until then, I was a breaker of hearts. Some good women with the best intentions got burned by this self-absorbed, free-spirited, *I gotta' ride the crest of the wave* thing I was on. I would throw my burning heart at whoever was attracted to the intensity, but the only thing that elicited a commitment from me was the drive to escape the ordinary and take the on-the-edge ride that made me feel alive. It was not from any malice that I left wreckage. It was just that this wild ride superseded everything and everyone, sometimes even decency. But I had outrun whatever maturity I had been sparingly afforded, and it could not prop up the results of my choices. Proportionate to the thickness of my skull, this rejection, this failure, was a lesson in a harsh language I finally understood. Thirty-eight gorgeous years with Beth could not have happened without it. Therapy didn't hurt, either.

Leaving Provincetown ostensibly spelled the end of my commercial fishing career. I made a trip on a scalloper out of Cape May, New Jersey, later that August (chronicled next) and one trip on a clammer out of Atlantic City three years later while working as a social worker. But it was really over when that plane left the tarmac in Provincetown. I felt noticeably better when the aircraft's wheels were no longer in contact with the ground like I had symbolically severed this sickened connection to Susan.

# Damned Yankee

**Finding myself back** at my mother's house in Atlantic City after being to the edge of endurance and even life was somewhat surreal. I had carved out a spot in Provincetown that I could have occupied comfortably for as long as I wished. It was now the last place in the world I wanted to be. I had to start over.

Mom was great. She was so supportive, but I got restless fast. My friend Tammi Pittaro drove me down to Cape May after a week. There was a decent commercial fleet down there, and I thought that if I hung around with my gear long enough, I might find myself a boat. Within two hours of my arrival, a big steel boat came in from sea. She was the *Billie Mae*, and the home port painted on her stern was Rockport, Texas. She was part of an extensive fisheries fleet, and I could see her scallop dredges from a distance. She looked a lot like those big steel-hulled sword fishers depicted in the film *The Perfect Storm*.

I approached her as she was tying up and saw two of the crew leaving the vessel with their gear. Seeing them unceremoniously off was a blonde guy in his early thirties. Once the two crew gained the pier and walked away, I asked if the captain was available.

"I'm the captain."

Seemed young and cocky. Dale Stockton was the youngest captain I had ever seen. He told me he just fired the two who had climbed off. It was obvious what I was here for, standing there on the pier with my boots and sea bag. The number should have tipped me off. *Two* crew being fired? One and you're thinking it must have been a crew shortcoming, but two and I should have been thinking it's a boat problem. But the *Billie Mae* would likely be the only scalloper putting in at Cape May that day.

There are no application forms when you are looking for a site on a boat. The captain will just ask you what you have done and listen for the language. You can claim anything, but you can only learn the language the hard way. He hired me.

Painted on her stern, Rockport, Texas, was her official home port, but the *Billie Mae*'s current home port was Newport News, Virginia. Her crew was all good ol' Virginia boys, and I was introduced as the replacement for the two worthless trash bags of excrement that had just exited.

Now the latest new kid on the block, the crew regarded me disdainfully and treated me like I was green, an indignity after all I had done to establish myself in Provincetown. *Not this again,* I thought, but there was another layer, more like a thick slab, to this. I realized I was on trial as a greenhorn until my actions redeemed me, but I was a *Yankee* greenhorn. This was far worse. It was the *Goddamned Yankee* this and the *Fucking Yankee* that. Bad enough being a greenhorn but, that I was from the North, I was greenhorn dipped in shit.

The *Billie Mae* was a floating hotel compared to the old wooden boats. There was running water, a shower, and a refrigerator/freezer. Nobody was going to tell me it was bad luck to practice good hygiene. We found bad luck in other ways. We headed southeast to the Baltimore Canyon area, where I demonstrated satisfactorily that I could pull my weight on the boat, however begrudgingly acknowledged. It was not good enough, though. I was still a fucking Yankee.

I was portside hookup man on this adventure. Captain Dale had found the mud, loading up both sides of the *Billie Mae* with a three-foot-high pile of it along with sand dollars (we called them "cookies") twelve feet long every tow. That meant that you had to claw through the tightly packed muck with your fingers, excavating scallops. You couldn't simply pick them up; you had to dig for them. There were not even enough to make it worthwhile—maybe a bushel or two.

I was on the port winch when we set the gear out. Shipmate David Lohse was the starboard hookup and on that winch. We muttered some uncomplimentary things about the captain regarding the half-ton of tight-packed mud being deposited on deck every twenty minutes. Our fingers were killing us from scratching through it for scallops. Mud has a way of suctioning to the deck and tenaciously fighting a shovel. Rocks are far easier.

I told David that we were getting so much mud because Dale was not setting out enough wire. If the cable is short, the dredge angles up during the tow, taking too big a bite out of the bottom. If we let out a little more wire, say ten fathoms, the dredge would lay down better, and we'd pick up less mud. Yeah. I learned that from Dickey, too.

That's what we did, stretching the captain's order by ten fathoms. Sure enough, after we hauled back, we had two bushels of scallops. Still not enough, but NO mud. We had the scallops picked up and shucked in fifteen minutes, leaving some hang-out time before the next haul back.

After seeing consecutive tows with no mud and us hanging out smoking cigarettes, Dale came down out of the wheelhouse and busted us, knowing we were letting out more wire. He hollered at us in a pricky way and told us to shorten it up next time. He liked to see us break our backs right up to the next haul back. So whaddya know, now we get a half-ton of mud and the same or a lesser amount of scallops, but now we have to work our asses off to get them. I somehow refrained from asking him how much a pound they were giving for mud at the wharf these days.

This nightmare lasted twenty-one days, the longest fishing trip of my short "career." But there was no Susan, no life in Provincetown waiting. On this inhospitable vessel, I had never felt more alone. We finally headed into the Chesapeake Bay and up the James River.

When we were taking out in Newport News, the guys in the packing shed sent back a bag of scallops they said had gone bad. In all the trips out of Provincetown, I had never seen a single scallop that had gone bad, but sure enough, there was a pocket about the size of a softball that looked gray turning to black and stunk like all hell. Someone had not iced the bag properly. There'd have been hell to pay for that if it happened in P'town. Dale ordered the whole bag dumped into the washer, where he added a box of baking soda. It was mixed around until the spoiled scallops lost their gray and stink, bagged up, and sent back up to the wharf where it passed inspection.

Bon a petit, scallop lovers.

## Chuckatuck Peanut Farm

**By the third** week at sea, I was on better terms with everyone on the vessel. It helped that I was willing to work hard and was semi-tolerable even though a Yank. And I made them laugh, a key which unlocks many doors.

When we finally put into port in Virginia, it was obvious this trip was a bust. Dale could not find any decent scallop beds, or he was under the impression that there was a good living in mud. At this point, I was hoping that I had at least made enough money to get me back to New Jersey. The fishery made us wait three days for our meager settlement. Wrong, but there it was. David lived on a peanut farm in Chuckatuck, a rural area between Richmond and Suffolk. He offered to let me stay there while we waited for our money.

Chuckatuck's claim to fame was that Confederate General George Pickett, who General Lee ordered to lead his ill-fated charge at Gettysburg, had a girl-friend in Chuckatuck where he visited whenever he could. David's place was a big, rambling white farmhouse. He took me out into the fields and pulled a peanut plant. The peanuts at this stage were all white. He demonstrated that you could eat them shell and all at this point. It was true. The shell was full of water like a snow pea shell.

There was no sleep in the house, being infested with fleas, so I slept outside under a tree. Then their dog was barking at something in the grass about ten feet from where I lay. I asked David what was up with the dog. He told me he barked like that at the rattlesnakes. I slept on the porch.

The next evening, some of the crew visited, and we were all drinking beer on the big wrap-around porch of the farmhouse. David brought out a semi-automatic 12-gauge shotgun. Now the evening's entertainment was shooting doves. There were a lot of them, and the boys picked them off in alarming numbers. When the surviving doves flew to a safer place, the boys switched to shooting tossed beer bottles.

"Let's see the Yank. You learn to shoot any up there in *New Jersey?*" He said "New Jersey" like it was an oozing venereal disease.

"Some," I said, getting up and taking the shotgun.

They smiled in anticipation of the northerner making a fool of himself.

"Throw two," I added. They did not know about my firearms experience in Nova Scotia.

"Whoa! Whoa! We got ourselves a real Yankee sharpshooter here!"

Yeah. They were breaking Yankee balls. I readied myself and gave the go-ahead. They threw two bottles at the same time. Pow! Pow! Both bottles practically vaporized. There were more "whoa's," but they had a decidedly different tone. Nice moment. Fucking Rebs.

The next day we went into Newport News and picked up our settlement. We made almost $300 per man in twenty-one days. Broker trip, baby. After visiting Uncle Joe and Aunt Pat in Baltimore, I made my way back to Atlantic City with a seabag full of failed marriage and a lot less to show for a three-week trip than I thought I'd have.

Night cometh.

## Two Ages

**I was 26** and had no idea what would come next. I could not know (in a sentence) that I would soon begin a career in psychiatric social work—working with people who suffer from schizophrenia and homelessness, or that I would learn swing guitar and play countless gigs with Bill, that I would be a working actor in New York City and become a member of the Screen Actors Guild, or that I would learn a new instrument, 5-string banjo, and study for over seven years with banjo wizard, Tony Trischka, touring and recording with two bluegrass bands; nor that I would meet my soul mate of thirty-eight years and counting, Beth, at my social work gig and become "Daddy" to an amazing little girl, Erin. I guess you only see what's directly in front of you at that age.

Fishing pounds you like a sparks-flying, hand-forged welding. If it takes, you are different, and every trial you face going forward is always measured against the yardstick of the many times you tip-toed the line between "maybe I'll make it" and "maybe I won't." You'll owe the best of it to guys like Richard Dickey, Rick O'Brian, George Hann, Gerald Costa, Wayne Costa, Skip Albanese, and Chris Scanlan, all of them generous with patience and kindness. And you'll even owe the guys who made it hard, for you'll find the defiance to succeed anyway.

I learned a lot about people confined in a small space in absurd conditions when things get feather white and staying alive is the only matter. It is still too easy to hear the winds shriek through the rigging and the seas breaking inches from the bunk on the other side of the hull, sleep music during off-watch. That I can muse about it at all owes to God.

The fishing chapter closed back in 1980, while the log cabin journal is still accepting new entries. Twice a year, I revisit this peace construct that even sustained me as a youngster, years before I built it. I love my "pile of sticks" in the woods . . . it does what eleven-year-old me had hoped it would. And even as an older feller, it feels a bit like living on the edge on that hill in a January deep freeze.

Author picking his banjo.

My father spoke to me across the gulf of years and insular walls. I found a birthday card, forgotten in the piles of papers I find nearly impossible to purge. Mom lay paralyzed in the hospital a little over a month after her broken neck in 1971, so it fell to him to handle my 18th birthday, the only time he had done so. He bought a card with a knight in armor on the cover, which probably was a convenient first or second card he saw. But inside, he had written what he was unable to say, in a fluid but masculine cursive, "Just stay as you are. Love, Dad." That he had liked me as I was never occurred to me. But here it was in writing.

Things would have turned out a lot differently if I had actually made it to the apple orchard in September of 1977, if that traffic light had turned green ten seconds before I entered the intersection, an army truck waiting at the red with the rack of moose horns strapped to the front grill.

I am grateful to have made it to my sixty-eighth birthday, considering having a thirtieth was a major accomplishment. I guess I managed to stir in a tablespoonful of growing up into this fun mixture I've been running on for so long and arrived at a tolerable concoction. I have yet to rue a birthday. Besides, there are only two ages: alive and dead.

# *About the Author*

MICKEY MAGUIRE has had such varied experiences, he was actually advised by a potential employer to merely state, "Jack of All Trades" on the previous jobs section of his psychiatric social worker employment application. Born in Atlantic City, New Jersey, he has been an off-shore scallop boat deckhand out of Provincetown, Cape Cod, ship's cook (a job he swears provided his most pertinent social work training), farm worker and blacksmith's apprentice in Nova Scotia where he built his own log cabin in 1974, banjo player for touring and recording bluegrass band James Reams & The Barnstormers and

Photo by Dorothy Kurzydlowski

New Jersey's String Fever, a working actor in New York City and Screen Actors Guild member, guitar player in a swing and country trio and, for thirty-three years, Assistant Program Director for the St. Francis Residences, a residential program providing permanent housing for homeless mentally ill individuals in Manhattan.

Graduating (barely) with an English Major from Rowan University (formerly Glassboro State College), Mickey balanced his education with the acquisition of land in Nova Scotia and building his hand-made log cabin. Throughout his artistic and philanthropic pursuits, Mickey has been a writer. Beginning with his first love, poetry, and shifting to articles, he has placed humorous pieces in trade magazine National Fisherman, Banjo Newsletter Magazine as well as a cover article in that publication on banjo legend Walter Hensley. *Feather White* was written with a great deal of reliance on the copious journal notes he kept during the 1970s.

Made in the USA
Middletown, DE
06 November 2021